Kids Win at Writing!

A Breakthrough Step-by-Step Guide to
Teaching Children How to Write, Spell and Read.

By Angela Marino

Founder and owner of Writing Wonders and Fun Writing Ideas

Charleston, SC

www.PalmettoPublishing.com

Kids Win at Writing!
A Breakthrough Step-by-Step Guide to Teaching Children How to Write, Spell and Read.

First Edition

Paperback ISBN: 978-1-63837-833-4
eBook ISBN: 978-1-63837-834-1

This book is dedicated to all teachers, parents and children.

CONTENTS

A NOTE FOR CLASSROOM TEACHERS: The activities listed in these sections support Common Core State Standards. The standards were taken from www.corestandards.org/ELA-Literacy/RF/, www.corestandards.org/ELA-Literacy/W/ and www.corestandards.org/ELA-Litearcy/L/ and are listed at the top of each activity and lesson when applicable.

ACKNOWLEDGMENTS

A special thanks to every student, every single one, that I have ever taught in a formal or informal setting. You helped me formulate the ideas in this book. You have shown me that these steps work. Your mere presence and participation encouraged me a great deal to finally finish this book.

I also want to thank my own 4 children. They actively completed each step of this book and also gave me so many ideas along the way. They have been by my side the most as I have worked out this project. They are, without hesitation, the most patient, forgiving and understanding children on the planet!

Thank you to my husband who makes us laugh, is a constant encouragement, and creates adventure in our everyday lives.

Thank you to my closest friends who have listened tirelessly to my on-going obsession with teaching writing. What a support, delight and dear presence you each are!

I owe an utmost gratitude to Kim, owner of Artzhub.com, whose invitation to teach summer camps with her set me on the track to teaching writing. Her business leadership, hard work, professionalism, reliability and resilience have made working with her an absolute joy. Her own method of teaching drawing through Artzhub.com produces phenomenal results in kids.

Thank you to Monica for taking the time to read through this and for giving your constructive advice. Thank you also to Carolyn and Paul for cheerfully and eagerly offering your input.

Lastly, I want to thank every teacher and parent who will embark on this step-by-step journey to teaching writing. Writing empowers students to communicate and convey their gifts to the world.

"One child, one teacher, one book, one pen can change the world."

Malala Yousafzai

"There is nothing like writing to force you to think and get your thoughts straight....
You have to be able to communicate in life...
If you can't talk to people or write, you're giving up your potential."

Warren Buffett

INTRODUCTION

Thank you so much for giving this book, *KIDS WIN AT WRITING!* a try and for your concerted effort to help build confident writers. I'm a licensed teacher with 22+ years of experience teaching language learners. For the past 8 years I've been teaching year-round writing classes to children ages 5–11 all the while homeschooling my own 4 children.

A few years ago, I began teaching writing every Friday morning at a homeschool co-op. After a couple weeks of classes, a parent sent me the following email. I decided to include it here as it completely encompasses my goal and passion for classroom teachers and homeschool families.

"(My 1st Grade son) was so proud of what he wrote and couldn't wait for me to read it! What a joy to see both boys (1st and 4th Grade) so thrilled with writing. Somehow you've made what was a dreaded thing fun! I'm so glad you're teaching this course. I was so concerned when I was told this year would be a writing class. I thought I'd have to drag the boys to co-op!"

Soon after, I completed courses from Professional Learning Board to renew my teaching license. Those courses absolutely solidified for me the importance of teaching writing, and focusing on it as early as possible.

Almost unanimously, parents and teachers will argue that writing is the most challenging piece of literacy. At the same time, writing is foundational for all other subjects. As a result, I propose we focus on it the most, and even first, **before** reading. Thus, this book is a step-by-step guide to teaching children how to write, spell and read. Children as young as 24 months can begin with step one. Moreover, children of **any** age or ability can begin and complete these steps at **any** time.

There are no grades, levels or races, just steps towards comfortable and confident writing. Each child completes the steps as slowly or as quickly as he or she is ready for. If a child appears to be moving through the steps quickly, make sure that they are doing so at mastery level. Mastering these simple steps is key to setting the child up for long term success in writing.

SECTION 1

8 Surprising Secrets to Building Confident Writers

Before I lay out the steps for you and your child or students to complete, it's paramount that I share with you these 8 secrets to building confident writers. These secrets help clarify expectations and demonstrate the positive tone necessary for directing students through each step.

SECRET #1: Start as Young as Possible

Children in general are geniuses! I don't think we give them enough credit. It's absolutely advantageous for them to start drawing and writing as early as possible. In Section 2 of this book, I spell out 12 steps to building strong writers. Step one can, and is recommended to, begin as early as 24 months.

To start, I am a HUGE proponent of drawing with young children for the following reasons. In the short term, it:

1. Builds strong fine motor skills

2. Creates quality time, memories and charming conversations with your child or students

3. Teaches children colors and shapes

4. Prepares children for "drawing" proper letter strokes, which leads to writing and reading

5. Guides children to draw independently for great lengths of time

Drawing with your young child can also have long term benefits. Children who have the patience and fine motor strength to draw pictures, typically have the focus and stamina to "draw" letters and eventually write words, sentences and stories.

These children often find handwriting and spelling to feel natural and "easy" rather than wearing or troublesome. In essence, they learn how to write before they ever hear that writing is "hard". This carries them through school with a relative amount of comfort and dexterity.

Secondly, in addition to the steps that I outline in Section 2, it's very important to expose children to letters and letter sounds early on. Enjoy reading ABC books and putting A–Z puzzles together with your child or students. As you and your child work with alphabet books and puzzles, sing or speak out the ABC song and point to the letters. Hearing these sounds and seeing the letters prepares them for drawing and writing them later on.

Thirdly, and surprisingly, putting puzzles together with young children can also set them up for writing success! Puzzles teach children to pay attention to details which in turn helps them notice differences in spelling patterns, as well as punctuation. Moreover, starting and finishing puzzles at an early age helps children gradually and naturally develop patience and perseverance which they will need to complete stories and writing assignments as they get older.

Conversely, I strongly recommend waiting as long as possible to introduce your children to I-Pads or Apps on your phone. It's so important for children to be handling markers, pens and paint brushes, drawing letters and writing words, as young as possible. While there's a plethora of "educational" games for small children, swiping a screen **cannot** replace the fundamental act of writing, nor can it solidify a child's ability to spell words. The physical act of writing out letters and words is crucial for strengthening fine motor skills, developing long attention spans and helping children learn to **write** and **spell**.

Any time my children accompany me to appointments, they bring a backpack, clipboard, paper, a box of markers and a couple of books to read. While we wait, they're drawing or reading. Occasionally, the office will have a TV and that is their treat. In other words, they don't expect, nor are they dependent on electronics to carry them through the wait time. Nevertheless, if electronics cannot be avoided in your situation, I would recommend the website, Starfall.com, and the app, Khan Academy Kids. They both support the literacy skills that your young children will be learning in Section 2 of this book.

Finally, while I highly advise parents and teachers to start teaching writing very early on, it's never too late to start! These secrets, and the steps laid out in this book, can work for your child right now, at whatever age or ability. They can work with language learners, late bloomers and even students with learning challenges.

One 5th Grader's Story

During the 2019–2020 school year, I had the absolute privilege of working with a 5th Grade boy who struggled terribly with writing. I only taught him for 50 minutes each week. At the beginning of the school year, he wasn't able to write a single word on his paper by himself. In fact, the only way I could get him to write anything was to stand next to him, ask him what he wanted to write and then verbally spell out each word for him. There were many times when I had to speak out proper letter strokes, as well, to help him along.

The general expectation that I have for 5th Graders who began writing at an early age and have progressed incrementally through the steps is to write about 25 sentences for each guided writing lesson. (You will learn how the guided writing lessons work in Section 4 of this book.)

So, at the beginning of the year, this student couldn't write one sentence independently. However, by the end of the year, he was able to write 10–15 sentences on his own. That's after only working with him less than one hour per week from September–March. Needless to say, I was so proud of him!

Most importantly, he is proof that the strategies behind the spelling activities in Section 3 and the guided writing lessons in Section 4 that I present in this book can work for even our most struggling writers. Additionally, my website www.funwritingideas.com has writing games that I used with this student. They also serve as an excellent support and intervention to strengthen older students' writing skills.

SECRET #2: Write With Your Child

Writing **with** your child in the beginning is critical to building a confident writer. It doesn't matter how old or young your child is. When you start to make writing a priority, it must be done together **with** the child.

The little time you spend drawing and writing **with** your child or students early on will save you SO much time in the future. Developing a young writer produces a strong reader. The early reader can in turn read instructions and complete school work independently as well as enjoy the mere act of reading many books.

Having a young independent reader and writer becomes golden when you have younger siblings to teach or care for. It's also so helpful in school, when you have struggling readers and writers that need more time and attention.

The 12 steps that I outline in Section 2 don't take long. As you work **with** the child on each step in the beginning, they quickly develop the ability to complete the steps independently.

For example, my 4½ year old gets out markers and paper and writes her ABCs all by herself because I have spent time sitting **with** her and teaching her how to draw them. My 2 year old now gets out markers and paper by herself to scribble and scrabble because I have spent time sitting next to her and showing her how to scribble and scrabble.

Right now, my 7 and 8 year old boys write without thinking too much. During the school year, I give them a guided writing lesson (discussed in Section 4) 1–2 times per week. They are able to complete it quickly and confidently. If they take a while to finish the task, it's because they are spending time creating a unique idea. At times, my oldest son will sit for a long time generating in his mind exactly what he wants to write. Then, once he gets started, he can finish writing out his sentences in a short amount of time. They are able to do this because, I walked them through the 12 steps outlined in Section 2. Additionally, I sat next to them when they were first learning how to complete sight word sentences explained in Section 3. Currently, I guide them to complete their 5 section essays and stories discussed in Section 4.

Writing With Older Children:

Again, if you are working with older students, you'll want to make sure that they can complete all 12 steps in Section 2. Then, you'll want them to move to Section 3 and show them how to complete sight word sentences. Lastly, you'll want to sit next to the child or students and guide them in writing 5 section essays and stories, which are outlined in Section 4 of this book. It's so important to work **with** the child with this mindset: It's not you, a parent or teacher, over a child's shoulder saying, "You're going to do this." Rather, it's you saying, "We have to do this. I'm here to help you."

When I teach large groups of students, ages 5–11, at my summer writing camps and year-round writing classes, I give the **same** guided writing lesson to the whole group. While the story line is similar, each child's completed story is unique.

Guiding them through a lesson becomes, "GAME ON!" as we write. Everyone is writing at the **same** time. I'm guiding the group through the 5 sections of the story. If anyone needs to know how to spell something or they don't know what to write, I'm right there to help them, by writing unknown words on the board and asking individual students questions to help them generate ideas.

I don't write **for** them on their paper. They write the entire story. But, I'm there **with** them, helping them as they need. As a result, students feel supported and encouraged and reach a finish, which ultimately helps build their confidence.

SECRET # 3: Fall Forward—No Erasing

The third secret is, "No erasing." Think of teaching your children or students to write the same way you would teach them how to walk. You're next to them. You help them. They are going to stumble and fall often. And when they get back up, they keep walking forward.

It's the same with writing. Children are going to make many mistakes. In my opinion, there's no need to erase. Just like we don't make a child learning to walk "go back" and redo those same steps again, we don't want to ask a child to go back and erase.

When I teach writing camps, my students use pens. At the beginning of each lesson I tell them, "If you write something you don't like, simply draw one line through it and keep going." If you've been asking your child or students to erase up to this point, no worries! Feel relieved that you don't ever have to do that again! Not erasing is particularly important when you first teach children how to draw, write their capital and lowercase letters, spell high frequency words and write sight word sentences. Consider these examples:

Letters

When you are teaching a student to draw the letter T, you will say and model:

"Draw down," for the first line.

If the child draws across, you simply repeat, "Draw down." Continue until the child can follow you and draw the line <u>down</u>. Then, say and model, "Draw a hat across the top". Watch the child draw a line, left to right, across the top of the vertical line.

If the child crosses the line or draws a line that doesn't touch the first line, keep moving forward, drawing down and crossing the top, until the child gets it right. Praise their effort and success.

Words

Let's talk about writing words which are discussed in Section 2 of this book. If you say the sounds, "C-A-T" and your child writes C-A-D. Point out the correct C and A, and follow with a sentence like, "You wrote the sounds, C, A, D. Let's try again to write the sounds, C-A-T." Continue until the child writes CAT correctly. Praise their effort and success.

Sentences

Next, let's talk about sentences (discussed in Section 3). Imagine that the child's weekly sight word sentence is, "I SEE A CAT." He or she has to write the sentence 3 times changing, and phonetically spelling, the underlined word. He or she might write:

I SEE A CAT.
I SEE A HORS.
I SE A BRD.

In this case, you would simply say, "Good job! You wrote, I SEE A CAT. I SEE A HORS. Let's look at the word, SEE, in the last sentence. What did you forget?" When the child finds the missing letter "E", respond, "Good job! Let's write that sentence one more time." Or, if you see that your child is getting tired, say, "Let's write the word, SEE, one more time."

Stories

After a child completes a story, enjoy reading it! Don't have the child erase or correct misspelled words in that story. Rather, in your own time, make a note of words that he or she consistently misspelled. Then, use these misspelled words to create your own sight word sentences which are explained in Section 3. Have the child practice writing these new sight word sentences the next couple of days.

Regarding punctuation, you can have your child slowly reread their story and try to find where the capital letters and punctuation should go. If they can't find these items, simply point them out and have them insert each.

SECRET #4: Use Motivating Materials

Because there's no need to erase, I strongly discourage using pencils. In fact, I highly recommend using all kinds of fun and motivating materials! My kids consistently have on hand and enjoy writing with:

Markers
Colored Pens
Gel Pens

There are so many more out there! Whatever you and your students like and can afford, by all means get them. Plus, these writing materials add color and charm to each child's writing activities.

Every now and then, my own kids will alternate colors as they write letters in a word or sentences in a story. I always let them. As long as they are writing, falling forward and completing their task, all is well! They can write it and complete it however they want.

Secondly, try to have many inexpensive materials to inspire and accompany your child's writing. Here's a list of materials that we have on hand continuously:

Stickers
Calendar Pictures
Googly Eyes
Watercolor Paint
Acrylic Paint

You can learn more about these materials that motivate children to write in Section 6 of this book.

SECRET # 5: Think Small

Less is more with writing! Somehow or somewhere, we've adopted this idea that children need to write a lot every day. I argue differently. Children need small, short, yet strong, increments of time to draw letters, write words, sentences and stories.

Imagine the following sequence of events for developing a confident writer early on. I list these steps in greater detail in Sections 2, 3 and 4 of this book.

2 years old:	Scribble and scrabble for 5 minutes, 1–3 x per week
2 ½ years old:	Draw counterclockwise circles for 5 minutes, 1–3 x per week
3 years old:	Draw capital letters for 5 minutes, 1–3 x per week
4 years old:	Write 3 letter words for 5–10 minutes, 1–3 x per week
4 ½ years old:	Phonetically label pictures for 10 minutes, 1–3 x per week
5 years old:	Copy one sight word sentence, 3–5x per week
6 years old:	Write 5 sentences about any one topic, 1–2x per week
7 years old:	Write 10 sentences about any one topic, 1–2x per week
11 years old	Write 25 sentences about any one topic, 1–2x per week

These activities truly don't take long. Yet, they set children up for comfortable and confident writing because children are learning the "hard" letter strokes, "difficult" spelling words and "long" compositions in short, manageable spurts of time and practice. This leads me to my next secret. Give clear expectations.

SECRET #6: Give Clear Expectations

The writing activities that I outline don't take long because the children don't have to write very much. Since they don't have to write very much, it's easy for me, as their parent or teacher, to hold them accountable. I often say the following sentences:

"We're going to practice 4 letters today, then we're done!"

"We're going to write the word "THE" 5 times and place a sticker next to it each time, then we're done!"

"You have to copy your sight word sentence 3 times, then you're done!"

"You have to write 1 sentence (K–1st Grade) for each section of the story, then you're done!"

"You have to write 5 sentences (5TH Grade) for each section of the story, then you're done!"

Setting clear and achievable expectations causes any one of these things to happen:

ONE: Children will finish with the feeling of "that was easy!" They finish feeling successful, happy and positive towards writing.

TWO: Children often want to do more. They want to write more letters, words or sentences.

THREE: Children who tend to dread writing get to feel successful often. They may not like the writing exercise, but they can see the end is near and finish it.

Again, I can't stress enough to start drawing and writing with your child as early as possible (Secret #1). The strategies that I use and present in this book and on the website, www.funwritingideas.com, were created to minimize, and even prevent all together, having children who "can't" or "won't" write.

If you have older students right now and are worried about their writing, plan to spend time writing **with** each child. In Section 3 of this book, I outline how to find out where older students are at with respect to spelling. There, you can find the sight word sentences that each child should start with. Then, regardless of their age, they can follow these steps:

1. On, Monday, Tuesday and Wednesday, they write their sight word sentences 3x each.

2. On Thursday and Friday, they write 1–5 sentences about any one topic, depending on their current ability.

In Section 4, I outline how to conduct guided writing lessons. Each lesson has 5 sections. These 5 sections help students organize their ideas and guide them to complete a beginning, middle and end. The **general** expectations that I set for students are:

K–1st Graders write 1 sentence per section, which amounts to 5 sentences total

2nd Graders write 2 sentences per section, which amounts to 10 sentences total

3rd Graders write 3 sentences per section, which amounts to 15 sentences total

4th Graders write 4 sentences per section, which amounts to 20 sentences total

5th Graders write 5 sentences per section, which amounts to 25 sentences total

However, if you are starting out with a struggling or reluctant writer, have them write 1 sentence per section, even if they are in 5th Grade. After a couple of weeks or months, work towards 2 sentences per section, then 3, and so on. The key is to set a clear and realistic expectation for each child and hold them accountable. Guide them to completion. Again, **sitting next to the child during these tough stages is really important (Secret #2).** Teachers and parents need to serve as a continual resource. It's okay, and even necessary, to help struggling writers with spelling and with generating ideas as they ask and need. This guides them towards comfortable, confident and independent writing. It's equally important to continually praise each child's efforts and successes.

SECRET #7: Keep the Topics Fun

As a child learns to write letters, words, sentences and stories, it really needs to be all about fun! Incorporate the students' interests as much as possible. They need to be writing about topics that they enjoy and know a lot about. Our goal is for children to WRITE. We want them to feel excited about what they're writing.

The fictional guided writing lessons that I include in Section 5 of this book and post on the website, www.funwritingideas.com are meant to be amusing. Students are free to let their imaginations soar and encouraged to make ANYTHING happen in their stories. The non-fiction guided writing lessons are meant to be personal. Students are given opportunities to write what they know and what they think.

Again, allow your children many opportunities to write about topics that interest them and make them laugh. It's so important to keep the environment cheerful and exciting in the early stages of learning to write. In this way, they can enjoy the process of learning proper letter strokes (Section 2) and how to spell tricky words (Section 3). They can laugh and have a good time while learning how to organize their ideas and finish their stories (Section 4).

THEN, when it comes time to write academically in later grades, they have the necessary tools to do so, which are handwriting, spelling, grammar and organization. The end goal is that by middle school and high school, the children have strong core writing skills and in turn, can focus their attention on writing more serious academic content.

SECRET #8: Praise Effort and Completion

Unfortunately, writing is a shuddered subject. So many children don't get an early start and wind up feeling defeated and frustrated. That's why it's important to focus on what each child **can** do, to start there, and positively build on those skills.

When I teach children to write, I figure out what each child knows as quickly as possible. Then, I find the step that they are on and go from there. The primary focus is helping them progress and move towards comfortable and confident writing.

During this process it's so important to praise each child liberally. Point out the successes. Reward them with positive words. As often as possible, give them time to add a simple art accent found in Section 6. The art accents add color and charm to their stories and reward them for their work!

Another way to honor completion is to slide each story into a plastic page protector and put it in a writing folder or binder. Each week of summer camp, my students store all of their stories in plastic page protectors and in writing folders that have center prongs.

Returning campers tell me time and time again that they still have their folders. My children at home store their protected stories in binders. These binders show a student's progress and become "books" that children get to reread. It's also common for children to show off their binders to grandparents, babysitters and visitors.

Lastly, by all means, treat your children and students generously for completing their writing tasks and stories. Stickers, simple snacks, extra free time, computer choice time, a run to the ice cream shop, are all ideas on how you can reward your writers.

Because writing is foundational for all other subjects, it's absolutely worth our time, effort and praise. Guiding our students and honoring their efforts and progress along the way will help them build confidence in writing! Now let's look at 12 steps that are key to building a strong foundation for long term writing.

12 Simple Steps to Building a Strong Foundation for Confident Writing

You'll be amazed at how early you can begin teaching your child how to write! These first years are spent building strong fine motor skills, long attention spans, phonemic awareness and proper letter strokes.

The activities listed in these 12 steps can be taught one on one with a child, in small groups, or with a classroom of children. For a classroom, I suggest modeling each step at the front of the room on chart paper or a whiteboard. Simultaneously, children can use clipboards and paper, or small whiteboards, to follow along and practice each step as you model it.

MATERIALS:

The materials that students need to complete these exercises are **a box of markers, a pack of white copy paper and stickers.** The materials that parents and teachers need to monitor each student's progress are:

1. A 3 ring binder (one for each child)

2. A 3 ring hole punch

3. Plastic page protectors (50–100 for each child)

4. A set of 12 charts for each child. (There is one chart for each step, so 12 charts for each child.)

5. A yellow marker or highlighter to fill in the charts.

Why Markers?

When working with toddlers and young children, we use markers because they are bigger for a comfortable handle-bar grip. They are also bolder in color and wash out. I find crayons to be messy. They break easily. The toddlers peel the paper and even eat them. Crayons also leave waxy crumbs. From the time my children and students have scribbled and scrabbled, we have only used markers.

Why Charts?

For each of the 12 steps, I explain the activities and include a chart. The charts are there for you to keep track of the exercises that each child completes. You can use a yellow marker to highlight the boxes to show which activity each child finishes.

Now let's look at the 12 steps!

STEP ONE: Scribble on paper and place stickers.

NOTE: This step can address the following Common Core State Standard: CCSS.RF.K.1.D.

1. First, sing the familiar ABC song to your child at any time throughout your days, in the car, while rocking, or playing, etc.

2. As early as 24 months, your child can begin to scribble on paper. Teach your child to hold the marker in the same way that you would hold the handlebar of a bicycle. Give him or her time to scribble and scrabble all over the paper. Children will want to draw on many places other than the paper, such as on themselves, the table, the floor, the wall, etc. Continually and patiently tell the child, "We only draw on paper. Stay on the paper."

3. Note that this activity will only last several minutes each time. Follow the interest of the child. When you see that your child is getting tired or uninterested, put the materials away and continue another day. Work on this simple activity 1–2x per week for 1–3 months.

4. Third, your child can begin placing stickers on paper. Teach them to remove a sticker using the thumb and index finger and place it on paper. This strengthens the fine motor skills in their thumb and first finger which sets them up for a proper pen and marker grip. Have the child fill the page with stickers. Sit with the child and place stickers yourself. Enjoy the time with your little one.

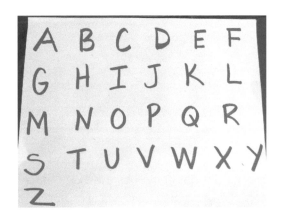

Sing the ABCs.

Scribble.

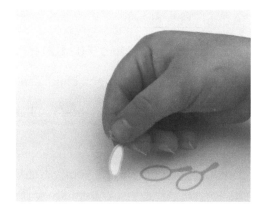

Place stickers.

On the next page, you'll find the chart that lists these activities. Use a yellow marker to highlight the activities that your child completes. You can even use a pen to write the date in the highlighted box if you want. The child should complete each activity at least once a week.

STEP ONE: Scribble on paper and place stickers.

MONTH 1	Monday	Tuesday	Wednesday	Thursday	Friday
	Sing the ABCs. The child scribbles using the handlebar grip.	Sing the ABCs. The child scribbles using the handlebar grip.	The child places stickers on paper.	The child places stickers on paper.	
Week 1					
Week 2					
Week 3					
Week 4					

MONTH 2	Monday	Tuesday	Wednesday	Thursday	Friday
	Sing the ABCs. The child scribbles using the handlebar grip.	Sing the ABCs. The child scribbles using the handlebar grip.	The child places stickers on paper.	The child places stickers on paper.	
Week 1					
Week 2					
Week 3					
Week 4					

MONTH 3	Monday	Tuesday	Wednesday	Thursday	Friday
	Sing the ABCs. The child scribbles using the handlebar grip.	Sing the ABCs. The child scribbles using the handlebar grip.	The child places stickers on paper.	The child places stickers on paper.	
Week 1					
Week 2					
Week 3					
Week 4					

STEP TWO: Color small sections and draw counterclockwise circles around stickers.

NOTE: This step can address and prepare the child for the following Common Core State Standards: CCSS.RF.K.1.D, L.K.1.A and L.1.1.A.

1. For step two, continue to sing the ABC song to your child often.

2. Next, teach your child to slow down and color in small sections. As your toddler gets used to scribbling and scrabbling, show your child how to draw slow scribbles as if they're coloring in a section of the paper. Most children will start off speed scribbling in a reckless manner all over the paper and off of it. That's okay for a while.

    As time goes on, gradually and patiently teach them to slow down. Be in charge in a gentle matter of fact way. Reward their cooperation with calm and sweet praise. If their drawings end with spots of color all over the paper, they've moved from scribbling all over to small concentrated spaces. This shows that the child has more control of the marker and is increasing in fine motor strength.

    Again, this activity will only take a few minutes each time. When you see that your child is getting tired or no longer interested, put the materials away and continue another day. Try to do this activity 1–2 x per week for 1–3 months.

3. Third, show your child how to draw a counterclockwise circle around a sticker. Gently take your child's hand, start at the **top** of the sticker and guide it to the **left** in order to draw a COUNTERCLOCKWISE CIRCLE. Drawing circles counterclockwise will foster proper letter strokes later on.

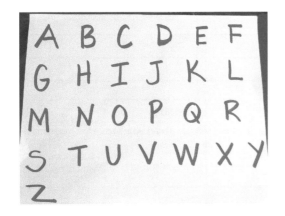

Sing the ABCs.   Color smaller spaces.   Circle stickers.

On the next page, you'll find the chart that lists these activities. Use a yellow marker to highlight the activities that your child completes. You can use a pen to write the date in the highlighted box as well, if you'd like. The child should complete each activity at least once a week.

STEP TWO: Color small sections and draw counterclockwise circles around stickers.

MONTH 1	Monday	Tuesday	Wednesday	Thursday	Friday
	Sing the ABCs. The child moves from scribbling to coloring small spaces.	Sing the ABCs. The child moves from scribbling to coloring small spaces.	Place stickers on paper. The child draws counter-clockwise circles around them.	Place stickers on paper. The child draws counter-clockwise circles around them.	
Week 1					
Week 2					
Week 3					
Week 4					

MONTH 2	Monday	Tuesday	Wednesday	Thursday	Friday
	Sing the ABCs. The child moves from scribbling to coloring small spaces.	Sing the ABCs. The child moves from scribbling to coloring small spaces.	Place stickers on paper. The child draws counter-clockwise circles around them.	Place stickers on paper. The child draws counter-clockwise circles around them.	
Week 1					
Week 2					
Week 3					
Week 4					

MONTH 3	Monday	Tuesday	Wednesday	Thursday	Friday
	Sing the ABCs. The child moves from scribbling to coloring small spaces.	Sing the ABCs. The child moves from scribbling to coloring small spaces.	Place stickers on paper. The child draws counter-clockwise circles around them.	Place stickers on paper. The child draws counter-clockwise circles around them.	
Week 1					
Week 2					
Week 3					
Week 4					

STEP THREE: Draw circles and straight lines.

NOTE: This step can address and prepare the child for the following Common Core State Standards: CCSS.RF.K.1.D, L.K.1.A and L.1.1.A.

1. Continue to sing the ABC song to your child. This time, write each capital letter, top to bottom, left to right, **as you slowly sing them.** It's important that you write the letters at this stage rather than simply point to them. Drawing out the letters while you sing them casually shows the child how the letters are formed. You can find the capital letters, A–Z, on page 36 to refer to if need be.

2. Continue to draw **counterclockwise** circles around stickers, or freely without stickers. Additional ideas for practicing **counterclockwise** circles are:

   Drawing circles around each Cheerio or pretzel before eating it

   Drawing 5 circles around a cookie before eating it

   Drawing circles in the sand, mud, shaving cream or in bath bubbles

   Using sidewalk chalk to draw circles

3. Third, on a piece of blank paper, place two stickers vertically apart from each other. The child uses a marker to draw a straight line, top to bottom, to connect the two stickers. Once a child is good at drawing vertical lines, you can place the stickers horizontally and diagonally apart. Each time, the child draws a line that connects the two stickers. This exercise strengthens fine motor skills while preparing children to draw lines that lead to writing capital letters later.

Write the ABCs as you sing them.

Circle a snack and eat it.

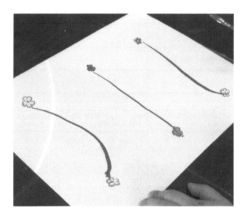

Draw straight lines between two stickers.

On the next page, you'll find the chart that lists these activities.

STEP THREE: Draw circles and straight lines.

MONTH 1	Monday	Tuesday	Wednesday	Thursday	Friday
	The adult sings and writes the ABCs. The child continues to draw counterclockwise circles around stickers.	The adult sings and writes the ABCs. The child continues to draw counterclockwise circles around stickers.	The adult places 2 stickers. The child draws a straight line vertically, horizontally or diagonally to connect them.	The adult places 2 stickers. The child draws a straight line vertically, horizontally or diagonally to connect them.	
Week 1					
Week 2					
Week 3					
Week 4					

MONTH 2	Monday	Tuesday	Wednesday	Thursday	Friday
	The adult sings and writes the ABCs. The child continues to draw counterclockwise circles around stickers.	The adult sings and writes the ABCs. The child continues to draw counterclockwise circles around stickers.	The adult places 2 stickers. The child draws a straight line vertically, horizontally or diagonally to connect them.	The adult places 2 stickers. The child draws a straight line vertically, horizontally or diagonally to connect them.	
Week 1					
Week 2					
Week 3					
Week 4					

MONTH 3	Monday	Tuesday	Wednesday	Thursday	Friday
	The adult sings and writes the ABCs. The child continues to draw counterclockwise circles around stickers.	The adult sings and writes the ABCs. The child continues to draw counterclockwise circles around stickers.	The adult places 2 stickers. The child draws a straight line vertically, horizontally or diagonally to connect them.	The adult places 2 stickers. The child draws a straight line vertically, horizontally or diagonally to connect them.	
Week 1					
Week 2					
Week 3					
Week 4					

STEP FOUR: Turn circles into objects.

NOTE: This step can address the following Common Core State Standard: CCSS.RF.K.1.D.

1. Continue to sing the ABC song and write each capital letter as you slowly sing them.

2. Have the child draw circles and start to color them in. Again, gently take your child's hand, start at the top, move the marker to the left, down and around to complete the **counterclockwise** circle. Then, have the child try to color inside the circle.

3. Third, show the child how to turn a circle into an object. When drawing circles with children, I like to start with the sun. I draw the circle. Then, I ask the child to draw the sun's rays on the circle. Next, I draw a second circle and ask the child to draw his or her **own** circle. Fourth, I draw rays on my sun and ask the child to try to draw rays on **his or her** sun. We follow the same steps to draw a balloon or smiley face.

    These activities usually only last a few minutes, but they are highly effective. When you see that your child is getting tired or is no longer interested, put the materials away and continue another day.

Write the ABCs as you sing them.

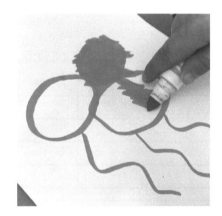
Color in circles.

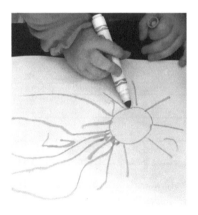
Turn circles into objects.

On the next page, you'll find the chart that lists these activities. Use a yellow marker to highlight the activities that your child completes. You can even use a pen to write the date in the highlighted box if you want. The child should complete each activity at least once a week.

STEP FOUR: Turn circles into objects.

MONTH 1	Monday	Tuesday	Wednesday	Thursday	Friday
	The adult sings and writes the ABCs. The child draws circles and tries to color them in.	The adult sings and writes the ABCs. The child draws circles and tries to color them in.	The adult and child draw circles and turn them into objects.	The adult and child draw circles and turn them into objects.	
Week 1					
Week 2					
Week 3					
Week 4					

MONTH 2	Monday	Tuesday	Wednesday	Thursday	Friday
	The adult sings and writes the ABCs. The child draws circles and tries to color them in.	The adult sings and writes the ABCs. The child draws circles and tries to color them in.	The adult and child draw circles and turn them into objects.	The adult and child draw circles and turn them into objects.	
Week 1					
Week 2					
Week 3					
Week 4					

MONTH 3	Monday	Tuesday	Wednesday	Thursday	Friday
	The adult sings and writes the ABCs. The child draws circles and tries to color them in.	The adult sings and writes the ABCs. The child draws circles and tries to color them in.	The adult and child draw circles and turn them into objects.	The adult and child draw circles and turn them into objects.	
Week 1					
Week 2					
Week 3					
Week 4					

STEP FIVE: Begin drawing capital letters.

NOTE: This step can address and prepare the child for the following Common Core State Standards: CCSS.RF.K.1.D, L.K.1.A and L.1.1.A.

1. Here, the parent can write out the 26 capital and lowercase letters on a piece of paper, or print the ones on page 37. Place this page in a plastic page protector. As you sing the ABC song, point to each letter so that the child can hear and see the letters at the same time. The lowercase letters are included on this page. This is one way to casually introduce the lowercase letters to toddlers for the first time.

2. Continue to draw circles with the child, turning them into objects such as a sun, balloon or smiley face.

3. Begin placing stickers and drawing lines that form capital letters. First, place two stickers for the first line. Then, add one sticker at a time until each line in the capital letter is complete. This activity works for the capital letters A, E, F, H, I, K, L, M, N, T, V, W, X, Y and Z. Each time the child writes a letter, have him or her say the name and sound of that letter.

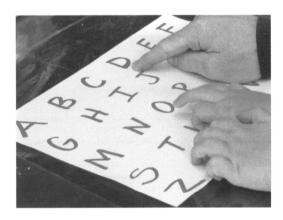

Point to the ABCs as
you sing them.

Turn circles into objects.

Connect stickers to
to form capital letters.

On the next page, you'll find the chart where you can highlight these activities as the child completes them.

STEP FIVE: Begin drawing capital letters.

MONTH 1	Monday	Tuesday	Wednesday	Thursday	Friday
	The adult sings and points to the ABCs. The child turns circles into objects.	The adult sings and points to the ABCs. The child turns circles into objects.	Place stickers so that the child can draw the following capital letters: F, E, H, L, I, T	Place stickers so that the child can draw the following capital letters: F, E, H, L, I, T	
Week 1					
Week 2					
Week 3					
Week 4					

MONTH 2	Monday	Tuesday	Wednesday	Thursday	Friday
	The adult sings and points to the ABCs. The child turns circles into objects.	The adult sings and points to the ABCs. The child turns circles into objects.	Place stickers so that the child can draw the following capital letters: A, N, M, K	Place stickers so that the child can draw the following capital letters: A, N, M, K	
Week 1					
Week 2					
Week 3					
Week 4					

MONTH 3	Monday	Tuesday	Wednesday	Thursday	Friday
	The adult sings and points to the ABCs. The child turns circles into objects.	The adult sings and points to the ABCs. The child turns circles into objects.	Place stickers so that the child can draw the following capital letters: V, W, X, Y, Z	Place stickers so that the child can draw the following capital letters: V, W, X, Y, Z	
Week 1					
Week 2					
Week 3					
Week 4					

STEP SIX: Draw side by side.

NOTE: This step can address the following Common Core State Standards: CCSS.RF.K.1.D, L.K.1.A and L.1.1.A.

1. Continue to sing and point to the ABCs as you sing them.

2. Begin drawing shapes and objects side by side. Sit next to the child. Make sure you and the child each have your own marker and drawing paper or white board. Draw lines to form shapes such as squares, rectangles, ovals and diamonds. Have the child draw the same shape. Name the shape each time you draw one. Then, turn the shapes into simple objects and pictures.

   As the child becomes more comfortable drawing simple shapes, ask the child what he or she would like to draw. Again, draw simple lines and shapes to form the picture. Have the child try to draw the same lines. This exercise strengthens their fine motor skills and ability to add finer details which in turn helps them draw their letters and words later on.

3. Third, sit side by side and guide the child in drawing 2–4 capital letters each week. Use the chart on page 23 to know which letters to practice. Show the child how to draw each capital letter top to bottom, left to right. Page 38 lists verbiage that you can use. The size of each letter is not important at this point. The child might write 1, 2 or 4 letters per page. Over time, the child's letters will get smaller. What matters is that the child is "drawing" proper letter strokes, starting at the top for each letter, drawing down, then left to right. Have the child say the name and sound of each letter that he or she writes.

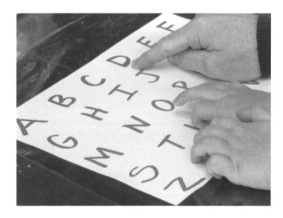

The adult points to the letters as he or she sings them.

Draw side by side. This child wanted to draw a treehouse.

Draw capital letters side by side.

On the next page, you'll find the chart that lists these activities.

STEP SIX: Draw side by side.

MONTH 1	Monday	Tuesday	Wednesday	Thursday	Friday
	The adult sings and points to the ABCs. The child and adult draw shapes and objects side by side.	The adult sings and points to the ABCs. The child and adult draw shapes and objects side by side.	Write any/all of the following capital letters side by side: F, E, H, L, I, T, A, N, M, K	Write any/all of the following capital letters side by side: F, E, H, L, I, T, A, N, M, K	
Week 1			F, E, H	F, E, H	
Week 2			L, I, T	L, I, T	
Week 3			A, N	A, N	
Week 4			M, K	M, K	

MONTH 2	Monday	Tuesday	Wednesday	Thursday	Friday
	The adult sings and points to the ABCs. The child and adult draw shapes and objects side by side.	The adult sings and points to the ABCs. The child and adult draw shapes and objects side by side.	Write any/all of the following capital letters side by side: V, W, X, Y, Z, J, U	Write any/all of the following capital letters side by side: V, W, X, Y, Z, J, U	
Week 1			V, W	V, W	
Week 2			X, Y	X, Y	
Week 3			Z, J	Z, J	
Week 4			U	U	

MONTH 3	Monday	Tuesday	Wednesday	Thursday	Friday
	The adult sings and points to the ABCs. The child and adult draw shapes and objects side by side.	The adult sings and points to the ABCs. The child and adult draw shapes and objects side by side.	Write any/all of the following capital letters side by side: O, Q, C, G, S, D, P, B, R	Write any/all of the following capital letters side by side: O, Q, C, G, S, D, P, B, R	
Week 1			O, Q	O, Q	
Week 2			C, G	C, G	
Week 3			S, D	S, D	
Week 4			P, B, R	P, B, R	

STEP SEVEN: Draw all 26 capital letters side by side.

NOTE: This step can address the following Common Core State Standards: CCSS.RF.K.1.D, L.K.1.A and L.1.1.A.

1. Continue to sing and point to the ABCs as you sing them.

2. Continue drawing simple pictures side by side with the child.

3. Begin drawing all 26 capital letters side by side, top to bottom, left to right, 1x per week. Continue to use the verbiage found on page 38, if you need it. Write all 26 letters in ABC order. Have the child say the name and sound of each letter as he or she writes them.

4. Meanwhile, teach the beginning sounds of each letter. First, teach children that letters are like animals. Just like each animal has a name and makes a sound, each letter has a name and makes a sound. To show this, make an A–Z binder. Get 26 pieces of plain white paper. Write one capital letter and one lower case letter on each page. Have the child add stickers and paste magazine pictures of things that start with each letter. Paste 2–10 pictures or stickers each time, depending on the interest and attention of the child.

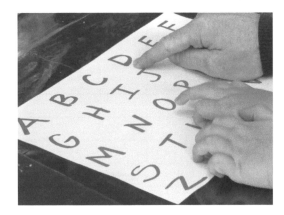   

| The adult points to the letters as he or she sings them. | Draw side by side. | Draw all 26 letters side by side. | Start an A–Z binder for placing stickers and magazine pictures. |

On the next page, you'll find the chart that lists the activities for Step 7. Use a yellow marker to highlight the activities that your child completes. You can even use a pen to write the date in the highlighted box if you want. The child should complete each activity at least once a week.

STEP SEVEN: Draw all 26 letters side by side.

MONTH 1	Monday	Tuesday	Wednesday	Thursday	Friday
	The adult sings and points to the ABCs. The adult and child draw all 26 capital letters side by side.	The adult sings and points to the ABCs. The adult and child draw all 26 capital letters side by side.	The adult and child add stickers and pictures to the A–Z pages.	The adult and child draw simple pictures side by side.	
Week 1					
Week 2					
Week 3					
Week 4					

MONTH 2	Monday	Tuesday	Wednesday	Thursday	Friday
	The adult sings and points to the ABCs. The adult and child draw all 26 capital letters side by side.	The adult sings and points to the ABCs. The adult and child draw all 26 capital letters side by side.	The adult and child add stickers and pictures to the A–Z pages.	The adult and child draw simple pictures side by side.	
Week 1					
Week 2					
Week 3					
Week 4					

MONTH 3	Monday	Tuesday	Wednesday	Thursday	Friday
	The adult sings and points to the ABCs. The adult and child draw all 26 capital letters side by side.	The adult sings and points to the ABCs. The adult and child draw all 26 capital letters side by side.	The adult and child add stickers and pictures to the A–Z pages.	The adult and child draw simple pictures side by side.	
Week 1					
Week 2					
Week 3					
Week 4					

STEP EIGHT: Write your name and label drawings and pictures.

NOTE: This step can address the following Common Core State Standards: CCSS.RF.K.1.D, RF.K.2.C, L.K.1.A and L.1.1.A.

1. Begin singing an ABC song that incorporates the name of the letter, the sound of the letter and an object that begins with that letter. Sing the song to the tune of "Frére Jaques." For example, in the ABC image below you would sing, "A-a-apple, B-b-bee, C-c-cat, D-d-dog, E-e-elephant, etc." There are many A–Z posters online and in stores. Find one that you like.

2. Continue to write all 26 capital letters side by side one time per week. Have the child say the name and sound of each letter as he or she writes it.

3. Continue to add stickers and pictures to the A–Z pages 1–2x per week.

4. Teach the child the letters in his or her name and have the child write his or her own name.

5. The child begins to label simple drawings, stickers, magazine pictures or calendar pictures by writing a capital letter for the first sound of each word.

| The adult sings the name, sound and object for each letter. | Write all 26 letters side by side. | Add stickers and pictures to each A–Z page. | Write the 1st letter of words in a picture. Above has E=ear, F=Fence, N=Nose, M=Mouth |

On the next page, you'll find the chart that lists these activities. Use a yellow marker to highlight the activities that your child completes. You can even use a pen to write the date in the highlighted box if you want. The child should complete each activity at least once a week.

STEP EIGHT: Write your name and label drawings and pictures.

MONTH 1	Monday	Tuesday	Wednesday	Thursday	Friday
	The adult sings the A–Z name, sound and object song and points to the pictures. The child and adult draw all 26 capital letters side by side.	The adult sings the A–Z name, sound and object song and points to the pictures. The child adds pictures to the A–Z binder.	The child writes his or her name and labels a drawing, sticker or picture by writing the first letter of the word.	The child writes his or her name and labels a drawing, sticker or picture by writing the first letter of the word.	
Week 1					
Week 2					
Week 3					
Week 4					

MONTH 2	Monday	Tuesday	Wednesday	Thursday	Friday
	The adult sings the A–Z name, sound and object song and points to the pictures. The child and adult draw all 26 capital letters side by side.	The adult sings the A–Z name, sound and object song and points to the pictures. The child adds pictures to the A–Z binder.	The child writes his or her name and labels a drawing, sticker or picture by writing the first letter of the word.	The child writes his or her name and labels a drawing, sticker or picture by writing the first letter of the word.	
Week 1					
Week 2					
Week 3					
Week 4					

MONTH 3	Monday	Tuesday	Wednesday	Thursday	Friday
	The adult sings the A–Z name, sound and object song and points to the pictures. The child and adult draw all 26 capital letters side by side.	The adult sings the A–Z name, sound and object song and points to the pictures. The child adds pictures to the A–Z binder.	The child writes his or her name and labels a drawing, sticker or picture by writing the first letter of the word.	The child writes his or her name and labels a drawing, sticker or picture by writing the first letter of the word.	
Week 1					
Week 2					
Week 3					
Week 4					

STEP NINE: Write words with the CVC pattern.

NOTE: This step can address the following Common Core State Standards: CCSS.RF.K.1.D, RF.K.2.C, RF.K.2.D, RF.1.2.C, L.K.1.A, L.K.2.C and L.1.1.A.

1. Continue to sing the ABC song that incorporates the name of the letter, the sound of the letter and an object that begins with that letter.

2. Continue to write all 26 capital letters side by side one time per week. Have the child say the name and sound of each letter as he or she writes it.

3. The child continues to write his or her name and draws side by side 1–2x per week.

4. Begin teaching and focusing on the short vowel sounds by writing words with the CVC pattern. CVC stands for Consonant-Vowel-Consonant. You can see the CVC pattern in the words: CAT, HAT, MAT, PAT, RAT and SAT.

   This spelling pattern is probably extremely familiar to you. However, you may not have heard it called the CVC pattern. Again, CVC means the word begins with a consonant (C), has a short vowel (V) in the middle and ends with another consonant (C).

   Begin by drawing, writing, showing and speaking, the 5 short vowel sounds. **Exaggerate** each short vowel sound as you say them: A-AAAA-APPLE, E-EEEE-EGG, I-IIII-IGLOO, O-OOOO-OCTOPUS and U-UUUU-UMBRELLA

I sketch the image above for the child as I say each letter, sound and word. They watch me draw it because doing so is more engaging to them than me pointing to a pre-drawn worksheet. You can also draw your own version and refer to it with the child each time he or she writes CVC words.

Next, have the child start writing CVC words. Students easily confuse the short A and E sounds, so I recommend teaching the CVC words in this order:

1. The short A as in CAT–HAT–RAT–SAT, MAN–PAN–RAN–VAN and DAD–HAD–MAD-SAD

2. The short I as in BIG-DIG-FIG-WIG, BIT-FIT-HIT-LIT and BIN-FIN-PIN-TIN

3. The short O as in DOT-HOT-NOT-POT, HOP-MOP-POP-TOP and MOM-BOX-FOX

4. The short U as in BUN-FUN-RUN-SUN, BUG-HUG-JUG-RUG and BUT-CUT-HUT-NUT

5. The short E as in BED-FED-RED-TED, DEN-HEN-MEN-TEN and LET-MET-NET-PET

As you work with the child, slowly say each sound of one word, C-A-T. The child writes each letter as you say its sound. In the beginning, the child may only write 1–2 words. The more they practice, the more words they can write at a time.

Here is a list of CVC words that you and your students can begin writing. Young students should still be writing capital letters at this point. Older students on this step may be using lowercase letters.

Cab	Wag	Pan	Cat	Fed	Ten	Fib	Dim	Rip	Bob	Fog	Cot	Hub	Gum	Cut
Lab	Bam	Ran	Fat	Led	Yes	Rib	Him	Sip	Cob	Hog	Dot	Rub	Hum	Gut
Dad	Ham	Tan	Hat	Red	Bet	Bid	Rim	Tip	Job	Jog	Got	Tub	Bun	Hut
Had	Jam	Cap	Mat	Ted	Get	Did	Tim	Bit	Lob	Log	Hot	Bud	Fun	Nut
Mad	Pam	Gap	Pat	Beg	Let	Hid	Bin	Fit	Rob	Mom	Lot	Mud	Gun	
Sad	Ram	Lap	Rat	Leg	Met	Lid	Fin	Hit	Sob	Tom	Not	Bug	Run	
Bag	Sam	Map	Sat	Peg	Net	Big	Pin	Lit	Cod	Bop	Pot	Hug	Sun	
Lag	Yam	Nap	Max	Ben	Pet	Dig	Tin	Pit	Nod	Cop	Rot	Jug	Cup	
Nag	Can	Rap	Wax	Den	Set	Fig	Win	Sit	Pod	Hop	Tot	Mug	Pup	
Rag	Dan	Sap	Deb	Hen	Wet	Pig	Dip	Fix	Rod	Mop	Box	Pug	Bus	
Sag	Fan	Tap	Web	Men	Yet	Rig	Hip	Mix	Sod	Pop	Fox	Rug	Gus	
Tag	Man	Bat	Bed	Pen	Bib	Wig	Lip	Six	Dog	Top	Cub	Tug	But	

| The adult sings the name, sound and object for each letter. | Draw all 26 letters side by side. | The child writes his or her name and draws a picture. (SHAY) | Write CVC words. |

Draw your own version of the short vowels found on p. 28. Place your page in a plastic protector. Refer to that page each time your child writes CVC words. On the next page, you'll find the chart that lists the activities in Step 9. Use a yellow marker to highlight the activities that your child completes. You can also use a pen to write the date in the highlighted box if you want. The child should complete each activity at least once a week.

STEP NINE: Write words with the CVC pattern.

MONTH 2	Monday	Tuesday	Wednesday	Thursday	Friday
	The adult sings the A–Z name, sound and object song while pointing to the letters and pictures. The adult and child draw all 26 capital letters side by side.	The adult sings the A–Z name, sound and object song while pointing to the letters and pictures. The child writes his or her name and draws side by side.	The child writes CVC words. Short A/I	The child writes CVC words. Short A/I	
Week 1					
Week 2					
Week 3					
Week 4					

MONTH 2	Monday	Tuesday	Wednesday	Thursday	Friday
	The adult sings the A–Z name, sound and object song while pointing to the letters and pictures. The adult and child draw all 26 capital letters side by side.	The adult sings the A–Z name, sound and object song while pointing to the letters and pictures. The child writes his or her name and draws side by side.	The child writes CVC words. Short O/U	The child writes CVC words. Short O/U	
Week 1					
Week 2					
Week 3					
Week 4					

MONTH 3	Monday	Tuesday	Wednesday	Thursday	Friday
	The adult sings the A–Z name, sound and object song while pointing to the letters and pictures. The adult and child draw all 26 capital letters side by side.	The adult sings the A–Z name, sound and object song while pointing to the letters and pictures. The child writes his or her name and draws side by side.	The child writes CVC words. Short E	The child writes CVC words. Short E	
Week 1					
Week 2					
Week 3					
Week 4					

STEP TEN: Write the words, A, THE, and AN.

NOTE: This step can address the following Common Core State Standards: CCSS.RF.K.1.D, RF.K.2.C, RF.K.2.D, RF.1.2.C, L.K.2.C and L.1.1.H.

1. Continue to sing the ABC song that incorporates the name of each letter, the sound of each letter and an object that begins with each letter.

2. The child continues to write his or her own name and draws simple pictures.

3. Continue to focus on the short vowel sounds by having the child write words with the CVC pattern.

4. Next, the child begins to write the words A, THE, and AN. After they write an article (A, THE, or AN), they get to place a sticker. Start with the article A. Teach the child that the letter A can be a **letter** OR a **word.** Show the child the words **A DOG** or **A CAT**. Have the child write the word "A", then place a sticker of a noun. Do this 3–5 times each sitting. After a month of writing and reading the word, "A", move to the words "THE" and "AN." Remember, words that follow "AN," need to begin with a vowel. Examples include: AN apple, AN elephant, AN igloo, AN octopus and AN umbrella.

The child writes the word A, THE, or AN, then, places a sticker of a noun.

In STEP 8, children learned to write the beginning sounds of words. You can take this activity a step further and have the child write the beginning sound of the sticker like the example above with the word "A.". Or you can leave this step out like the samples above with the words "THE" and "AN." Work according to the interest and stamina of the child. On the next page, you'll find the chart that lists these activities. The child should complete each activity at least once a week.

STEP TEN: Write the words, A, THE, and AN.

MONTH 1	Monday	Tuesday	Wednesday	Thursday	Friday
	The adult sings the A–Z name, sound and object song while pointing to the letters and pictures. The child writes his or her name and draws a picture.	The adult sings the A–Z name, sound and object song while pointing to the letters and pictures. The child writes 2–3 CVC words.	The child writes the word A, and places a sticker.	The child writes the word A, and places a sticker.	
Week 1					
Week 2					
Week 3					
Week 4					

MONTH 2	Monday	Tuesday	Wednesday	Thursday	Friday
	The adult sings the A–Z name, sound and object song while pointing to the letters and pictures. The child writes his or her name and draws a picture.	The adult sings the A–Z name, sound and object song while pointing to the letters and pictures. The child writes 2–3 CVC words.	The child writes the word THE, and places a sticker.	The child writes the word THE, and places a sticker.	
Week 1					
Week 2					
Week 3					
Week 4					

MONTH 3	Monday	Tuesday	Wednesday	Thursday	Friday
	The adult sings the A–Z name, sound and object song while pointing to the letters and pictures. The child writes his or her name and draws a picture.	The adult sings the A–Z name, sound and object song while pointing to the letters and pictures. The child writes 2–3 CVC words.	The child writes the word AN, and places a sticker.	The child writes the word AN, and places a sticker.	
Week 1					
Week 2					
Week 3					
Week 4					

STEP ELEVEN: Phonetically spell and write words.

NOTE: This step can address and prepare the child for the following Common Core State Standards: CCSS.RF.K.1.B, RF.K.1.D, RF.K.2, RF.K.2.C, RF.K.2.D, RF.K.3, RF.K.3.A, RF.1.2.B, RF.1.2.C, RF.1.2.D, RF.1.3, RF.1.3.B, L.K.2.C, L.K.2.D, L.1.2.D, L.1.2.E, L.2.2.D, L.3.2.F and L.4.2.D.

1. Here, the child can try to sing and point to each capital letter as he or she sings the <u>traditional</u> ABC song. Next, the child can try to sing the 2nd song, singing the name, sound and object while pointing to each letter.

2. The child continues to focus on the short vowel sounds by writing words with the CVC pattern. He or she also continues to write the words A, THE, or AN, and places a sticker or draws a picture. At this point, the child can try to combine these two skills and write two words together, such as "THE CAT" or "A DOG". They can write these words to go along with a sticker, drawing, magazine picture or old calendar picture.

3. Finally, the child can begin to phonetically write longer words. Phonetic spelling means that the child writes all of the sounds that he or she hears in a word. The words most likely won't be spelled correctly. The goal is for the child to slowly say each word and write the sounds that he or she hears. For example, in the word PEPPERS, a child might only write PPRS, or PEPRS.

   Have the child phonetically write words for stickers or pictures in their A–Z binder. They can also phonetically write words for their own drawings or calendar pictures. Start off by writing 1–2 words at a time and work up to 3–4 words at a time.

The child points to the ABCs as he or she sings them.

The child points and sings the name, sound and object of each letter.

The child writes A or THE with a CVC word

The child phonetically writes longer words.

On the next page, you'll find the chart that lists these activities. The child should complete each activity at least once a week.

STEP ELEVEN: Phonetically spell and write words.

MONTH 1	Monday	Tuesday	Wednesday	Thursday	Friday
	The child sings and points to the ABCs. The child phonetically writes 1–2 words in the A–Z binder.	The child sings the A–Z name, sound and object song while pointing to the letters and pictures. The child phonetically writes 1–2 words in the A–Z binder.	The child writes the word A, THE, or AN, and places a sticker or draws a picture.	The child writes the word A, or THE + a CVC word. The child places a sticker, draws a picture or pastes the words to a picture.	
Week 1					
Week 2					
Week 3					
Week 4					

MONTH 2	Monday	Tuesday	Wednesday	Thursday	Friday
	The child sings and points to the ABCs. The child phonetically writes 1–2 words in the A–Z binder.	The child sings the A–Z name, sound and object song while pointing to the letters and pictures. The child phonetically writes 1–2 words in the A–Z binder.	The child writes the word A, THE, or AN, and places a sticker or draws a picture.	The child writes the word A, or THE + a CVC word. The child places a sticker, draws a picture or pastes the words to a picture.	
Week 1					
Week 2					
Week 3					
Week 4					

MONTH 3	Monday	Tuesday	Wednesday	Thursday	Friday
	The child sings and points to the ABCs. The child phonetically writes 1–2 words in the A–Z binder.	The child sings the A–Z name, sound and object song while pointing to the letters and pictures. The child phonetically writes 1–2 words in the A–Z binder.	The child writes the word A, THE, or AN, and places a sticker or draws a picture.	The child writes the word A, or THE + a CVC word. The child places a sticker, draws a picture or pastes the words to a picture.	
Week 1					
Week 2					
Week 3					
Week 4					

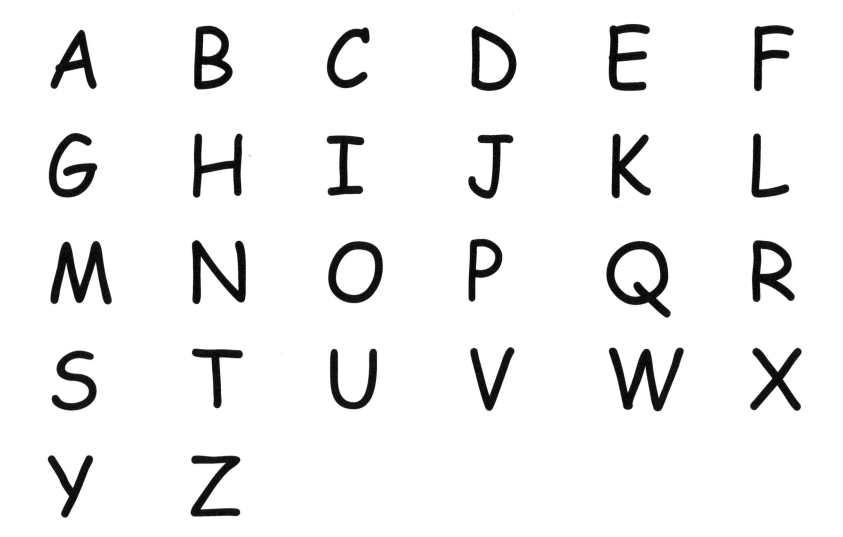

Aa   Bb   Cc   Dd   Ee

Ff   Gg   Hh   Ii   Jj

Kk   Ll   Mm   Nn   Oo

Pp   Qq   Rr   Ss   Tt

Uu   Vv   Ww   Xx   Yy

Zz

TEACHING CHILDREN HOW TO WRITE UPPER CASE (CAPITAL) LETTERS

It's important to teach children to draw **counterclockwise** circles and write the other letters, **top to bottom, left to right**. I recommend teaching the capital letters in the following order:

F—down, across from the top, across from the middle
E—down, across from the top, across from the middle, across from the bottom
H—down, down, across the middle
L—down, across
I—down, draw a hat across the top, shoes across the bottom (make sure the top and bottom lines are drawn left to right only)
T—down, draw a hat across the top (make sure the top line is drawn left to right only)

A—slide to the left, slide to the right, across the middle
N—down, back to the top, slide down to the right, up
M—down, back to the top, slide down to the right, slide up to the right, down
K—down, slide to the middle, slide to the right

V—slide down to the right, slide up to the right
W—slide down to the right, slide up to the right, slide down to the right, slide up to the right
X—slide to the right, slide to the left crossing at the middle
Y—slide to the right, slide to the left crossing at the bottom
Z—pull to the right, slide to the left, pull to the right (a left handed child will push to the right, slide to the left, push to the right)
J—down and hook to the left, draw a hat across the top (make sure the top line is drawn left to right only)
U—down and back up

O—start at the top, push your circle all the way around (a left handed child will pull the circle).
Q—start at the top, push your circle all the way around, (a left handed child will pull the circle). Start in the middle and slide to the right.
C—start at the top, push your 'C' around to the bottom (a left handed child will pull the C)
G—start at the top, push your G around to the bottom and up to the middle, back to the left (a left-handed child will pull the G)
S—start at the top, make a c, continue down and back

D—down, back to the top, curve to the bottom
P—down, back to the top, curve to the middle
B—down, back to the top, curve to the middle, curve to the bottom
R—down, back to the top, curve to the middle, slide to the right

STEP TWELVE: REVIEW and MASTER the following skills: This step assesses several Common Core State Standards noted below.

Have the child complete each step below one more time. When you know the child can complete a step easily and confidently, highlight the box next to it and write the date. If there is a step that a child cannot complete, focus on that step continually until the child has mastered it.

As soon as the child has mastered all 14 exercises, move on to Section 3 and have the child begin writing Sight Word Sentences.

ACTIVITY	COMPLETED	DATE
1. Place stickers on paper using the thumb and index finger.		
2. Color in simple shapes and spaces.		
3. Start at the top and draw a **counterclockwise** circle around a sticker.		
4. Draw a **counterclockwise** circle and turn it into an object such as a sun, balloon or face.		
5. Draw a straight line between two stickers.		
6. Draw straight lines between stickers to form a capital letter, such as an N.		
7. Side by side, draw the shapes square, triangle, rectangle and diamond.		
8. Write all 26 capital letters correctly, top to bottom, left to right. (CCSS.L.K.1.A and L.1.1.A)		
9. Say the names and sounds of all 26 letters. (CCSS.RF.K.1.D)		
10. Write his or her name using capital letters.		
11. Label simple pictures with the first letter of a word. (CCSS.RF.K.2.C)		
12. Write 2 different words that have the CVC pattern (Consonant-Vowel-Consonant), such as CAT, DAD, PEN, BIG, MOM or BUG. (CCSS.RF.K.2.C, RF.K.2.D and RF.1.2.C)		
13. Write the word A, THE, and AN, and place a sticker or draw a picture next to each word. (CCSS.L.1.1.H)		
14. Phonetically spell 2 different words found in simple drawings or pictures. (CCSS.RF.K.1.B, RF.K.2, RF.K.2.C, RF.1.2.B, RF.1.2.D, RF.1.3., RF.1.3.B, L.K.2.D, L.1.2.D, L.1.2.F, L.2.2.D, L.3.2.D and L.4.2.D)		

Note for #12: Students will continue to practice the CVC pattern in Section 3 when writing out sentences. They don't have to be able to spell every CVC word, but they should know the 5 vowel sounds well enough to write out at least 2 CVC words to move on to Section 3 of this book.

After completing these 14 tasks, reward the child liberally with praise and celebration!

SECTION 3

An Easy and On-Going Spelling Strategy

If your child or students have successfully completed the foundational Steps 1–12 that are outlined in Section 2, then they are ready to begin writing sentences! It's important to note that sight word sentences should be taught *after* a child has learned the names and sounds of the letters in the alphabet. Once children know the letter names and sounds, we can show them how those **letters** work together to form **words,** which we started to do in Section 2, Steps 8, 9, 10 and 11 of this book. Next, children can begin writing sight word sentences to see how **words** work together to form **sentences.**

Generally, around age 5, children can begin this easy and on-going spelling strategy and use it continuously throughout elementary school. It consists of children learning to **spell and read** by writing sight word sentences.

A NOTE FOR CLASSROOM TEACHERS:

Before I explain what sight word sentences are, it's important to note that throughout this spelling strategy, the following Common Core State Standards can be addressed:

1. Demonstrate understanding of the organization and basic features of print: CCSS.RF.K.1 and RF.1.1

2. Demonstrate understanding of spoken words, syllables and sounds (phonemes): CCSS.RF.K.2 and RF.1.2

3. Know and apply grade level phonics and word analysis skills in decoding words: CCSS.RF.K.3, RF.1.3, RF.2.3, RF.3.3, RF.4.3 and RF.5.3

4. Read common high frequency words by sight: CCSS.RF.K.3.C, RF.1.3.G, RF.2.3.E, RF.2.3.F and RF.3.3.D

5. Associate the long and short vowels with the common spellings (graphemes) for the five major vowels: CCSS.RF.K.3.B, RF.1.2.A, RF.1.3.C, RF.2.3.A and RF.2.3.B

6. Phonetic Spelling: CCSS.RF.K.1.B, RF.K.3, RF.K.3.A, RF.1.2.B, RF.1.2.D, RF.1.3, RF.1.3.G, RF.2.3, RF.3.3, RF.4.3, L.K.2.D, L.1.2.D, L.1.2.E, L.2.2.D, L.3.2.D and L.4.2.D

7. Reading: RF.K.4

8. Demonstrate command of the conventions of Standard English grammar and usage when writing or speaking: CCSS.L.K.1, L.1.1, L.2.1, L.3.1, L.4.1 and L.5.1

9. Demonstrate command of the conventions of standard English capitalization, punctuation and spelling when writing: CCSS.RF.1.1A, L.K.2, L.1.2, L.2.2, L.3.2, L.4.2 and L.5.2

Additional Common Core State Standards taken from www.corestandards.org/ELA-Literacy/RF/, www.corestandards.org/ELA-Literacy/W/ and www.corestandards.org/ELA-Litearcy/L/ are noted later as specific sentences, or lists of sentences, incorporate them.

Now, let's look at what sight word sentences are and how to use them!

WHAT ARE SIGHT WORD SENTENCES?

Sight word sentences are made up of high frequency words (also known as sight words). Sight words are words that are used often, but in many cases are not spelled the way that they sound. The word CAT is spelled the way that it sounds, C-A-T. The word FROM is not. If you ask an early learner how to write FROM, they will probably write F-R-U-M, the way that it sounds.

Sight words are also words that don't typically fall into a **word family**. A word family is a list of words that have the same spelling pattern, such as BAKE, CAKE and RAKE. FROM is not spelled the way that it sounds, nor does it fall into a **word family.** So it's a sight word. It is a word that students learn by writing and reading frequently.

Learning to spell by writing sight word sentences is great for **five reasons:**

1. First, children learn sight words **in context.**

2. Second, there is often one word in the sentence that can be used to teach a **spelling pattern** (or word family).

3. Third, the sentences are structured so that one word can be replaced with a related word to **build vocabulary.**

4. Fourth, they incorporate **capitalization and punctuation.**

5. Last, children learn to **read** by writing these sentences.

Because these sentences incorporate sentence structure, spelling patterns, vocabulary, capitalization and punctuation, they are especially great for English language learners.

Let's look at these five reasons in greater detail by using the sample sight word sentence:

I LIKE TO PLAY.

1. IN CONTEXT

In this example, children first learn the correct use of each word, I LIKE TO PLAY. Learning to spell these words in the context of a sentence helps students distinguish and remember **when** and **how** to use each word. Words such as "WERE, WHERE and WE'RE" are easily confused if students learn them in a list of words rather than in the context of a sentence.

2. SPELLING PATTERNS

Secondly, in the sample, I LIKE TO PLAY, children learn the spelling pattern -IKE by replacing the first letter to form new words such as bike, hike and Mike. Sight words sentences incorporate CVC word families discussed in Section 2. Subsequently, they introduce spelling patterns that make the **long vowel** sounds.

Thus, this is when I begin teaching the CVCE (consonant-vowel-consonant-silent e) and CVVC (consonant-vowel-vowel-consonant) patterns. Let's take a moment and look at these two spelling patterns since they are so common.

First, is the CVCE pattern. Here, the E at the end of the word is silent and the 1st vowel makes a LONG sound. Examples are, MADE, HERE, KITE, ROPE and CUTE.

You can teach the child or students to say, "Cover the silent E, say A---M-A-D-E. Cover the silent E, say E---H-E-R-E. Cover the silent E, say I---K-I-T-E. Cover the silent E, say O—R-O-P-E. Cover the silent E, say U—C-U-T -E," etc.

You can also show children the change from short to long vowel sounds using these pairs of words:

CAP	CAPE
PET	PETE
KIT	KITE
HOP	HOPE
CUT	CUTE

Here is a list of CVCE words that you can begin writing with your students:

Abe	Cage	Male	Mane	Vase	Gave	Eve	Life	Dime	Ripe	Robe	Bone	Sore	Rude	Muse
Gabe	Page	Pale	Vane	Ate	Pave	Ice	Wife	Lime	Wipe	Code	Cone	Tore	Huge	Cute
Ace	Bake	Sale	Cape	Date	Rave	Dice	Bike	Mime	Fire	Rode	Tone	Wore	Mule	Mute
Face	Cake	Tale	Tape	Fate	Save	Lice	Hike	Time	Hire	Poke	Zone	Hose	Rule	
Lace	Fake	Came	Bare	Gate	Wave	Mice	Like	Dine	Tire	Woke	Hope	Nose	Dune	
Pace	Make	Fame	Care	Hate	Daze	Nice	Mike	Fine	Wire	Cole	Mope	Rose	June	
Race	Rake	Name	Dare	Late	Gaze	Rice	Pike	Line	Wise	Hole	Rope	Note	Tune	
Fade	Sake	Same	Hare	Mate	Maze	Hide	File	Mine	Bite	Mole	Bore	Vote	Cure	
Made	Take	Tame	Mare	Nate	Zeke	Ride	Mile	Nine	Kite	Pole	Core	Doze	Lure	
Wade	Wake	Cane	Rare	Rate	Gene	Side	Nile	Pine	Mite	Role	Fore	Cube	Pure	
Safe	Bale	Dane	Base	Cave	Here	Tide	Pile	Vine	Size	Dome	More	Tube	Use	
Age	Kale	Lane	Case	Dave	Pete	Wide	Tile	Pipe	Lobe	Home	Pore	Dude	Fuse	

Second, is the CVVC pattern. Here, the 1st vowel makes a LONG sound. The 2nd vowel is silent. Examples are RAIN, MEAT, PIES, COAT, and SUIT. You can teach the children this traditional phrase, "The 1st vowel TALKS, the 2nd vowel WALKS (and is silent)."

Here is a list of CVVC words that you can begin writing with your students.

Maid	Tail	Pair	Peak	Bean	Hear	Neat	Seed	Peel	Deer	Tied	Oak	Boar	Foes	
Paid	Aim	Bait	Weak	Jean	Gear	Seat	Weed	Seem	Bees	Dies	Soak	Roar	Goes	
Raid	Gain	Wait	Deal	Lean	Near	Bee	Beef	Seen	Fees	Lies	Coal	Soar	Toe	
Fail	Main	Bead	Heal	Mean	Rear	Fee	Reef	Beep	Sees	Pies	Foal	Oat	Toes	
Hail	Pain	Lead	Meal	Heap	Tear	Lee	Peek	Deep	Beet	Ties	Goal	Boat	Suit	
Mail	Rain	Read	Seal	Leap	Eat	See	Seek	Jeep	Feet	Load	Foam	Coat		
Pail	Fair	Leaf	Teal	Reap	Beat	Deed	Week	Peep	Meet	Road	Loan	Goat		
Rail	Hair	Beak	Beam	Dear	Heat	Feed	Feel	Seep	Died	Toad	Moan	Moat		
Sail	Lair	Leak	Team	Fear	Meat	Need	Heel	Weep	Lied	Loaf	Soap	Foe		

The truth is, MANY words (such as said and does) will **NOT** follow these CVC, CVCE, CVVC patterns or "rules". Still, the CVCE and CVVC patterns give us a context for teaching those tricky words.

For example, I will often say, "SAID looks and is spelled like sAid (making a long A sound), but it sounds like SED. The child will often laugh when I use SAID in a sentence with the Long A sound, "Come here," I sAid. ☺ This joke helps them remember to spell said using the CVVC pattern (SAID) rather than the way that it sounds (SED).

I've used the same joke for the word DOES. I'll say, "DOES looks and is spelled like dOes (making the long O sound like in the word TOES), but it sounds like DUZ." Again, the child will chuckle when I use DOES in a sentence with the long O sound, "My mom dOes not like fish." The students laugh and remember to spell does using the CVVC pattern (DOES) rather than the way that it sounds (DUZ).

So, learning the common CVC, CVCE and CVVC patterns gives us a context for teaching words that DON'T follow spelling "rules". When students write out sight word sentences, it helps them to spell, remember and read those tricky words.

Again, after you show the new sentence to students, you will introduce the spelling pattern listed in the chart. Do this by writing a list of words that follow the pattern, such as LIKE, BIKE, HIKE, MIKE, PIKE and STRIKE. Talk about the sounds in the spelling pattern. Refer to this list throughout the week. If the child is having trouble learning the spelling pattern, have them write out the list of words themselves. Additionally, you can have the child spell the words in the list using plastic letters where they are moving and positioning the letters with their hands.

Finally, when you're introducing the spelling pattern, students do not necessarily need to know the meaning of each word in a spelling pattern. In fact, to be fun, you can add made up words! A sample list of real and made up words could be: BIKE, HIKE, JIKE, KIKE, LIKE, MIKE, PIKE, RIKE, SIKE, TIKE, WIKE, and ZIKE. Children often laugh at these silly words and in turn enjoy the process of learning the spelling pattern. In conclusion, the main purpose for showing the spelling pattern is to teach the **sounds**, not the meaning of the words.

Again, learning to spell using sight word sentences is good because children first learn the use of each word **in context**. Secondly, they learn a specific **spelling pattern** that they can use in their independent writing. Thirdly, they learn a list of vocabulary that can be used in the sentence.

3. BUILDING VOCABULARY

In the sentence, I LIKE TO <u>PLAY,</u> the underlined word <u>PLAY</u> can be replaced with various verbs to **build vocabulary**. For example, the child can write I LIKE TO RUN. I LIKE TO JUMP. I LIKE TO CLIMB. In this strategy, the children copy and write "I LIKE TO" correctly. Then, they **phonetically spell** the new words that replace PLAY. To phonetically spell means that they write the sounds that they hear. As a result, the vocabulary words that they write to replace PLAY do **not** need to be spelled correctly.

This third step is so critical! Providing the sentence to copy gives children the confidence to start writing. Allowing them the opportunity to replace one word with a new word gives them choice. This choice motivates them to write new sentences and rewards them for their work. Children enjoy sharing their sentences and emphasizing the new words that they chose to write!

Additionally, allow students to make their sentences silly. This encourages them and makes writing enjoyable for them. If a child writes, I LIKE TO SPIT, smile with them. Praise their participation and performance. Of course, use your discretion to make sure their sentences remain appropriate. As much as possible, though, let their sentences be silly. Have fun and laugh with them!

4. CAPITALIZATION and PUNCTUATION

Fourth, by using sight word sentences to teach children how to spell, they develop capitalization and punctuation skills in the process. For the first list of sight word sentences found on pages 56–69 and 86, I have students write their sentences using all capital letters. We focus primarily on making sure that our sentences end with a period. Meanwhile, as the students work through the sentences from LIST 1, I teach them how to write their lowercase letters.

Note, many teachers argue that we should teach children how to write lowercase letters first, since that's what students see the most when they are reading books. I propose differently.

To start, it's easier for young children to "draw" the capital letters first. Secondly, using the strategies found in this book, we are teaching students to write and then read what **they** have written. Essentially, the children aren't reading books or popular print at this point. They are just reading the words that **they** are writing, or words that you, the teacher or instructor, are writing. As a result, it works to have children write upper case letters first, then, lowercase letters later.

So, again, I suggest that the students begin writing sight word sentences using all capital letters. Meanwhile, as we work through the first list of sight word sentences, we spend one day a week learning how to write lowercase letters. You will see these lowercase letters noted next to Thursday on the charts that begin on page 56. On the next page, I list the verbiage that I use when teaching children how to write lowercase letters.

Lastly, when we start SENTENCES LIST 2, I guide the students to move from writing all capital letters to simply capitalizing the first letter and writing lowercase letters for everything else. This is a gradual process that students master over time. Finally, we begin teaching children to capitalize proper nouns in SENTENCES LIST 3–12 found on pages 88–107.

TEACHING CHILDREN HOW TO WRITE LOWER CASE LETTERS

First, I remind students to draw <u>counterclockwise</u> circles and write the remaining letters <u>**top to bottom, left to right**</u>. Secondly, I don't teach lowercase letters in ABC order, but rather in the order listed below. Thirdly, when I initially teach children how to draw lowercase letters we write them on one line. I point out that the **letters should sit on the line like birds on a wire and not float off the line like bubbles.** The letters that cross the bottom line "dangle their feet". Later, if a child is still struggling with the height or position of letters, we will practice writing those letters on notebook paper where there is a top, middle and bottom line. (See page 49) Again, if a child writes a letter incorrectly, have them simply move forward and try again. Finally, I recommend using the following verbiage:

SMALL (not tall) COUNTERCLOCKWISE CIRCLES: Starting in the middle of the space

c—start at the top, push your curve up, down and around (a left handed child pulls it)

o—start at the top, push your circle up all the way around (a left-handed child pulls it)

a—start at the top, push your circle all the way around, draw a short stick

d—start at the top, push your circle all the way around, top-down, or DONUT-DUNK-D

g—start at the top, push your circle around, draw down past the line, hook left

q—start at the top, push your circle around, draw down past the line, hook right

u—"q and u stick together like glue", start at the middle, draw down, curve up, down

SMALL (not tall) LETTERS: Starting in the middle of the space

p---draw down past the line, back to the top, curve down to the line

j—draw down past the line, hook left, dot above the top

i---draw down, dot above the top

r—draw down, back up the same line, hook right

n—draw down, back up the same line, draw a tunnel

m—draw down, back up the same line, draw a tunnel, tunnel

v—slide down to the line, slide up to the right

w—slide down to the line, slide up to the right, slide down to the line, slide up to right

x—slide down to the line, slide down to the left crossing at the middle of the first line

y—slide down to the line, slide down to the left crossing at the bottom of the first line

z—pull to the right, slide to the left, pull to the right

A left handed child will push to the right, slide to the left, push to the right

e—pull to the right, push up and around like a 'c'

A left handed child will push to the right, pull up and around like a 'c'

s—start at the top, make a c, continue around, down and back

TALL (not small) LETTERS: Starting at the top of the space

l—start tall, draw down

t—start tall, draw down, cross at the middle

h—start tall, draw down, back up to the middle, tunnel

b—start tall, draw down, back up to the middle, curve to the bottom, or BACK-BELLY-B

k—start tall, draw down, slide down to the left, slide down to the line

f—start high, push up to the left, around, down to the line, cross at the middle

A left handed child will pull up to the left.

Here, a 6 year old and I wrote all 26 lowercase letters side by side on one line and on notebook paper:

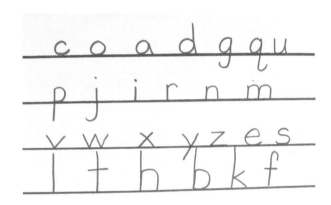

My letters

A 6 year old writing on one line

My letters

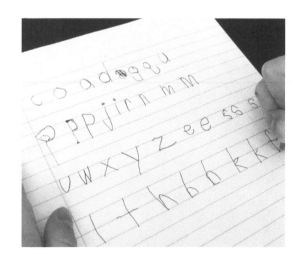

A six year old writing on notebook paper

5. CHILDREN LEARN TO READ

Fifth and finally, writing sight word sentences teaches children how to **read**. As a child learns to **write**, I LIKE TO PLAY, they learn how to spell I LIKE TO PLAY. Once they know how to **spell** I LIKE TO PLAY, they will be able to recognize I, LIKE, TO and PLAY in books and ultimately **read** those words!

The kinesthetic act of writing out the sentence slows the child down and causes them to produce the word. If they can produce the word and put it on paper, it will be easier for them to recognize and read the word when they see it in books. Because of this, I strongly suggest that you KEEP each child's writing for them to read regularly. After a child has written a sentence, put it in a plastic page protector and into a 3 ring-binder. 1−3x per week, have the child open his or her binder and read the sentences that he or she has written. Fundamentally, this binder will be the first "book" that the child reads!

Without hesitation, I strongly recommend that you focus solely on writing before reading. Doing so helps cement a child's literacy skills from the very beginning. Have them read what **they** have written or books that contain the words that they are writing.

Moreover, you, the instructor, can write simple sentences using the same sight words that the students are learning to write. The greatest advantage to this strategy is that you can incorporate the interests of each child, whether it be Star Wars, cheetahs, sharks, Dude Perfect, Elsa, what have you!!

A 5 ½ year old working on
SENTENCES LIST 1.

A 6 ½ year old working on
SENTENCES LIST 3.

Once you've written sentences for the child to read, you can have the child highlight the sight words that he or she knows. The child can read the highlighted words, while the parent or teacher reads the plain words. Additionally, the child can search for and highlight words that he or she knows in books that you own. When the child is done, he or she can read the highlighted words while the teacher or parent reads the plain words.

Now that we know why and how writing sight words sentences helps children learn to write, spell and read, let's look at how to logistically teach these sight word sentences and use them with your child or students!

TEACHING SIGHT WORD SENTENCES

MATERIALS:

The materials each student needs to complete these exercises are:

1. White copy paper and markers

2. A three ring binder and plastic page protectors

3. Stickers, calendar pictures or magazine pictures

PACE:

Students who have completed the foundational Steps 1–12 from Section 2 of this book are most likely starting to write sentences for the 1st time. For this reason, it's important to go slow in the beginning. Consider spending 2 weeks on one sentence. As the children strengthen their phonemic awareness, get used to tricky spelling and grow more comfortable writing sentences, they can speed up to 1 sentence per week.

For this reason, I chart how to use these sentences day by day and week by week for SENTENCES LIST 1 and 2. These charts begin on page 56. On pages 54–55, I outline how to use these sentences with older students.

FOR EACH SENTENCE:

1. **Introduce the new sentence.**
   The first thing that you will do is write and read the new sentence to the child or group of students. Point to each word as you read it. Lastly, if you are working with language learners, verbally translate the sentence in their native language, if possible.

2. **Introduce the spelling pattern.**
   Next, you will point out and discuss the spelling pattern for the week. You will notice that these sight word sentences give students an opportunity to continue practicing the CVC (consonant-short vowel-consonant) pattern that was introduced in Step 9 on pages 28–30. Additionally, the sentences will introduce spelling patterns that make the long vowel sounds.

3. **Introduce the vocabulary.**
   The 3rd step in teaching a new sight word sentence is to introduce a list of words that fit the vocabulary theme (i.e. colors, people, objects, verbs, etc.) Talk about words that the students know and are interested in as well as words that they may not know yet. This is the time to focus on the MEANINGS of words. When teaching vocabulary, it's important to incorporate lots of drawings and pictures. Children need to SEE the words that they are learning.

4. **Teach students correct capitalization and punctuation.**
   The fourth step in introducing a new sight word sentence to children is teaching them capitalization and punctuation rules. For LIST 1, students will write their sentences in capital letters and include a period. In LIST2, you can start teaching that the first letter of the sentence is capitalized and the rest of the letters are lowercase. It's normal for children to mix capital letters for a while.

   Further along in LISTS 3–12, (found on pages 88–107), there will be opportunities to teach proper nouns that are capitalized, as well as other punctuation, such as question marks (?), exclamation marks (!), commas (,), apostrophes (') and quotation marks (").

5. **Have the students write and read.**
   Finally, have each child copy his or her sentence 1–3 times. Make sure they read their sentences after they write them.

STARTING SIGHT WORD SENTENCES WITH OLDER STUDENTS

If you want to use sight word sentences with older students, the first thing you need to do is find out which words each child can already spell. Follow the steps below to find out which list of sentences the child should start on:

MATERIALS

You'll need white copy paper and a marker or pen.

WRITING WORDS

1. Print WORDS LIST 1 (found at the bottom of page 86).

2. Read off one word at a time.

3. The child writes each word that you say on a separate sheet of paper.

4. Highlight each word on the list that the child spells correctly. If the child spells all of the words correctly on WORDS LIST 1, move to WORDS LIST 2 on the next page. This can be done in the same sitting or on another day. Continue until the child cannot spell all of the words correctly on a list. If the child can't spell all the words on LIST 1, then, the child will begin writing sentences from SENTENCES LIST 1. If the child can spell all of the words through list 3 correctly, but not all of the words on LIST 4, then, he or she will begin with SENTENCES LIST 4, and so on.

WRITING SENTENCES

Second, go to the SENTENCES LIST 1–12 (found on pages 86–107). Find the list that the child needs to start on.

You, the teacher or parent, write out the first sentence from the SENTENCES LIST on a piece of white copy paper or in a notebook. Point out the noted spelling pattern and discuss new vocabulary. Then, the child copies the sentence **3 times.** The 2nd and 3rd time that the child copies the sentence, he or she changes the underlined word to a new word. Every word needs to be written correctly **except** the underlined word. If the child doesn't know how to spell the new underlined word, he or she spells it phonetically by writing the sounds that he or she hears in the word. (Phonetic spelling is discussed on pages 34–35.) For example, if the child's sentence is I LIKE TO PLAY, he or she might write, I LIKE TO <u>PLAY</u>, I LIKE TO <u>KLIM</u>, I LIKE TO <u>DANS</u>.

Thus, the words that replace the underlined word **do not** need to be spelled correctly.

When your child writes the sentences, **each sentence should have nice handwriting, a capital letter at the beginning, spaces, correct spelling and punctuation at the end**. If your child writes a sentence incorrectly or sloppily, simply have him or her write it one more time. If possible, allow your child to write using pen or marker to make it more colorful and visible.

A WEEKLY SCHEDULE FOR OLDER STUDENTS

If you are working with older students, I suggest using the following schedule each week to complete these sight word sentences.

1. On, Monday, Tuesday and Wednesday, write the sentence on a piece of paper or in the child's notebook. Point out the spelling pattern and discuss any new vocabulary. The child writes the sentence 3 times, changing the underlined word each time.

2. On Thursday and Friday, the child can write freely about ANY one topic that interests him or her. Topics can include Non-Fiction Facts, Personal Narratives, How-To Instructions, Opinions, Persuasions, Letters, Summaries or Creative Stories. A general expectation for each grade is:

> K—1st Graders should try to write at least 5 sentences per topic
>
> 2nd Graders should try to write at least 10 sentences per topic
>
> 3rd Graders should try to write at least 15 sentences per topic
>
> 4th Graders should try to write at least 20 sentences per topic
>
> 5th Graders should try to write at least 25 sentences per topic

However, an older student who is working on LIST 1 or 2 will probably only write 5 sentences per topic. That child will gradually work up to 15—25 sentences as he or she moves through the lists of sentences and learns to spell more words.

If your child or students are having trouble thinking of topics to write about on Thursdays and Fridays, or if they are having trouble organizing their ideas when they write, turn to Section 4 of this book. There, I outline how to guide children to completing stories and essays. Then, in Section 5, I include an academic year's worth of guided writing lessons for you to use and choose from. Furthermore, you can find complete guided writing lessons on my website, www.funwritingideas.com.

THE FOLLOWING WEEK

The following Monday, introduce the **next sentence** from the SENTENCES LIST. Write the sentence on a piece of paper or in the child's notebook. The child copies the new sentence **3 times on Monday, 3 times on Tuesday and 3 times on Wednesday.** On **Thursday and Friday,** the child writes freely about ANY one topic. Continue this pattern week after week progressing through the sentences.

If you see that the child is learning to spell the words and sentences quickly, you can have him or her cover 2—3 sentences per week. Or, the child can cover one sentence from the list and 1—2 sentences that you create based on words that the child misspells in his or her free writing. For example, if the child misspells "LERN" in free writing. You can create the sentence, "I want to learn about <u>bears</u>." Copy and use the following chart to keep track of each child's progress.

An Easy and On-Going Spelling Strategy

NAME: _____   MONTH/YEAR: _____   AGE/GRADE: _____

	Monday _co-op_	Tuesday _class_	Wednesday _class_	Thursday _sentence_	Friday _free_
	COPY SIGHT WORD SENTENCES			**WRITE FREELY**	
WEEK 1	Copy this sentence 3 times: Teach this spelling pattern:	Copy this sentence 3 times: Review the spelling pattern. Teach this vocabulary:	Copy this sentence 3 times: Review the spelling pattern. Review the vocabulary:	TOPIC: # of sentences:	TOPIC: # of sentences:
WEEK 2	Copy this sentence 3 times: Teach this spelling pattern:	Copy this sentence 3 times: Review the spelling pattern. Teach this vocabulary:	Copy this sentence 3 times: Review the spelling pattern. Review the vocabulary:	TOPIC: # of sentences:	TOPIC: # of sentences:
WEEK 3	Copy this sentence 3 times: Teach this spelling pattern:	Copy this sentence 3 times: Review the spelling pattern. Teach this vocabulary:	Copy this sentence 3 times: Review the spelling pattern. Review the vocabulary:	TOPIC: # of sentences:	TOPIC: # of sentences:
WEEK 4	Copy this sentence 3 times: Teach this spelling pattern:	Copy this sentence 3 times: Review the spelling pattern. Teach this vocabulary:	Copy this sentence 3 times: Review the spelling pattern. Review the vocabulary:	TOPIC: # of sentences:	TOPIC: # of sentences:

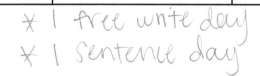

* 1 free write day
* 1 sentence day

Now, let's start with **SENTENCES LIST 1!**

Remember, if your child or students have successfully completed the foundational Steps 1–12 that are outlined in Section 2 of this book, then they are ready to begin writing sentences! These sentences can be used with one child or with a class of students. Thus, when I write out the instructions for each day, I will refer to a single child or a group of students interchangeably.

Additional Common Core State Standards that these activities can address are CCSS.L.K.1.A, L.K.2.A, L.1.1.A, RF.K.2.A, RF.K.2.C, RF.K.2.D, RF.K.3.D, RF.K.2.E and RF.1.2.C

SENTENCE #1	I AM (CHILD'S NAME).	
SPELLING PATTERN: _____ AM	FOCUS VOCABULARY:	NAMES
MONDAY	Using all capital letters, write the sentence **I AM <u>(CHILD'S NAME)</u>.** on a piece of paper. The child copies the sentence **ONE TIME.** Make sure they write the period. Add a picture of the child! (optional)	
TUESDAY	Write out and say the sounds for the word family, _AM, HAM, JAM, PAM, RAM, SAM The child writes the sentence I AM <u>(NAME)</u>. **ONE TIME.** Make sure they write the period at the end.	
WEDNESDAY	Write out and say the sounds for the word family, __AM, HAM, JAM, PAM, RAM, SAM The child writes the sentence I AM <u>(NAME)</u>. **ONE TIME.** Make sure they write the period at the end.	
THURSDAY	Review the word family, _AM, HAM, JAM, PAM, RAM, SAM Using the verbiage on page 48, the teacher and child write each lowercase letter **c, o,** and **a** side by side **5–10 times.**	
FRIDAY	Review the word family, _AM, HAM, JAM, PAM, RAM, SAM The child draws a picture, then labels it with beginning sounds or phonetic spelling.	
MONDAY	Using all capital letters, write the sentence **I AM <u>(CHILD'S NAME)</u>.** on a piece of paper. The child copies the sentence **ONE TIME** and draws a picture. Make sure they write the period at the end. Review the word family, _AM, HAM, JAM, PAM, RAM, SAM	
TUESDAY	Teach the names of people the child knows: DAD, MOM, TOM, DEB, etc. The child writes, I AM <u>(name)</u>. **ONE TIME.** The child writes, I AM <u>(and phonetically spells the name of someone he or she knows)</u>. **1–2 times**	
WEDNESDAY	Talk about the names of family, classmates and friends that the child knows. The child writes, I AM <u>(name)</u>. **ONE TIME.** The child writes: I AM <u>(and phonetically spells the name of someone he or she knows)</u>. **1–2 times**	
THURSDAY	Review the word family, _AM, HAM, JAM, PAM, RAM, SAM and names of people. Using the verbiage on page 48, the teacher and child write each lowercase letter **c, o,** and **a** side by side **5-10 times.**	
FRIDAY	Review the word family, _AM, HAM, JAM, PAM, RAM, SAM and names of people. The child draws a picture of anything, then labels it with beginning sounds and phonetic spelling.	

NOTE: Place the child's writing in plastic page protectors and a 3 ring binder for reading and review. **Again, I strongly recommend that you focus solely on writing at this stage.** If the children read anything, have them read what they have written. In addition to reading their sight word sentences, they can read simple sentences that you write. Be sure and write sentences that include the words they have learned to write as well as topics that interest them.

An Easy and On-Going Spelling Strategy

Additional Common Core State Standards that these activities can address are CCSS.L.K.1.A, L.K.2.A, L.1.1.A, RF.K.2.A, RF.K.2.C, RF.K.2.D, RF.K.3.D, RF.K.2.E and RF.1.2.C

SENTENCE #2	I AM SAD.	
SPELLING PATTERN: _____ AD	FOCUS VOCABULARY: FEELINGS	
MONDAY	Using all capital letters, write the sentence **I AM SAD.** on a piece of paper. Emphasize the period at the end. The child copies the sentence **ONE TIME** and draws a picture of a sad face. Review the word family, _AM, HAM, JAM, PAM, RAM, SAM	
TUESDAY	Review the word family, _AM, HAM, JAM, PAM, RAM, SAM Write and say the sounds for the word family, _AD, BAD, DAD, HAD, GLAD, MAD, SAD The child writes the sentence I AM SAD. **ONE TIME** and draws a picture of a sad face.	
WEDNESDAY	Review the word families AM, HAM, JAM, PAM, RAM, SAM and BAD, DAD, HAD, GLAD, MAD, SAD The child copies the sentence I AM SAD. **ONE TIME** and draws a picture of a sad face.	
THURSDAY	Review the word families AM, HAM, JAM, PAM, RAM, SAM and BAD, DAD, HAD, GLAD, MAD, SAD Using the verbiage on page 48, the teacher and child write each lowercase letter **c, o, a, d** and **g** side by side **5–10 times.**	
FRIDAY	Review the word families AM, HAM, JAM, PAM, RAM, SAM and BAD, DAD, HAD, GLAD, MAD, SAD The child draws a picture, then, labels it with beginning sounds or phonetic spelling.	
MONDAY	Using all capital letters, write the sentence **I AM SAD** on a piece of paper. The child copies the sentence **ONE TIME** and draws a picture of a sad face. Review the word families AM, HAM, JAM, PAM, RAM, SAM and BAD, DAD, HAD, GLAD, MAD, SAD	
TUESDAY	Teach feelings vocabulary: SAD, MAD, GLAD, HAPPY, HUNGRY, TIRED, etc. The child writes: I AM SAD. ONE TIME The child writes: I AM (and phonetically spells a feeling word). **1–2 times,** then, draws a picture	
WEDNESDAY	Teach feelings vocabulary: SAD, MAD, GLAD, HAPPY, HUNGRY, TIRED, etc. The child writes: I AM SAD. **ONE TIME** The child writes: I AM (and phonetically spells a feeling word). **1–2 times,** then, draws a picture	
THURSDAY	Review the word families AM, HAM, JAM, PAM, RAM, SAM and BAD, DAD, HAD, GLAD, MAD, SAD and feelings vocabulary. Using the verbiage on page 48, the teacher and child write each lowercase letter **c, o, a, d** and **g** side by side **5–10 times.**	
FRIDAY	Review the word families _AM, HAM, JAM, PAM, RAM, SAM and BAD, DAD, HAD, GLAD, MAD, SAD and feelings vocabulary. The child draws a picture of anything, then labels it with beginning sounds and phonetic spelling	

NOTE: Place the child's writing in plastic page protectors and a 3 ring binder for reading and review. Again, I strongly recommend that you focus solely on writing at this stage. If the children read anything, have them read what they have written. In addition to reading their sight word sentences, they can read simple sentences that you write. Be sure and write sentences that include the words they have learned to write as well as topics that interest them.

Additional Common Core State Standards that these activities can address are CCSS.L.K.1.A, L.K.2.A, L.1.1.A, RF.K.2.A, RF.K.2.C, RF.K.2.D, RF.K.3.D, RF.K.2.E and RF.1.2.C

SENTENCE #3	I AM A <u>CAT</u>.	
SPELLING PATTERN: _____ AT	FOCUS VOCABULARY: ANIMALS	
MONDAY	Using all capital letters, write the sentence **I AM A <u>CAT</u>.** on a piece of paper. Emphasize the period at the end. The child copies the sentence **ONE TIME** and adds a sticker or pastes the sentence to a picture of a cat. Review the word families, _AM, HAM, JAM, PAM, RAM, SAM and BAD, DAD, HAD, GLAD, MAD, SAD	
TUESDAY	Review the word families, _AM, HAM, JAM, PAM, RAM, SAM and BAD, DAD, HAD, GLAD, MAD, SAD Write and say the sounds for the word family, _AT, BAT, CAT, FAT, HAT, MAT, RAT, SAT The child writes the sentence I AM A CAT. **ONE TIME** and adds a sticker, calendar picture or drawing of a cat.	
WEDNESDAY	Review the word families _AM, HAM, JAM, RAM, SAM, _AD, BAD, DAD, HAD, MAD, SAD, and _AT, BAT, CAT, HAT, MAT, RAT, SAT The child copies the sentence I AM A CAT. **ONE TIME** and adds a sticker, calendar picture or drawing of a cat.	
THURSDAY	Review the word families _AM, HAM, JAM, RAM, SAM, _AD, BAD, DAD, HAD, MAD, SAD, and _AT, BAT, CAT, HAT, MAT, RAT, SAT Using the verbiage on page 48, the teacher and child write each lowercase letter **c, o, a, d, g, q, u** and **p** side by side **5–10 times.**	
FRIDAY	Review the word families _AM, HAM, JAM, RAM, SAM, _AD, BAD, DAD, HAD, MAD, SAD, and _AT, BAT, CAT, HAT, MAT, RAT, SAT The child draws a picture, then labels it with beginning sounds or phonetic spelling.	
MONDAY	Using all capital letters, write the sentence **I AM A <u>CAT</u>.** on a piece of paper. The child copies the sentence **ONE TIME.** Add a sticker or paste the sentence to a picture of a cat. Review the word families _AM, HAM, JAM, RAM, SAM, _AD, BAD, DAD, HAD, MAD, SAD, and _AT, BAT, CAT, HAT, MAT, RAT, SAT	
TUESDAY	Teach animal vocabulary: CAT, RAT, HEN, FISH, PIG, DOG, COW, PUP, etc. The child writes: I AM A CAT. **ONE TIME** The child writes: I AM A <u>(and phonetically spells an animal word)</u>. **1–2 times** The child adds a sticker, calendar picture or drawing of the animal.	
WEDNESDAY	Teach animal vocabulary: CAT, RAT, HEN, FISH, PIG, DOG, COW, PUP, etc. The child writes: I AM A CAT. **ONE TIME** The child writes: I AM <u>(and phonetically spells an animal word)</u>. **1–2 times** The child adds a sticker, calendar picture or drawing of the animal.	
THURSDAY	Review the word families for _AM, __AD and __AT and animal vocabulary. Using the verbiage on page 48, the teacher and child write each lowercase letter **c, o, a, d, g, q, u** and **p** side by side **5–10 times.**	
FRIDAY	Review the word families for _AM, __AD and __AT and animal vocabulary. The child draws a picture of anything, then labels it with beginning sounds and phonetic spelling.	

NOTE: Place the child's writing in plastic page protectors and a 3 ring binder for reading and review. Again, I strongly recommend that you focus solely on writing at this stage. If the children read anything, have them read what they have written. In addition to reading their sight word sentences, they can read simple sentences that you write. Be sure and write sentences that include the words they have learned to write as well as topics that interest them.

An Easy and On-Going Spelling Strategy

Additional Common Core State Standards that these activities can address are CCSS.L.K.1.A, L.K.2.A, L.1.1.A, RF.K.2.A, RF.K.2.C, RF.K.2.D, RF.K.3.D, RF.K.2.E and RF.1.2.C

SENTENCE #4	I SEE A <u>DOG</u>.
SPELLING PATTERN: _____ OG	FOCUS VOCABULARY: ANIMALS
MONDAY	Using all capital letters, write the sentence **I SEE A <u>DOG.</u>** on a piece of paper. Emphasize the period at the end. The child copies the sentence **ONE TIME** and adds a sticker or pastes the sentence to a picture of a dog. Write and say the sounds for the word family, _OG, DOG, FOG, FROG, HOG, LOG.
TUESDAY	Write and say the sounds for the word family, _OG, DOG, FOG, FROG, HOG, LOG The child writes the sentence I SEE A DOG. **ONE TIME.** The child adds a sticker, calendar picture or drawing of a dog.
WEDNESDAY	Write and say the sounds for the word family, _OG, DOG, FOG, FROG, HOG, LOG The child writes the sentence I SEE A DOG. **ONE TIME.** The child adds a sticker, calendar picture or drawing of a dog.
THURSDAY	Review the word family, _OG, DOG, FOG, FROG, HOG, LOG Using the verbiage on page 48, the teacher and child write each lowercase letter **q, u, p, j, i, r, n** and **m** side by side **5-10 times.**
FRIDAY	Review the word family, _OG, DOG, FOG, FROG, HOG, LOG The child draws a picture, then labels it with beginning sounds or phonetic spelling.
MONDAY	Using all capital letters, write the sentence **I SEE A <u>DOG.</u>** on a piece of paper. Emphasize the period at the end. The child copies the sentence **ONE TIME.** Add a sticker or paste the sentence to a picture of a dog. Review the word family, _OG, DOG, FOG, FROG, HOG, LOG
TUESDAY	Teach animal vocabulary: BEAR, CUB, HORSE, DOLPHIN, LIZARD, SHARK, etc. The child writes: I SEE A DOG. **ONE TIME** The child writes: I SEE A (and phonetically spells an animal word). **1–2 times** The child adds a sticker, calendar picture or drawing of the animal.
WEDNESDAY	Teach animal vocabulary: BEAR, CUB, HORSE, DOLPHIN, LIZARD, SHARK, etc. The child writes: I SEE A DOG. **ONE TIME** The child writes: I SEE A (and phonetically spells an animal word). **1–2 times** The child adds a sticker, calendar picture or drawing of the animal.
THURSDAY	Review the word family, _OG, DOG, FOG, FROG, HOG, LOG and animal vocabulary. Using the verbiage on page 48, the teacher and child write each lowercase letter **q, u, p, j, i, r, n** and **m** side by side **5–10 times.**
FRIDAY	Review the word family, _OG, DOG, FOG, FROG, HOG, LOG and animal vocabulary. The child draws a picture, then labels it with beginning sounds or phonetic spelling.

NOTE: Place the child's writing in plastic page protectors and a 3 ring binder for reading and review. Again, I strongly recommend that you focus solely on writing at this stage. If the children read anything, have them read what they have written. In addition to reading their sight word sentences, they can read simple sentences that you write. Be sure and write sentences that include the words they have learned to write as well as topics that interest them

Additional Common Core State Standards that these activities can address are CCSS.L.K.1.A, L.K.2.A, L.1.1.A, RF.K.2.A, RF.K.2.C, RF.K.2.D, RF.K.3.D, RF.K.2.E and RF.1.2.C

SENTENCE #5	THE WIG IS <u>RED</u>
SPELLING PATTERN: _____ IG and _____ ED	FOCUS VOCABULARY: COLORS

MONDAY	Using all capital letters, write the sentence THE WIG IS <u>RED.</u> on a piece of paper. Emphasize the period at the end. The child copies the sentence **ONE TIME** and draws a picture of a red wig. Write and say the sounds for the word family, BIG, DIG, FIG, PIG, TWIG, WIG.
TUESDAY	Write and say the sounds for the word family, BIG, DIG, FIG, PIG, TWIG, WIG The child writes the sentence THE WIG IS RED. **ONE TIME**
WEDNESDAY	Write and say the sounds for the word family, RED, BED, FED, LED, NED, TED, WED The child writes the sentence THE WIG IS RED. **ONE TIME** The child draws a wig on red construction paper, cuts it out and pastes it to a picture of an animal.
THURSDAY	Review the word families, BIG, DIG, FIG, PIG, TWIG, WIG and RED, BED, FED, LED, NED, TED, WED Using the verbiage on page 48, the teacher and child write each lowercase letter **i, r, n, m, v, w, x** and **y** side by side **5–10 times.**
FRIDAY	Review the word families, BIG, DIG, FIG, PIG, TWIG, WIG and RED, BED, FED, LED, NED, TED, WED The child draws a picture, then labels it with beginning sounds or phonetic spelling.
MONDAY	Using all capital letters, write the sentence **THE WIG IS <u>RED.</u>** on a piece of paper. Emphasize the period at the end. The child copies the sentence **ONE TIME** and draws a picture of a red wig. Review the word families, BIG, DIG, FIG, PIG, TWIG, WIG and RED, BED, FED, LED, NED, TED, WED
TUESDAY	Teach color vocabulary: RED, ORANGE, YELLOW, GREEN, BLUE, PURPLE, BLACK, etc. The child writes: THE WIG IS RED. **ONE TIME** The child writes: THE WIG IS <u>(and phonetically spells a color word)</u>. **1–2 times** The child draws wigs on construction paper, cuts them out and pastes them to pictures of animals.
WEDNESDAY	Teach color vocabulary: BROWN, GRAY, PINK, WHITE, etc. The child writes: THE WIG IS RED. **ONE TIME** The child writes: THE WIG IS <u>(and phonetically spells a color word)</u>. **1–2 times** The child draws wigs on construction paper, cuts them out and pastes them to pictures of animals.
THURSDAY	Review the word families, BIG, DIG, FIG, PIG, TWIG, WIG and RED, BED, FED, LED, NED, TED, WED and color vocabulary. Using the verbiage on page 48, the teacher and child write each lowercase letter **i, r, n, m, v, w, x** and **y** side by side **5–10 times.**
FRIDAY	Review the word families, BIG, DIG, FIG, PIG, TWIG, WIG and RED, BED, FED, LED, NED, TED, WED and color vocabulary. The child draws a picture, then labels it with beginning sounds or phonetic spelling.

NOTE: Place the child's writing in plastic page protectors and a 3 ring binder for reading and review. Again, I strongly recommend that you focus solely on writing at this stage. If the children read anything, have them read what they have written. In addition to reading their sight word sentences, they can read simple sentences that you write. Be sure and write sentences that include the words they have learned to write as well as topics that interest them

Additional Common Core State Standards that these activities can address are CCSS.L.K.1.A, L.K.1.B, L.K.2.A, L.1.1.A, RF.K.2.A, RF.K.2.C, RF.K.2.D, RF.K.3.D, RF.K.2.E and RF.1.2.C

SENTENCE #6	I CAN RUN.	
SPELLING PATTERN: _____ AN and _____ UN	FOCUS VOCABULARY: VERBS	
MONDAY	Using all capital letters, write the sentence **I CAN RUN.** on a piece of paper. Emphasize the period at the end. The child copies the sentence **ONE TIME** and draws a picture. Write and say the sounds for the word family, CAN, DAN, FAN, MAN, PAN, RAN, TAN	
TUESDAY	Write and say the sounds for the word family, CAN, DAN, FAN, MAN, PAN, RAN, TAN The child writes the sentence I CAN RUN. **ONE TIME** and draws a picture.	
WEDNESDAY	Write and say the sounds for the word family, RUN, BUN, FUN, GUN, SUN The child writes the sentence I CAN RUN. **ONE TIME** and draws a picture.	
THURSDAY	Review the word families CAN, DAN, FAN, MAN, PAN, RAN, TAN and RUN, BUN, FUN, GUN, SUN Using the verbiage on page 48, the teacher and child write each lowercase letter **v, w, x, y, z, e** and **s** side by side **5–10 times.**	
FRIDAY	Review the word families CAN, DAN, FAN, MAN, PAN, RAN, TAN and RUN, BUN, FUN, GUN, SUN The child draws a picture, then labels it with beginning sounds or phonetic spelling.	
MONDAY	Using all capital letters, write the sentence **I CAN RUN.** on a piece of paper. Emphasize the period at the end. The child copies the sentence **ONE TIME** and draws a picture. Review the word families CAN, DAN, FAN, MAN, PAN, RAN, TAN and RUN, BUN, FUN, GUN, SUN	
TUESDAY	Teach the children that a verb is an action word. It's something that they can *do.* Discuss and write a list of verbs: RUN, HOP, JUMP, SING, DANCE, SIT, NOD, etc. The child writes: I CAN RUN. **ONE TIME** The child writes: I CAN (and phonetically spells a verb). **1–2 times,** then, draws a picture.	
WEDNESDAY	Teach the children that a verb is an action word. It's something that they can *do.* Discuss and write a list of verbs: RUN, HOP, JUMP, SING, DANCE, SIT, NOD, etc. The child writes: I CAN RUN. **ONE TIME** The child writes: I CAN (and phonetically spells a verb). **1–2 times,** then, draws a picture.	
THURSDAY	Review the word families CAN, DAN, FAN, MAN, PAN, RAN, TAN and RUN, BUN, FUN, GUN, SUN and verbs. Using the verbiage on page 48, the teacher and child write each lowercase letter **v, w, x, y, z, e** and **s** side by side **5–10 times.**	
FRIDAY	Review the word families CAN, DAN, FAN, MAN, PAN, RAN, TAN and RUN, BUN, FUN, GUN, SUN and verbs The child draws a picture, then labels it with beginning sounds or phonetic spelling.	

NOTE: Place the child's writing in plastic page protectors and a 3 ring binder for reading and review. Again, I strongly recommend that you focus solely on writing at this stage. If the children read anything, have them read what they have written. In addition to reading their sight word sentences, they can read simple sentences that you write. Be sure and write sentences that include the words they have learned to write as well as topics that interest them.

Kids Win at Writing!

Additional Common Core State Standards that these activities can address are CCSS.L.K.1.A, L.K.1.B, L.K.2.A, RF.K.3.B, RF.1.2.A, RF.1.3.C, RF. 2.3.A and RF.2.3.B

SENTENCE #7	I LIKE TO <u>PLAY</u>.	
SPELLING PATTERN: _____ IKE	FOCUS VOCABULARY: VERBS	
MONDAY	Using all capital letters, write the sentence **I LIKE TO <u>PLAY.</u>** on a piece of paper. Emphasize the period at the end. The child copies the sentence **ONE TIME** and draws a picture. Write and say the sounds for the word family, LIKE, BIKE, HIKE, MIKE, PIKE, STRIKE	
TUESDAY	Write and say the sounds for the word family, LIKE, BIKE, HIKE, MIKE, PIKE, STRIKE Here, the child learns the silent E that makes the "I" a LONG I sound. Teach the child to "cover the silent E and say I---L-I-K-E, cover the silent E, say I---B-I-K-E," etc. The child writes the sentence I LIKE TO PLAY. **ONE TIME** and draws a picture.	
WEDNESDAY	Review the sounds for the word family, LIKE, BIKE, HIKE, MIKE, PIKE, STRIKE Again, teach the child to "cover the silent E and say I---L-I-K-E, cover the silent E, say I---B-I-K-E," etc. The child writes the sentence I LIKE TO PLAY. **ONE TIME** and draws a picture.	
THURSDAY	Review the word family, LIKE, BIKE, HIKE, MIKE, PIKE, STRIKE Using the verbiage on page 48, the teacher and child write each lowercase letter **z, e, s, l, t** and **h** side by side **5–10 times.**	
FRIDAY	Review the word family, LIKE, BIKE, HIKE, MIKE, PIKE, STRIKE The child draws a picture, then labels it with beginning sounds or phonetic spelling.	
MONDAY	Using all capital letters, write the sentence **I LIKE TO <u>PLAY.</u>** on a piece of paper. Emphasize the period at the end. The child copies the sentence **ONE TIME** and draws a picture. Review the word family, LIKE, BIKE, HIKE, MIKE, PIKE, STRIKE	
TUESDAY	Remind the children that a verb is an action word. It's something that you can *do*. Discuss and write a list of verbs: BAKE, CLIMB, HIT, JOG, MAKE, RIDE, SWIM, etc. The child writes: I LIKE TO PLAY. **ONE TIME** The child writes: I LIKE TO <u>(and phonetically spells a verb)</u>. **1–2 times,** then, draws a picture.	
WEDNESDAY	Remind the children that a verb is an action word. It's something that you can *do*. Discuss and write a list of verbs: BAKE, CLIMB, HIT, JOG, MAKE, RIDE, SWIM, etc. The child writes: I LIKE TO PLAY. **ONE TIME** The child writes: I LIKE TO <u>(and phonetically spells a verb)</u>. **1–2 times,** then draws a picture.	
THURSDAY	Review the word family, LIKE, BIKE, HIKE, MIKE, PIKE, STIKE and verbs. Using the verbiage on page 48, the teacher and child write each lowercase letter **z, e, s, l, t** and **h** side by side **5– 10 times.**	
FRIDAY	Review the word family, LIKE, BIKE, HIKE, MIKE, PIKE, STIKE and verbs. The child draws a picture, then labels it with beginning sounds or phonetic spelling.	

NOTE: Place the child's writing in plastic page protectors and a 3 ring binder for reading and review. Again, I strongly recommend that you focus solely on writing at this stage. If the children read anything, have them read what they have written. In addition to reading their sight word sentences, they can read simple sentences that you write. Be sure and write sentences that include the words they have learned to write as well as topics that interest them.

An Easy and On-Going Spelling Strategy

Additional Common Core State Standards that these activities can address are CCSS.L.K.1.A, L.K.1.B, L.K.2.A, L.1.1.A, RF.K.2.A, RF.K.2.C, RF.K.2.D, RF.K.3.D, RF.K.2.E and RF.1.2.C

SENTENCE #8	I LIKE TO PLAY AND HOP.	
SPELLING PATTERN: _____ AY (Long A) and _____ OP		FOCUS VOCABULARY: VERBS
MONDAY	Using all capital letters, write the sentence **I LIKE TO PLAY AND** <u>HOP.</u> on a piece of paper. Emphasize the period at the end. The child copies the sentence **ONE TIME** and draws a picture. Write and say the sounds for the word family, PLAY, BAY, DAY, MAY, PAY, RAY, SAY, TRAY, WAY.	
TUESDAY	Write and say the sounds for the word family PLAY, BAY, DAY, MAY, PAY, RAY, SAY, TRAY, WAY Teach the child that the AY makes a LONG A sound. The child writes the sentence I LIKE TO PLAY AND HOP. **ONE TIME** and draws a picture.	
WEDNESDAY	Write and say the sounds for the word family HOP, BOP, FLOP, MOP, POP, STOP, TOP Teach the child that the AY makes a LONG A sound. The child writes the sentence I LIKE TO PLAY AND HOP. **ONE TIME** and draws a picture.	
THURSDAY	Review the word families PLAY, BAY, DAY, MAY, PAY, RAY, SAY, WAY and HOP, BOP, FLOP, MOP, POP, STOP, TOP Using the verbiage on page 48, the teacher and child write each lowercase letter **l, t, h, b, k** and **f** side by side **5–10 times.**	
FRIDAY	Review the word families PLAY, BAY, DAY, MAY, PAY, RAY, SAY, WAY and HOP, BOP, FLOP, MOP, POP, STOP, TOP The child draws a picture, then labels it with beginning sounds or phonetic spelling.	
MONDAY	Using all capital letters, write the sentence **I LIKE TO PLAY AND** <u>HOP.</u> on a piece of paper. Point out the period. The child copies the sentence **ONE TIME** and draws a picture. Review the word families PLAY, BAY, DAY, MAY, PAY, RAY, SAY, WAY and HOP, BOP, FLOP, MOP, POP, STOP, TOP	
TUESDAY	Remind the children that a verb is an action word. It's something that they can *do*. Discuss and write a list of verbs: BUILD, CUT, GLUE, FEED, HELP, READ, WALK, etc. The child writes: I LIKE TO PLAY AND HOP. **ONE TIME** The child writes: I LIKE TO PLAY AND <u>(and phonetically spells a verb)</u>. **1–2 times,** then draws a picture.	
WEDNESDAY	Remind the children that a verb is an action word. It's something that they can *do*. Discuss and write a list of verbs: BUILD, CUT, GLUE, FEED, HELP, READ, WALK, etc. The child writes I LIKE TO PLAY AND HOP. **ONE TIME** The child writes: I LIKE TO PLAY AND <u>(and phonetically spells a verb)</u>. **1–2 times, then,** draws a picture.	
THURSDAY	Review the word families PLAY, BAY, DAY, MAY, PAY, RAY, SAY, WAY and HOP, BOP, FLOP, MOP, POP, STOP, TOP and verbs. Using the verbiage on page 48, the teacher and child write each lowercase letter **l, t, h, b, k** and **f** side by side **5–10 times.**	
FRIDAY	Review the word families PLAY, BAY, DAY, MAY, PAY, RAY, SAY, WAY and HOP, BOP, FLOP, MOP, POP, STOP, TOP and verbs. The child draws a picture, then labels it with beginning sounds or phonetic spelling.	

NOTE: Place the child's writing in plastic page protectors and a 3 ring binder for reading and review. Again, I strongly recommend that you focus solely on writing at this stage. If the children read anything, have them read what they have written. In addition to reading their sight word sentences, they can read simple sentences that you write. Be sure and write sentences that include the words they have learned to write as well as topics that interest them.

Kids Win at Writing!

NOTE: At this point, many students will be used to the format of these sentences and only need one week to learn each sentence. Decide to spend 1 or 2 weeks on each sentence based on each child's needs. Beginning with SENTENCE #9, I'm only going to include one week of plans. If you need two weeks, simply repeat these plans twice.

Additional Common Core State Standards that these activities can address are CCSS.L.K.1.A and L.K.1.B.

SENTENCE #9	LOOK AT ME JUMP!
SPELLING PATTERN: _____ AT and _____ OOK	FOCUS VOCABULARY: VERBS
MONDAY	Using all capital letters, write the sentence **LOOK AT ME JUMP!** on a piece of paper. Show the students the exclamation mark at the end of the sentence. Explain that it means strong emotion like excitement, anger or fear. The child copies the sentence **ONE TIME** and draws a picture. Review the word family, _AT, BAT, CAT, FAT, HAT, MAT, RAT, SAT Write and say the sounds for the word family BOOK, COOK, HOOK, LOOK, TOOK
TUESDAY	Review the word families _AT, BAT, CAT, FAT, HAT, MAT, RAT, SAT and BOOK, COOK, HOOK, LOOK, TOOK Remind the children that a verb is an action word. It's something that they can *do.* Discuss and write a list of verbs: JUMP, BUMP, CLEAN, COOK, DRAW, DUNK, FOLD, PAINT, etc. The child writes: LOOK AT ME JUMP! **ONE TIME** The child writes: LOOK AT ME (and phonetically spells a verb)! **1–2 TIMES** and draws a picture of the verbs.
WEDNESDAY	Review the word families _AT, BAT, CAT, FAT, HAT, MAT, RAT, SAT and BOOK, COOK, HOOK, LOOK, TOOK Remind children that a verb is an action word. It's something that they can *do.* Discuss and write a list of verbs: JUMP, BUMP, CLEAN, COOK, DRAW, DUNK, FOLD, PAINT, etc. The child writes: LOOK AT ME JUMP! **ONE TIME** The child writes: LOOK AT ME (and phonetically spells a verb)! **1–2 TIMES** and draws a picture of the verbs.
THURSDAY	Review the word families _AT, BAT, CAT, FAT, HAT, MAT, RAT, SAT and BOOK, COOK, HOOK, LOOK, TOOK The teacher and child write all 26 lowercase letters side by side If a letter is still difficult for the child, have the child write that letter **5 times.**
FRIDAY	Review the word families _AT, BAT, CAT, FAT, HAT, MAT, RAT, SAT and BOOK, COOK, HOOK, LOOK, TOOK The child uses sight words and phonetic spelling to write **1–2 sentences** about a drawing, sticker, calendar picture or magazine picture.

Place the child's writing in plastic page protectors and a 3 ring binder for reading and review. Again, I strongly recommend that you focus solely on writing at this stage. If the children read anything, have them read what they have written. In addition to reading their sight word sentences, they can read simple sentences that you write. Be sure and write sentences that include the words they have learned to write as well as topics that interest them.

NOTE: This is a good time to start looking for simple books for each child to read. Try to find books that contain the words that the child has learned from these sight word sentences.

Additional Common Core State Standards that these activities can address are CCSS.L.K.1.A, L.K.1.B and L.1.1.A.

SENTENCE #10	THIS IS MY <u>BOOK</u>!	
SPELLING PATTERN: TH_____ and _____OOK		FOCUS VOCABULARY: NOUNS-THINGS
MONDAY	Using all capital letters, write the sentence **THIS IS MY <u>BOOK</u>!** on a piece of paper. Point out the exclamation mark. The child copies the sentence **ONE TIME,** then places a sticker of a book or draws a picture. Point out the word THIS. Teach the child the TH sound. Talk about other words that have the "TH" sounds like, THE, THAT, THEM, THEN Point out the word, MY. Teach the child that the Y makes a Long i Sound. A fun way to remember that there is a "Y" and not an "I" is to say, "Why does MY have a Y?" Review the sounds for the word family BOOK, COOK, HOOK, LOOK, TOOK	
TUESDAY	Review words that begin with TH like THE, THAT and THIS and the word family BOOK, COOK, HOOK, LOOK, TOOK Teach that a NOUN is a person, place or thing. Discuss and write a list of nouns that are THINGS: BOOK, PEN, MARKER, GLUE, BOX, DESK, etc. The child writes: THIS IS MY BOOK! **ONE TIME** The child writes: THIS IS MY <u>(and phonetically spells an object word)</u>! **TWO TIMES** The child draws a picture of the objects.	
WEDNESDAY	Review words that begin with TH like THE, THAT and THIS and the word family BOOK, COOK, HOOK, LOOK, TOOK Teach that a NOUN is a person, place or thing. Discuss and write a list of nouns that are THINGS: BOOK, PEN, MARKER, GLUE, BOX, DESK, etc. The child writes: THIS IS MY BOOK! **ONE TIME** The child writes: THIS IS MY <u>(and phonetically spells an object word)</u>! **TWO TIMES** The child draws a picture of the objects.	
THURSDAY	Review words that begin with TH like THE, THAT and THIS and the word family BOOK, COOK, HOOK, LOOK, TOOK The teacher and child write all 26 lowercase letters side by side. If a letter is still difficult for the child, have the child write that letter **5 times.**	
FRIDAY	Review words that begin with TH like THE, THAT and THIS and the word family BOOK, COOK, HOOK, LOOK, TOOK The child uses sight words and phonetic spelling to write **1–2 sentences** about a drawing, sticker, calendar picture or magazine picture.	

Place the child's writing in plastic page protectors and a 3 ring binder for reading and review. Again, I strongly recommend that you focus solely on writing at this stage. If the children read anything, have them read what they have written. In addition to reading their sight word sentences, they can read simple sentences that you write. Be sure and write sentences that include the words they have learned to write as well as topics that interest them.

NOTE: This is also a good time to start looking for simple books for each child to read. Try to find books that contain the words that the child has learned from these sight word sentences.

Additional Common Core State Standards that these activities can address are CCSS.L.K.1.A, L.K.1.B, L.1.1.A and RF.1.2.A.

SENTENCE #11	THIS IS MY <u>FISH</u>.
SPELLING PATTERN: TH and SH	FOCUS VOCABULARY: NOUNS-THINGS
MONDAY	Using all capital letters, write the sentence **THIS IS MY <u>FISH</u>.** on a piece of paper. Point out the period. The child copies the sentence **ONE TIME** and adds a sticker or pastes the sentence to a picture of a fish. Review the word THIS. Talk about other words that have the "TH" sound like, THE, THAT, THEM, THEN, THIS Review the word, MY. Teach the child that the Y makes a Long i Sound. A fun way to remember that there is a "Y" and not an "I" is to say, "Why does MY have a Y?" Point out the word FISH. Write and say the sounds for the words, FISH, DISH and WISH Talk about words that begin with the SH sound, like, SHED, SHOT, SHUT, SHAPE, SHEEP, SHY and SHOE.
TUESDAY	Review words that begin with TH-THE, THAT, THIS and SH-SHED, SHOT, SHUT, SHAPE, SHEEP, SHY, SHOE Remind the children that a NOUN is a person, place or thing. Discuss and write a list of nouns that have SH in it: DISH, WISH, SHARK, SHELL, SHEEP, SHED, SHOP, etc. The child writes: THIS IS MY FISH. **ONE TIME** The child writes: THIS IS MY <u>(and phonetically spells a noun that has SH in it)</u>. **TWO TIMES** The child draws a picture or glues the sentence to a picture of the objects.
WEDNESDAY	Review words that begin with TH-THE, THAT, THIS and SH-SHED, SHOT, SHUT, SHAPE, SHEEP, SHY, SHOE Teach that a NOUN is a person, place or thing. Discuss and write a list of nouns that have SH in it: DISH, WISH, SHARK, SHELL, SHEEP, SHIRT, SHOE, SHOP The child writes: THIS IS MY FISH. **ONE TIME** The child writes: THIS IS MY <u>(and phonetically spells a noun that has SH in it)</u>. **TWO TIMES** The child draws a picture or glues the sentence to a picture of the objects.
THURSDAY	Review words that begin with TH-THE, THAT, THIS and SH-SHED, SHOT, SHUT, SHAPE, SHEEP, SHY, SHOE The teacher and child write all 26 lowercase letters side by side. If a letter is still difficult for the child, have the child write that letter **5 times.**
FRIDAY	Review words that begin with TH-THE, THAT, THIS and SH-SHED, SHOT, SHUT, SHAPE, SHEEP, SHY, SHOE The child uses sight words and phonetic spelling to write **1–2 sentences** about a drawing, sticker, calendar picture or magazine picture.

Place the child's writing in plastic page protectors and a 3 ring binder for reading and review. Again, I strongly recommend that you focus solely on writing at this stage. If the children read anything, have them read what they have written. In addition to reading their sight word sentences, they can read simple sentences that you write. Be sure and write sentences that include the words they have learned to write as well as topics that interest them.

An Easy and On-Going Spelling Strategy

NOTE: This is also a good time to start looking for simple books for the child to read. Try to find books that contain the words that the child has learned from these sight word sentences.

Additional Common Core State Standards that these activities can address are CCSS.L.K.1.A, L.K.1.B, L.K.2.A, L.1.1.A, RF.K.2.A, RF.K.2.C, RF.K.2.D, RF.K.3.D, RF.K.2.E and RF.1.2.C

SENTENCE #12	IT IS NOT IN THE <u>BOX</u>.		
SPELLING PATTERN: _____ IT and _____ OT	FOCUS VOCABULARY: NOUNS-THINGS-PLACES		
MONDAY	Using all capital letters, write the sentence **IT IS IN THE <u>BOX</u>.** on a piece of paper. Point out the period. The child copies the sentence **ONE TIME** and draws a picture of a box. Teach the sounds for the word family IT, BIT, FIT, HIT, LIT, KNIT, PIT, SIT Teach the sounds for the word family NOT, DOT, GOT, HOT, LOT, POT, ROT You can also teach the sounds for the words BOX and FOX as well as IN, BIN, FIN, PIN, TIN, WIN
TUESDAY	Review the word families IT, BIT, FIT, HIT, LIT, KNIT, PIT, SIT and NOT, DOT, GOT, HOT, LOT, POT, ROT Remind the students that a NOUN is a person, place or thing. Discuss and write a list of nouns that are THINGS and PLACES: BOX, BIN, CLOSET, BATHROOM, KITCHEN, BEDROOM, DRAWER, etc. The child writes: IT IS IN THE BOX. **ONE TIME** The child writes: IT IS IN THE (and phonetically spells an object/room word). **TWO TIMES** The child draws a picture of the object or room.
WEDNESDAY	Review the word families IT, BIT, FIT, HIT, LIT, KNIT, PIT, SIT and NOT, DOT, GOT, HOT, LOT, POT, ROT Remind the students that a NOUN is a person, place or thing. Discuss and write a list of nouns that are THINGS and PLACES: BOX, BIN, CLOSET, BATHROOM, KITCHEN, BEDROOM, DRAWER, etc. The child writes: IT IS IN THE BOX. **ONE TIME** The child writes: IT IS IN THE (and phonetically spells an object/room word). **TWO TIMES** The child draws a picture of the object or room.
THURSDAY	Review the word families IT, BIT, FIT, HIT, LIT, KNIT, PIT, SIT and NOT, DOT, GOT, HOT, LOT, POT, ROT The teacher and child write all 26 lowercase letters side by side. If a letter is still difficult for the child, have the child write that letter **5 times.**
FRIDAY	Review the word families IT, BIT, FIT, HIT, LIT, KNIT, PIT, SIT and NOT, DOT, GOT, HOT, LOT, POT, ROT The child uses sight words and phonetic spelling to write **1–2 sentences** about a drawing, sticker, calendar picture or magazine picture.

Place the child's writing in plastic page protectors and a 3 ring binder for reading and review. Again, I strongly recommend that you focus solely on writing at this stage. If the children read anything, have them read what they have written. In addition to reading their sight word sentences, they can read simple sentences that you write. Be sure and write sentences that include the words they have learned to write as well as topics that interest them.

NOTE: This is also a good time to start looking for simple books for each child to read. Try to find books that contain the words that the child has learned from these sight word sentences.

Additional Common Core State Standards that these activities can address are CCSS.L.K.1.A, L.K.2.A, L.1.1.A, RF.K.2.A, RF.K.2.C, RF.K.2.D, RF.K.3.D, RF.K.2.E and RF.1.2.C

SENTENCE #13	WE CAN GO <u>UP</u>.
SPELLING PATTERN: _____ AN and _____ UP	FOCUS VOCABULARY: DIRECTIONAL WORDS

MONDAY	Using all capital letters, write the sentence **WE CAN GO UP**. on a piece of paper. Emphasize the period at the end. The child copies the sentence **ONE TIME** and draws a picture. Point out the word WE. Teach the students that it has a LONG E sound as in WE, ME, HE and SHE. Review the sounds for the word family, CAN, DAN, FAN, MAN, PAN, RAN, TAN Point out the word GO. Teach the students that it has a LONG O sound. Write and say the sounds for the word family, UP, CUP, PUP
TUESDAY	Review the word families, CAN, DAN, FAN, MAN, PAN, RAN, TAN and UP, CUP, PUP Teach directional words: UP, DOWN, IN, OUT, UNDER, BEHIND and AROUND The child writes: WE CAN GO UP. **ONE TIME** The child writes: WE CAN GO <u>(and phonetically spells a directional word)</u>. **TWO TIMES** The child draws a picture of the direction.
WEDNESDAY	Review the word families, CAN, DAN, FAN, MAN, PAN, RAN, TAN and UP, CUP, PUP Teach directional words: UP, DOWN, IN, OUT, UNDER, BEHIND and AROUND The child writes: WE CAN GO UP. **ONE TIME** The child writes: WE CAN GO <u>(and phonetically spells a directional word)</u>. **TWO TIMES** The child draws a picture of the direction.
THURSDAY	Review the word families, CAN, DAN, FAN, MAN, PAN, RAN, TAN and UP, CUP, PUP The teacher and child write all 26 lowercase letters side by side. If a letter is still difficult for the child, have the child write that letter **5 times.**
FRIDAY	Review the word families, CAN, DAN, FAN, MAN, PAN, RAN, TAN and UP, CUP, PUP The child uses sight words and phonetic spelling to write **1–2 sentences** about a drawing, sticker, calendar picture or magazine picture.

Place the child's writing in plastic page protectors and a 3 ring binder for reading and review. Again, I strongly recommend that you focus solely on writing at this stage. If the children read anything, have them read what they have written. In addition to reading their sight word sentences, they can read simple sentences that you write. Be sure and write sentences that include the words they have learned to write as well as topics that interest them.

NOTE: This is also a good time to start looking for simple books for each child to read. Try to find books that contain the words that the child has learned from these sight word sentences.

Additional Common Core State Standards that these activities can address are CCSS.L.K.1.B and L.K.2.A.

SENTENCE #14	I HAVE A <u>PEN</u>.	
SPELLING PATTERN: _____ EN	FOCUS VOCABULARY: NOUNS-THINGS	
MONDAY	Using all capital letters, write the sentence, **I HAVE A <u>PEN</u>.** on a piece of paper. Emphasize the period at the end. The child copies the sentence **ONE TIME** and draws a picture or places a sticker of a pen. Point out the word HAVE. Teach that the word looks like the CVCE pattern where we say, "Cover the silent E, say A—H-A-V-E," with a long A sound. Show that it's spelled HAVE, but it sounds like, "HAV." To emphasize how "HAVE" looks, show the word family, CAVE, DAVE, GAVE, PAVE, SAVE, WAVE. Make the kids laugh by saying, "I HAVE (with a LONG A) A PEN. Remind them that HAVE sounds like HAV, but is spelled like HAVE and needs a silent E on the end. Teach the sounds for the word family BEN, DEN, HEN, MEN, PEN, TEN	
TUESDAY	Review the spelling of HAVE and that it looks like the word family CAVE, DAVE, GAVE, PAVE, SAVE, WAVE Review the word family BEN, DEN, HEN, MEN, PEN, TEN Remind the students that a NOUN is a person, place or thing. Discuss and write a list of nouns that are THINGS: TOY, CAR, TRUCK, ROBOT, DOLL, NET, etc. The child writes: I HAVE A PEN. **ONE TIME** The child writes: I HAVE A <u>(and phonetically spells an object)</u>. **TWO TIMES** The child draws a picture of the objects.	
WEDNESDAY	Review the spelling of HAVE and that it looks like the word family CAVE, DAVE, GAVE, PAVE, SAVE, WAVE Review the word family BEN, DEN, HEN, MEN, PEN, TEN Remind the students that a NOUN is a person, place or thing. Discuss and write a list of nouns that are THINGS: TOY, CAR, TRUCK, ROBOT, DOLL, NET, etc. The child writes: I HAVE A PEN. **ONE TIME** The child writes: I HAVE A <u>(and phonetically spells an object)</u>. **TWO TIMES** The child draws a picture of the objects.	
THURSDAY AND FRIDAY	Informal Assessment: Copy WORDS LIST 1 on page . Say each word. The child writes the word (or verbally spells it). Highlight each word on the list that the child spells correctly. Have the child continue to practice any misspelled words from LIST 1. Then, start LIST 2.	

Place the child's writing in plastic page protectors and a 3 ring binder for reading and review. Again, I strongly recommend that you focus solely on writing at this stage. If the children read anything, have them read what they have written. In addition to reading their sight word sentences, they can read simple sentences that you write. Be sure and write sentences that include the words they have learned to write as well as topics that interest them.

NOTE: This is also a good time to start looking for simple books for each child to read. Try to find books that contain the words that the child has learned from these sight word sentences.

SENTENCES LIST 2

NOTE: At this point, start showing the child that the first letter of the sentence is capital while the rest are lowercase. When you write the sentence on the child's paper, write it using correct capitalization. Children will continue to use capital letters throughout their sentences a lot. Each week, remind them to try to use lowercase letters. Little by little, over time, they will learn and remember to capitalize the first letter and use lowercase for the rest of the sentence.

Further along, in LISTS 3–12, there will be opportunities to teach proper nouns that are capitalized, as well as other punctuation like question marks (?), exclamation marks (!), commas (,), apostrophes (') and quotation marks (").

Additional Common Core State Standards that these activities can address are CCSS.L.K.1.A, L.K.1.B, L.K.2.A and L.1.1.A.

SENTENCE #1	You are my <u>friend</u>.
SPELLING PATTERN: FRI-END and _____ END	FOCUS VOCABULARY: NOUNS-PEOPLE
MONDAY	Using capital and lowercase letters, write, **You are my** <u>friend.</u> on a piece of paper. Emphasize the period at the end. The child copies the sentence **TWO TIMES** and draws a picture. Teach that the word "friend" is spelled like "FRI-END." It has 6 letters. Teach the sounds for the word family, BEND, LEND, MEND, SEND and TEND.
TUESDAY	Review the spelling of FRIEND, that it looks like FRI-END and has 6 letters Review the word family, BEND, LEND, MEND, SEND and TEND. Remind the students that a NOUN is a person, place or thing. Review and discuss a list of nouns that are PEOPLE: MOM, DAD, BROTHER, SISTER, TEACHER, DOCTOR, NEIGHBOR, ETC. The child writes, You are my friend. **ONE TIME** The child writes, You are my <u>(and phonetically spells a person word)</u>. **TWO TIMES** and draws a picture.
WEDNESDAY	Review the spelling of FRIEND and the word family, BEND, LEND, MEND, SEND and TEND. Teach that a NOUN is a person, place or thing. Review and discuss a list of nouns that are PEOPLE: MOM, DAD, BROTHER, SISTER, TEACHER, DOCTOR, NEIGHBOR, ETC. The child writes, You are my friend. **ONE TIME** The child writes, You are my <u>(and phonetically spells a person word)</u>. **TWO TIMES** and draws a picture.
THURSDAY	Review the spelling of FRIEND and the word family, BEND, LEND, MEND, SEND and TEND. The teacher and child write all 26 lowercase letters side by side. If a letter is still difficult for the child, have the child write that letter **5 times.** Write the blends **bl** and **br**. Have the students **say** words that begin with each blend. Write their words down to read and review. Add words that you think of. Point out long and short vowels sounds.
FRIDAY	Review the spelling of FRIEND and the word family, BEND, LEND, MEND, SEND and TEND. The child uses sight words and phonetic spelling to write **2–3 sentences** about a drawing, sticker, calendar picture or magazine picture.

Additional Common Core State Standards that these activities can address are CCSS.L.K.1.A, L.K.2.A, L.1.1.A and L.1.2.A.

SENTENCE #2	Come with me, <u>Tom</u>.	
SPELLING PATTERN: COME/WITH/ME	FOCUS VOCABULARY: CAPITALIZE NAMES	
MONDAY	Write the sentence **Come with me, <u>Tom</u>**. on a piece of paper. Teach and emphasize the comma and period. The child copies the sentence **TWO TIMES** and draws a picture. Point out the word COME. Teach that the word looks like the CVCE pattern where we say, "Cover the silent E, say O--C-O-M-E, with a long O sound, like in the word HOME." It sounds like "KUM", but is spelled, C-O-M-E. Point out the word WITH. Say each sound in the word, "W-I-TH." Show the students that the word only has 4 letters and makes the SHORT I sound. (Older students that I work with often write WHITH. We want to prevent this habit early on.) Point out the word ME. Remind the child that the E makes a LONG E sound as in ME, HE, SHE and WE. Write and say the sounds for the words ME, HE, SHE and WE.	
TUESDAY	Review the spelling of the words COME, WITH and ME. Teach that the first letter in someone's name starts with a capital letter. Talk about names that the child knows. The child writes, Come with me, Tom. **ONE TIME** The child writes, Come with me, <u>(and phonetically spells a person's name)</u>. **TWO TIMES** and draws a picture.	
WEDNESDAY	Review the spelling of the words COME, WITH and ME. Teach that the first letter in someone's name starts with a capital letter. Talk about names that the child knows. The child writes, Come with me, Tom. **ONE TIME** The child writes, Come with me, <u>(and phonetically spells a person's name)</u>. **TWO TIMES** and draws a picture.	
THURSDAY	Review the spelling of the words COME, WITH and ME. The teacher and child write all 26 lowercase letters side by side. If a letter is still difficult for the child, have the child write that letter **5 times.** Write the blends **cl**, **cr** and **dr.** Have the students **say** words that begin with each blend. Write their words down to read and review. Add words that you think of. Point out long and short vowels sounds.	
FRIDAY	Review the spelling of the words COME, WITH and ME. The child uses sight words and phonetic spelling to write **2–3 sentences** about a drawing, sticker, calendar picture or magazine picture.	

NOTE: Place the child's writing in plastic page protectors and a 3 ring binder for reading and review. At this point, children will be able to start reading easy readers found in libraries and book stores. Look for books that have words similar to the ones the child is writing in these sentences.

Additional Common Core State Standards that these activities can address are CCSS.L.K.1.A, L.K.2.A, L.1.1.A, L.1.2.A, L.3.2.C and L.4.2.B.

SENTENCE #3	"Come here," <u>Deb</u> said.	
SPELLING PATTERN: COME/HERE/SAID	FOCUS VOCABULARY: QUOTATION PUNCTUATION	
MONDAY	Write the sentence **"Come here," <u>Deb</u> said.** on a piece of paper. Teach the quotation marks, comma and period. The child copies the sentence **TWO TIMES** and draws a picture. Spend time talking about the 4 letter words COME, HERE and SAID. Review the word COME. Point out the word HERE. It follows the CVCE pattern, where we "Cover the silent E and say, E—H—E—R—E." Point out the word SAID. It looks like it follows the CVVC pattern where the 1st vowel talks and the 2nd vowel walks and is silent. Make the kids laugh by reading the sentence, "COME HERE," I SAID pronouncing SAID with a long A sound. Remind the students that SAID sounds like SED, but looks like, "sAid" so it's spelled with a long A and silent I. Remind the students that SAID has 4 letters.	
TUESDAY	Review the spelling of the words COME, HERE and SAID Review that the first letter in someone's name starts with a capital letter. Talk about names that the child knows. Point out the quotation marks, comma and period in the sentence, "Come here," <u>Deb</u> said. The child writes, "Come here," <u>Deb</u> said. **ONE TIME** The child writes, "Come here," <u>(and phonetically spells a person's name)</u> said. **TWO TIMES** and draws a picture.	
WEDNESDAY	Review the spelling of the words COME, HERE and SAID Review that the first letter in someone's name starts with a capital letter. Talk about names that the child knows. Point out the quotation marks, comma and period in the sentence, "Come here," <u>Deb</u> said. The child writes, "Come here," <u>Deb</u> said. **ONE TIME** The child writes, "Come here," <u>(and phonetically spells a person's name)</u> said. **TWO TIMES** and draws a picture.	
THURSDAY	Review the spelling of the words COME, HERE and SAID The teacher and child write all 26 lowercase letters side by side. If a letter is still difficult for the child, have the child write that letter **5 times.** Write the blends **fl** and **fr**. Have the students **say** words that begin with each blend. Write their words down to read and review. Add words that you think of. Point out long and short vowels sounds.	
FRIDAY	Review the spelling of the words COME, HERE and SAID The child uses sight words and phonetic spelling to write **2—3 sentences** about a drawing, sticker, calendar picture or magazine picture.	

NOTE: Place the child's writing in plastic page protectors and a 3 ring binder for reading and review. At this point, children will be able to start reading easy readers found in libraries and book stores. Look for books that have words similar to the ones the child is writing in these sentences.

Additional Common Core State Standards that these activities can address are CCSS.L.K.1.A, L.K.1.B, L.K.2.A, L.2.1.D, RF.K.3.B, RF.1.2.A, RF.1.3.C, RF. 2.3.A and RF.2.3.B

SENTENCE #4	He ate his <u>chips</u>.	
SPELLING PATTERN: _____ ATE and CH_____	FOCUS VOCABULARY: NOUNS-FOOD	
MONDAY	Write the sentence **He ate his <u>chips</u>.** on a piece of paper. Emphasize the period at the end. The child copies the sentence **TWO TIMES** and draws a picture or places a sticker. Point out the word ATE. Show the silent E that makes the "A" a LONG A sound. Teach the sounds for the word family ___ATE, DATE, GATE, LATE, MATE, PLATE, STATE Teach the child to "cover the silent E and say, A---D-A-T-E, cover the E, say, A---G-A-T-E," etc. Teach the "CH" sound in CHIPS. Talk about other words that start with CH, such as CHAT, CHICKEN, CHOP, CHAIR, and CHEEK.	
TUESDAY	Review the word family ATE, DATE, GATE, LATE, MATE, PLATE, STATE and words that begin with CH. Remind the students that a NOUN is a person, place or thing. Discuss and write a list of nouns that are FOODS: SANDWICH, BANANA, APPLE, CHIPS, COOKIE, CARROTS, RICE, ETC. The child writes, He ate his chips. **ONE TIME** The child writes, He ate his <u>(and phonetically spells a food word)</u>. **TWO TIMES** The child draws a picture or places stickers.	
WEDNESDAY	Review the word family ATE, DATE, GATE, LATE, MATE, PLATE, STATE and words that begin with CH. Remind the students that a NOUN is a person, place or thing. Discuss and write a list of nouns that are FOODS: SANDWICH, BANANA, APPLE, CHIPS, COOKIE, CARROTS, RICE, ETC. The child writes, He ate his chips. **ONE TIME** The child writes, He ate his <u>(and phonetically spells a food word)</u>. **TWO TIMES** The child draws a picture or places stickers.	
THURSDAY	Review the word family ATE, DATE, GATE, LATE, MATE, PLATE, STATE and words that begin with CH. The teacher and child write all 26 lowercase letters side by side. If a letter is still difficult for the child, have the child write that letter **5 times.** Write the blends **gl** and **gr**. Have the students **say** words that begin with each blend. Write their words down to read and review. Add words that you think of. Point out long and short vowels sounds.	
FRIDAY	Review the word family ATE, DATE, GATE, LATE, MATE, PLATE, STATE and words that begin with CH. The child uses sight words and phonetic spelling to write **2–3 sentences** about a drawing, sticker, calendar picture or magazine picture.	

NOTE: Place the child's writing in plastic page protectors and a 3 ring binder for reading and review. At this point, children will be able to start reading easy readers found in libraries and book stores. Look for books that have words similar to the ones the child is writing in these sentences.

Additional Common Core State Standards that these activities can address are CCSS.L.K.1.A, L.K.1.B, L.K.2.A, L.2.1.D, RF.K.3.B, RF.1.2.A, RF.1.3.C, RF. 2.3.A and RF.2.3.B

SENTENCE #5	She ate her <u>meat</u>.	
SPELLING PATTERN: _____ ATE and _____ EAT	FOCUS VOCABULARY: NOUNS-FOOD	
MONDAY Jax Ellie	Write the sentence **She ate her <u>meat</u>.** on a piece of paper. Emphasize the period at the end. The child copies the sentence **TWO TIMES** and draws a picture. Review the word ATE and word family ATE, DATE, GATE, HATE, LATE, NATE, PLATE, STATE Teach the long E sounds in the word family __EAT, BEAT, HEAT, MEAT, SEAT, TREAT Talk about how it follows the CVVC pattern where the 1st vowel talks and the 2nd vowel walks and is silent. The E makes the long E sound. The A is silent.	
TUESDAY	Review the word families ATE, DATE, GATE, HATE, LATE and EAT, BEAT, HEAT, MEAT, SEAT TREAT Remind the students that a NOUN is a person, place or thing. Discuss and write a list of nouns that are FOODS: BREAD, BAGEL, CHICKEN, DONUT, FRIES, HOT DOG, NUGGETS, PIZZA, PRETZELS, ETC. The child writes, She ate her meat. **ONE TIME** The child writes, She ate her <u>(and phonetically spells a food word)</u>. **TWO TIMES** The child draws a picture.	
WEDNESDAY	Review the word families ATE, DATE, GATE, HATE, LATE and EAT, BEAT, HEAT, MEAT, SEAT TREAT Remind the students that a NOUN is a person, place or thing. Discuss and write a list of nouns that are FOODS: BREAD, BAGEL, CHICKEN, DONUT, FRIES, HOT DOG, NUGGETS, PIZZA, PRETZELS, ETC. The child writes, She ate her meat. **ONE TIME** The child writes, She ate her <u>(and phonetically spells a food word)</u>. **TWO TIMES** The child draws a picture.	
THURSDAY	Review the word families ATE, DATE, GATE, HATE, LATE and EAT, BEAT, HEAT, MEAT, SEAT TREAT The teacher and child write all 26 lowercase letters side by side. If a letter is still difficult for the child, have the child write that letter **5 times.** Write the blends **pl** and **pr**. Have the students **say** words that begin with each blend. Write their words down to read and review. Add words that you think of. Point out long and short vowels sounds.	
FRIDAY	Review the word families ATE, DATE, GATE, HATE, LATE and EAT, BEAT, HEAT, MEAT, SEAT TREAT The child uses sight words and phonetic spelling to write **2–3 sentences** about a drawing, sticker, calendar picture or magazine picture.	

NOTE: Place the child's writing in plastic page protectors and a 3 ring binder for reading and review. At this point, children will be able to start reading easy readers found in libraries and book stores. Look for books that have words similar to the ones the child is writing in these sentences.

Additional Common Core State Standards that these activities can address are CCSS.L.K.1.A, L.K.1.B, L.K.2.A, L.2.1.D, RF.K.3.B, RF.1.2.A, RF.1.3.C, RF. 2.3.A and RF.2.3.B

SENTENCE #6	We went to the <u>fair.</u>	
SPELLING PATTERN: _____ ENT and _____ AIR		FOCUS VOCABULARY: NOUNS-PLACES
MONDAY	Write the sentence **We went to the** <u>fair.</u> on a piece of paper. Emphasize the period at the end. The child copies the sentence **TWO TIMES** and draws a picture. Point out the word WENT. Say each sound in the word, "W-E-N-T. Show the students that the word only has 4 letters and makes the SHORT E sound. (Older students that I work with often write WHENT. We want to prevent this habit early on.) Teach the sounds for the word family __ENT, BENT, DENT, RENT, SENT, TENT Teach the sounds for the word family AIR, CHAIR, FAIR, HAIR, LAIR, PAIR Talk about how it follows the CVVC pattern where the 1st vowel talks and the 2nd vowel walks and is silent. The A makes the long A sound. The I is silent.	
TUESDAY	Review the word families BENT, DENT, RENT, SENT, TENT and AIR, CHAIR, FAIR, HAIR, LAIR, PAIR Remind the students that a NOUN is a person, place or thing. Discuss and write a list of nouns that are PLACES: MALL, MUSEUM, PARK, RESTAURANT, ZOO, ETC. The child writes, We went to the fair. **ONE TIME** The child writes, We went to the <u>(and phonetically spells a place word).</u> **TWO TIMES** The child draws a picture, places a sticker or pastes the sentence to a picture of a place.	
WEDNESDAY	Review the word families BENT, DENT, RENT, SENT, TENT and AIR, CHAIR, FAIR, HAIR, LAIR, PAIR Remind the students that a NOUN is a person, place or thing. Discuss and write a list of nouns that are PLACES: MALL, MUSEUM, PARK, RESTAURANT, ZOO, ETC. The child writes, We went to the fair. **ONE TIME** The child writes, We went to the <u>(and phonetically spells a place word).</u> **TWO TIMES** The child draws a picture, places a sticker or pastes the sentence to a picture of a place.	
THURSDAY	Review the word families BENT, DENT, RENT, SENT, TENT and AIR, CHAIR, FAIR, HAIR, LAIR, PAIR The teacher and child write all 26 lowercase letters side by side. If a letter is still difficult for the child, have the child write that letter **5 times.** Write the blends **qu** and **squ**. Have the students **say** words that begin with each blend. Write their words down to read and review. Add words that you think of. Point out long and short vowels sounds.	
FRIDAY	Review the word families BENT, DENT, RENT, SENT, TENT and AIR, CHAIR, FAIR, HAIR, LAIR, PAIR The child uses sight words and phonetic spelling to write **2–3 sentences** about a drawing, sticker, calendar picture or magazine picture.	

NOTE: Place the child's writing in plastic page protectors and a 3 ring binder for reading and review. At this point, children will be able to start reading easy readers found in libraries and book stores. Look for books that have words similar to the ones the child is writing in these sentences.

Additional Common Core State Standards that these activities can address are CCSS.L.K.1.A, L.K.1.B, L.K.2.A, L.2.1.D, L.4.1.G, RF.K.3.B, RF.1.2.A, RF.1.3.C, RF. 2.3.A and RF.2.3.B

SENTENCE #7	They came to the <u>fair</u> too.	
SPELLING PATTERN:	____ AME and ____ AIR	FOCUS VOCABULARY: NOUNS-PLACES
MONDAY	Write the sentence **They came to the <u>fair</u> too.** on a piece of paper. Emphasize the period at the end. The child copies the sentence **TWO TIMES** and draws a picture. Point out the word THEY. Show the children that it makes a long A sound, but is spelled with an E. (Older students that I work with often write THAY. We want to prevent this habit early on.) Teach the sounds for the word family CAME, FLAME, FRAME, GAME, NAME, SAME, TAME Here the child learns that the silent E makes the A, a long A sound. Teach the child to "cover the silent E and say A---C-A-M-E, cover the silent E, say A---G-A-M-E," etc. Review the word family AIR, CHAIR, FAIR, HAIR, LAIR, PAIR Point out the word TOO. Show the children the two o's. Tell them to imagine that the two o's are friends. If one O goes. The other O wants to go TOO, me TOO, you TOO. This TOO is spelled with 2 Os.	
TUESDAY	Review the word families CAME, FLAME, FRAME, GAME, NAME, SAME and AIR, CHAIR, FAIR, HAIR, LAIR, PAIR Remind the students that a NOUN is a person, place or thing. Discuss and write a list of nouns that are PLACES: MALL, MUSEUM, PARK, RESTAURANT, ZOO, ETC. The child writes, They came to the <u>fair</u> too. **ONE TIME** The child writes, They came to the (<u>phonetically spell the name of a place</u>) too. **TWO TIMES** and draws a picture.	
WEDNESDAY	Review the word families CAME, FLAME, FRAME, GAME, NAME, SAME and AIR, CHAIR, FAIR, HAIR, LAIR, PAIR Remind the students that a NOUN is a person, place or thing. Discuss and write a list of nouns that are PLACES: MALL, MUSEUM, PARK, RESTAURANT, ZOO, ETC. The child writes, They came to the <u>fair</u> too. **TWO TIMES** The child writes, They came to the (<u>phonetically spell the name of a place</u>) too. **TWO TIMES** and draws a picture.	
THURSDAY	Review the word families CAME, FLAME, FRAME, GAME, NAME, SAME and AIR, CHAIR, FAIR, HAIR, LAIR, PAIR The teacher and child write all 26 lowercase letters side by side. If a letter is still difficult for the child, have the child write that letter **5 times.** Write the blends **sc, sk** and **scr**. Have the students **say** words that begin with each blend. Write their words down to read and review. Add words that you think of. Point out long and short vowels sounds.	
FRIDAY	Review the word families CAME, FLAME, FRAME, GAME, NAME, SAME and AIR, CHAIR, FAIR, HAIR, LAIR, PAIR The child uses sight words and phonetic spelling to write **2–3 sentences** about a drawing, sticker, calendar picture or magazine picture.	

NOTE: Place the child's writing in plastic page protectors and a 3 ring binder for reading and review. At this point, children will be able to start reading easy readers found in libraries and book stores. Look for books that have words similar to the ones the child is writing in these sentences.

An Easy and On-Going Spelling Strategy

Additional Common Core State Standards that these activities can address are CCSS.L.K.1.A, L.K.1.B, L.K.1.C, L.K.2.A, L.1.1.A, L3.1.B, L.2.1.D and RF.K.2.C.

SENTENCE #8	We took our <u>coats</u>.	
SPELLING PATTERN: _____ OOK and _____ OAT		FOCUS VOCABULARY: PLURAL NOUNS-THINGS
MONDAY	Write the sentence **We took our** <u>coats</u>. on a piece of paper. Emphasize the period at the end. The child copies the sentence **TWO TIMES** and draws a picture or places a sticker. Review the word family BOOK, COOK, LOOK, HOOK, SHOOK, TOOK Teach the sounds for the word family OATS, BOATS, COATS, GOATS, MOATS, Talk about how it follows the CVVC pattern where the 1st vowel talks and the 2nd vowel walks and is silent. The O makes the long O sound. The A is silent.	
TUESDAY	Review the word families BOOK, COOK, LOOK, HOOK, SHOOK, TOOK and OATS, BOATS, COATS, GOATS, MOATS Remind students that a NOUN is a person, place or thing. Teach the students that if there is more than one thing, they have to add an "S" and that these nouns are called PLURAL NOUNS. Discuss and write a list of nouns that are THINGS that people can "take": MAPS, BAGS, BACKPACKS, KEYS, TICKETS, etc. The child writes, We took our coats. **ONE TIME** The child writes, We took our <u>(and phonetically spells an object word)</u>. **TWO TIMES** The child draws a picture or places stickers.	
WEDNESDAY	Review the word families BOOK, COOK, LOOK, HOOK, SHOOK, TOOK and OATS, BOATS, COATS, GOATS, MOATS Remind students that a NOUN is a person, place or thing. Teach the students that if there is more than one NOUN, it's called a PLURAL NOUN. Plural nouns end with an "S." Discuss and write a list of nouns that are THINGS that people can "take": MAPS, BAGS, BACKPACKS, KEYS, TICKETS, etc. The child writes, We took our coats. **ONE TIME** The child writes, We took our <u>(and phonetically spells an object word)</u>. **TWO TIMES** The child draws a picture or places stickers.	
THURSDAY	Review the word families BOOK, COOK, LOOK, HOOK, SHOOK, TOOK and OATS, BOATS, COATS, GOATS, MOATS The teacher and child write all 26 lowercase letters side by side. If a letter is still difficult for the child, have the child write that letter **5 times.** Write the blends **sl, sm** and **sn**. Have the students **say** words that begin with each blend. Write their words down to read and review. Add words that you think of. Point out long and short vowels sounds.	
FRIDAY	Review the word families BOOK, COOK, LOOK, HOOK, SHOOK, TOOK and OATS, BOATS, COATS, GOATS, MOATS The child uses sight words and phonetic spelling to write **2–3 sentences** about a drawing, sticker, calendar picture or magazine picture.	

NOTE: Place the child's writing in plastic page protectors and a 3 ring binder for reading and review. At this point, children will be able to start reading easy readers found in libraries and book stores. Look for books that have words similar to the ones the child is writing in these sentences.

Additional Common Core State Standards that these activities can address are CCSS.L.K.1.A, L.K.1.C, L.K.2.A, L.1.1.A, L.2.1.D and L.3.1.B.

SENTENCE #9	We saw two <u>slides</u>.
SPELLING PATTERN: ONE, TWO, SIX, TEN	**FOCUS VOCABULARY: PLURAL NOUNS-THINGS**

MONDAY	Write the sentence **We saw two <u>slides</u>.** on a piece of paper. Emphasize the period at the end. The child copies the sentence **TWO TIMES** and draws a picture or places stickers. Teach the sounds for the word family CAW, LAW, PAW, RAW, SAW and add HAWK, LAWN, YAWN Teach the CVCE sounds for the word family BRIDE, HIDE, RIDE, SIDE, SLIDE, TIDE, WIDE Remind the students to cover the silent "E", say the vowel I-SL-I-D-E.
TUESDAY	The child writes **We saw two snakes.** on a piece of paper **ONE TIME.** Teach the students how to spell the number words that have 3 letters: ONE, TWO, SIX and TEN. First, show the number words SIX and TEN that follow the CVC pattern and have SHORT vowel sounds. Next, point out the word ONE. Teach that the word looks like the CVCE pattern where we say, "Cover the silent E, say O--O-N-E with a long O sound, as in the word CONE." It's spelled ONE, but it sounds like "WUN." Last, point out the number word TWO. Show the children the 3 letters. (For some, the acronym, Two With One, helps them remember the three letters, TWO.) Have children write TWO and place 2 stickers of something, like a ball. Then, the child reads, "TWO slides" or "TWO cakes" or "TWO cats," etc. Continue to practice the words SIX, TEN and ONE in the same way.
WEDNESDAY	Review the number words SIX, TEN, ONE and TWO. Remind students that a NOUN is a person, place or thing and that if there is more than one NOUN, it's called a PLURAL NOUN. Plural nouns end with an "S." Discuss and write a list of plural nouns that are THINGS: SLIDES, RIDES, WHEELS, GAMES, BUILDINGS, PRIZES, etc. You can teach adding "ES", "changing the Y to I and adding "ES" and "changing F to V and adding ES". Sample words that show students these rules are: BOXES, BRUSHES, BUNNIES, BERRIES, LEAVES and SHELVES. The child writes, We saw two slides. **ONE TIME** The child writes, We saw two <u>(and phonetically spells a plural noun)</u>. **TWO TIMES**
THURSDAY	Review the number words SIX, TEN, ONE and TWO. The teacher and child write all 26 lowercase letters side by side. If a letter is still difficult for the child, have the child write that letter **5 times.** Write the blends **sp, spl** and **spr.** Have the students **say** words that begin with each blend. Write their words down to read and review. Add words that you think of. Point out long and short vowels sounds.
FRIDAY	Review the number words SIX, TEN, ONE and TWO. The child uses sight words and phonetic spelling to write **2—3 sentences** about a drawing, sticker, calendar picture or magazine picture.

NOTE: Place the child's writing in plastic page protectors and a 3 ring binder for reading and review. At this point, children will be able to start reading easy readers found in libraries and book stores. Look for books that words similar to the ones the child is writing in these sentences.

Additional Common Core State Standards that these activities can address are CCSS.L.K.1.A, L.K.1.C, L.K.2.A, L.1.1.A, L.2.1.D and L.3.1.B.

SENTENCE #10	There were four <u>rides</u>.	
SPELLING PATTERN: FOUR, FIVE, NINE	**FOCUS VOCABULARY: PLURAL NOUNS-THINGS**	
MONDAY	Write the sentence **There were four <u>rides</u>.** on a piece of paper. Emphasize the period at the end. The child copies the sentence **TWO TIMES** and draws a picture or places stickers. Point out the words THERE and WERE. Show the students that they both end in –ERE. Review the CVCE sounds for the word family BRIDE, HIDE, RIDE, SIDE, TIDE, WIDE	
TUESDAY	The child writes **There were four rocks.** on a piece of paper **ONE TIME**. Teach the students how to spell the number words that have 4 letters: FOUR, FIVE and NINE. Point out that the word FOUR, has 4 letters. This helps them remember the U. Point out that FIVE and NINE follow the CVCE pattern and have the long I sound. Students can say, "Cover the silent E, say I---F-I-V-E. Cover the silent E, say I---N-I-N-E." Have children write FOUR and place 4 stickers or draw four of something, like rocks. Then, the child reads, "FOUR rides" or "FOUR slides" or "FOUR games," etc. Continue to practice the words FIVE and NINE in the same way.	
WEDNESDAY	Review the number words SIX, TEN, ONE, TWO, FOUR, FIVE and NINE. Remind students that a NOUN is a person, place or thing and that if there is more than one NOUN, it's called a PLURAL NOUN. Plural nouns end with an "S." Discuss and write a list of plural nouns that are THINGS: CARS, TRUCKS, BIKES, BALLS, BATS, DOLLS You can teach adding "ES", "changing the Y to I and adding "ES" and "changing F to V and adding ES". Sample words that show students these rules are: DRESSES, LUNCHES, PONIES, CHERRIES, ELVES and WOLVES. The child writes, There were four rides. **ONE TIME** The child writes, There were four <u>(and phonetically spells a plural noun)</u>. **TWO TIMES** The child draws a picture or places stickers.	
THURSDAY	Review the number words SIX, TEN, ONE, TWO, FOUR, FIVE and NINE. The teacher and child write all 26 lowercase letters side by side. If a letter is still difficult for the child, have the child write that letter **5 times**. Write the blends **st** and **str**. Have the students **say** words that begin with each blend. Write their words down to read and review. Add words that you think of. Point out long and short vowels sounds.	
FRIDAY	Review the number words SIX, TEN, ONE, TWO, FOUR, FIVE and NINE. The child uses sight words and phonetic spelling to write **2–3 sentences** about a drawing, sticker, calendar picture or magazine picture.	

NOTE: Place the child's writing in plastic page protectors and a 3 ring binder for reading and review. At this point, children will be able to start reading easy readers found in libraries and book stores. Look for books that have words similar to the ones the child is writing in these sentences.

Additional Common Core State Standards that these activities can address are CCSS.L.K.1.A, L.K.1.C, L.K.2.A, L.1.1.A, L.2.1.D and L.3.1.B.

SENTENCE #11	There were three <u>sheep</u>.
SPELLING PATTERN: THREE, SEVEN, EIGHT	FOCUS VOCABULARY: PLURAL NOUNS-ANIMALS

MONDAY	Write the sentence **There were three <u>sheep</u>.** on a piece of paper. Emphasize the period at the end. The child copies the sentence **TWO TIMES** and draws a picture or places stickers. Review the words THERE and WERE. Point out the word SHEEP. Remind the students that the two "E"s make a long E sound as in BEEP, DEEP, JEEP, KEEP, PEEP
TUESDAY	Teach the students how to spell the number words that have 5 letters: THREE, SEVEN, EIGHT You can sing the BINGO song with them, for each number using these lyrics: There was a farmer who had a dog, and THREE was his number: T-H-R-E-E, T-H-R-E-E, T-H-R-E-E and THREE was his number. Sing the same song using the numbers SEVEN and EIGHT. Have children write THREE and place 3 stickers or draw three of something, like cars. Then, the child reads, "THREE cars" or "THREE trucks" or "THREE hats," etc. Continue to practice the words SEVEN and EIGHT in the same way.
WEDNESDAY	Review the number words SIX, TEN, ONE, TWO, FOUR, FIVE, NINE, THREE, SEVEN and EIGHT Review that a NOUN is a person, place or thing and that a PLURAL NOUN means more than one. Remind the students that if there is more than one thing, they have to add an "S". Discuss and write a list of plural nouns that are ANIMALS: SNAKES, RATS, BUGS, CATS, DOGS, BEARS, ETC. Again, you can teach adding "es" and "changing f to v and adding es". Animals that follow these rules are: FOXES and WOLVES. The child writes, There were three cars. **ONE TIME** The child writes, There were three <u>(and phonetically spells a plural noun)</u>. **TWO TIMES**
THURSDAY	Review the number words SIX, TEN, ONE, TWO, FOUR, FIVE, NINE, THREE, SEVEN and EIGHT Play the NUMBER WORDS GAME (The instructions are found on the next page.)
FRIDAY	Review the number words SIX, TEN, ONE, TWO, FOUR, FIVE, NINE, THREE, SEVEN and EIGHT Play the NUMBER WORDS GAME (The instructions are found on the next page.)

NOTE: Place the child's writing in plastic page protectors and a 3 ring binder for reading and review. At this point, children will be able to start reading easy readers found in libraries and book stores. Look for books that have words similar to the ones the child is writing in these sentences.

LET'S PRACTICE SPELLING NUMBER WORDS ONE to TEN!

Setting up the game:

1. You'll need one dice (or magnetic spinner).

2. Write each word (one to ten) on the side of a whiteboard.

3. If you are using a magnetic spinner, draw a circle in the center of the whiteboard and divide it into 3 sections. Write the numbers 3, 4 and 5. Hang the magnetic spinner in the center of the circle.

How to play:

1. A child rolls the dice, or spins. The child has to write all of the number words that have the # spun of letters.

   For example:
   If the child rolls or spins the number 3, he or she writes: one, two, six and ten.
   If the child rolls or spins the number 4, he or she writes: four, five and nine.
   If the child rolls or spins the number 5, he or she writes: three, seven and eight.

   If the child rolls a 1, he or she writes the word ONE.
   If the child rolls a 2, he or she writes the word TWO.
   If the child rolls a 6, he or she writes the word SIX.

2. Continue rolling the dice or spinning in order to complete these tasks:
   The 1st time the child spins the # 3, he or she writes the list of 3 letter words, then **ERASES** those words from the list!
   The 2nd time the child spins the #3, he or she has to write the list of 3 letter words without seeing the words.
   The 3rd time the child spins the # 3, he or she has to verbally spell the 3 letter words without seeing the words.

3. Continue to play until the child has spun each number three times OR the allotted time runs out!

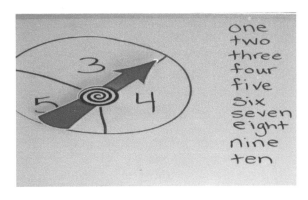

Additional Common Core State Standards that these activities can address are CCSS.L.K.1.A, L.K.2.A, L.K.5.B, L.1.1.A, L.1.1.F and L.2.1.D

SENTENCE #12	One red car was for my friend.
SPELLING PATTERN: _____ AR and _____ OR	FOCUS VOCABULARY: ADJECTIVES-COLORS

MONDAY	Write the sentence **One red car was for my friend**. on a piece of paper. Emphasize the period at the end. The child copies the sentence **TWO TIMES** and draws a picture or pastes the sentences to a picture of a car. Point out the word WAS. It sounds like WUZ, but is spelled WAS. Point out the word CAR. Teach and write the sounds for the word family BAR, CAR, FAR, JAR, STAR, TAR Write a list of words that have the AR sound in the middle as in BARN, CARD, DART, FARM, HARD, PARK, YARD Point out the word FOR. Talk about and write a list of words that have OR in them as in BORN, CORN, FORT, NORTH, FORK, YORK, MORE, WORE. Some students may be ready to learn POOR, DOOR, FLOOR and FOUR and POUR. Lastly, review the word FRIEND. It looks like FRI-END and has 6 letters.
TUESDAY	Review words that have AR and OR in them. Review that a noun is a person, place or thing. Then, teach that an adjective is a word that describes a noun. Explain that an adjective can describe how a noun looks, sounds, smells, tastes or feels. Explain that all colors are adjectives. Discuss and write a list of adjectives that are colors: RED, ORANGE, YELLOW, GREEN, BLUE, PURPLE, etc. The child writes, One red car was for my friend. **THREE TIMES** replacing the underlined word with a color word. Have the child draw a picture of each car or paste the sentences to pictures of cars.
WEDNESDAY	Review words that have AR and OR in them. Review that a noun is a person, place or thing. Then, teach that an adjective is a word that describes a noun. Explain that an adjective can describe how a noun looks, sounds, smells, tastes or feels. Explain that all colors are adjectives. Discuss and write a list of adjectives that are colors: BLACK, WHITE, GRAY, BROWN, PINK, etc. The child writes, One red car was for my friend. **THREE TIMES** replacing the underlined word with a color word. Have the child draw a picture of each car or paste the sentences to pictures of cars.
THURSDAY	Review words that have AR and OR in them. The teacher and child write all 26 lowercase letters side by side. If a letter is still difficult for the child, have the child write that letter **5 times**. Write the blends **w** and **wh**. Have the students **say** words that begin with each blend. Write their words down to read and review. Add words that you think of. Point out long and short vowels sounds.
FRIDAY	Review words that have AR and OR in them. The child uses sight words and phonetic spelling to write **2–3 sentences** about a drawing, sticker, calendar picture or magazine picture.

NOTE: Place the child's writing in plastic page protectors and a 3 ring binder for reading and review. At this point, children will be able to start reading easy readers found in libraries and book stores. Look for books that have words similar to the ones the child is writing in these sentences.

Additional Common Core State Standards that these activities can address are CCSS.L.K.1.A, L.K.1.C, L.K.2.A, L.1.1.A, L.1.1.F, L.2.1.D and L.3.1.B.

SENTENCE #13	<u>Three</u> birds were hurt.	
SPELLING PATTERN: _____ ER _____ IR _____ UR	FOCUS VOCABULARY: ADJECTIVES-NUMBERS	
MONDAY	Write the sentence <u>**Three birds were hurt.**</u> on a piece of paper. Emphasize the period at the end. The child copies the sentence **TWO TIMES** and draws a picture or pastes the sentences to a picture of birds. Point out the words BIRDS and WERE. Teach the students that the letters IR and ER in these words make the same sound "ER". Talk about and write lists of words for each: BIRD, CHIRP, DIRT, FIRST, GIRL, SHIRT, THIRD AND HER, VERB, TIGER, LADDER, etc. Next, point out the word HURT. Explain that the letters UR also make the sound "ER". Talk about and write a list of words that have UR: BLUR, BURP, BURN, CURL, CURB, FUR, HURT, TURN, etc.	
TUESDAY	Review words that have the letters ER, IR and UR in them. Review that a noun is a person, place or thing and that an adjective describes how a noun looks, sounds, smells, tastes or feels. Explain to students that numbers are also adjectives because they tell us how many nouns. Review how to spell the numbers SIX, TEN, ONE, TWO, FOUR, FIVE, NINE, THREE, SEVEN and EIGHT. The child writes, <u>Three</u> birds were hurt. **THREE TIMES** replacing the number word each time. Have the child draw pictures, place stickers or paste the sentences to pictures of birds.	
WEDNESDAY	Review words that have the letters ER, IR and UR in them. Review that a noun is a person, place or thing and that an adjective describes how a noun looks, sounds, smells, tastes or feels. Explain to students that numbers are also adjectives because they tell us how many nouns. Review how to spell the numbers SIX, TEN, ONE, TWO, FOUR, FIVE, NINE, THREE, SEVEN and EIGHT. The child writes, <u>Three</u> birds were hurt. **THREE TIMES** replacing the number word each time. Have the child draw pictures, place stickers or paste the sentences to pictures of birds.	
THURSDAY	Review words that have the letters ER, IR and UR and in them. The teacher and child write all 26 lowercase letters side by side. If a letter is still difficult for the child, have the child write that letter **5 times**. Write the blends **tr** and **wr**. Have the students **say** words that begin with each blend. Write their words down to read and review. Add words that you think of. Point out long and short vowels sounds.	
FRIDAY	Review words that have the letters ER, IR and UR in them. The child uses sight words and phonetic spelling to write **2–3 sentences** about a drawing, sticker, calendar picture or magazine picture.	

NOTE: Place the child's writing in plastic page protectors and a 3 ring binder for reading and review. At this point, children will be able to start reading easy readers found in libraries and book stores. Look for books that have words similar to the ones the child is writing in these sentences.

Additional Common Core State Standards that these activities can address are CCSS.L.K.1.A, L.K.2.A, L.1.1.A, L.1.1.F and L.2.1.D

SENTENCE #14	All of the balls were too <u>small</u>.
SPELLING PATTERN: _____ALL	FOCUS VOCABULARY: ADJECTIVES

MONDAY	Write the sentence **All of the balls were too <u>small</u>.** on a piece of paper. Emphasize the period at the end. The child copies the sentence **TWO TIMES** and draws a picture or add stickers of balls. Write and say the sounds for the word family ALL, BALL, CALL, FALL, HALL, MALL, STALL, WALL Point out the word OF. Tell students that it sounds like "UV", but it's spelled OF. Point out the word TOO. Show the children the two o's. Tell them to imagine that something is TOOOOOOOOOOOO HOT, TOOOOOOOOO COLD or TOOOOOOOO FAR. The exaggerations helps them remember to write TWO "O"s.
TUESDAY	Review the word families ALL, BALL, CALL, FALL, HALL, MALL, STALL, WALL and BIG, DIG, FIG, PIG, TWIG, WIG Review that a noun is a person, place or thing. Then, teach that an adjective is a word that describes a noun. Explain that an adjective can describe how a noun looks, sounds, smells, tastes or feels. Discuss and write a list of adjectives that describe nouns: BIG, SMALL, SHORT, TALL, FUN, FLAT, HOT, WET, etc. The child writes, All of the balls were too <u>small</u>. **ONE TIME** The child writes, All of the balls were too <u>(and phonetically spells an adjective)</u>. **TWO TIMES** Have the child draw a picture of the balls or place stickers of balls.
WEDNESDAY	Review the word families ALL, BALL, CALL, FALL, HALL, MALL, STALL, WALL and BIG, DIG, FIG, PIG, TWIG, WIG Review that a noun is a person, place or thing. Then, teach that an adjective is a word that describes a noun. Explain that an adjective can describe how a noun looks, sounds, smells, tastes or feels. Discuss and write a list of adjectives that describe nouns: BIG, SMALL, SHORT, TALL, FUN, FLAT, HOT, WET, etc. The child writes, All of the balls were too <u>small</u>. **ONE TIME** The child writes, All of the balls were too <u>(and phonetically spells an adjective)</u>. **TWO TIMES** Have the child draw a picture of the balls or place stickers of balls.
THURSDAY	Review the word family ALL, BALL, CALL, FALL, HALL, MALL, STALL, WALL The teacher and child write all 26 lowercase letters side by side. If a letter is still difficult for the child, have the child write that letter **5 times**. Write the blends **w** and **wh**. Have the students **say** words that begin with each blend. Write their words down to read and review. Add words that you think of. Point out long and short vowels sounds.
FRIDAY	Review the word family ALL, BALL, CALL, FALL, HALL, MALL, STALL, WALL The child uses sight words and phonetic spelling to write **2—3 sentences** about a drawing, sticker, calendar picture or magazine picture.

NOTE: Place the child's writing in plastic page protectors and a 3 ring binder for reading and review. At this point, children will be able to start reading easy readers found in libraries and book stores. Look for books that have words similar to the ones the child is writing in these sentences.

CONTINUING THROUGH SENTENCES LIST 3–12

Now that the child has the hang of this on-going strategy you can continue to move through the lists of sentences. Copy this chart to keep track of the child's progress each week. You can follow this same schedule through lists 3–12 which are found on pages 86–107.

NAME: _____   MONTH/YEAR: _____   AGE/GRADE: _____

	Monday	Tuesday	Wednesday	Thursday	Friday
	COPY SIGHT WORD SENTENCES			WRITE FREELY	
WEEK 1	Copy this sentence 3 times: Teach this spelling pattern:	Copy this sentence 3 times: Review the spelling pattern. Teach this vocabulary:	Copy this sentence 3 times: Review the spelling pattern. Review the vocabulary:	TOPIC: # of sentences:	TOPIC: # of sentences:
WEEK 2	Copy this sentence 3 times: Teach this spelling pattern:	Copy this sentence 3 times: Review the spelling pattern. Teach this vocabulary:	Copy this sentence 3 times: Review the spelling pattern. Review the vocabulary:	TOPIC: # of sentences:	TOPIC: # of sentences:
WEEK 3	Copy this sentence 3 times: Teach this spelling pattern:	Copy this sentence 3 times: Review the spelling pattern. Teach this vocabulary:	Copy this sentence 3 times: Review the spelling pattern. Review the vocabulary:	TOPIC: # of sentences:	TOPIC: # of sentences:
WEEK 4	Copy this sentence 3 times: Teach this spelling pattern:	Copy this sentence 3 times: Review the spelling pattern. Teach this vocabulary:	Copy this sentence 3 times: Review the spelling pattern. Review the vocabulary:	TOPIC: # of sentences:	TOPIC: # of sentences:

NOTE: Regarding the free writing on Thursday and Friday, you can turn to SECTION 4 of this book to learn more about completing stories and compositions

Remember, once a child has learned the names and sounds of each letter, you can begin teaching him or her how to write and read these sentences.
The suggested time for each sentence is 1–2 weeks. Students learn how to spell the sight words, a spelling pattern and new vocabulary.
The child should know how to spell _all_ of the sight words in one sentence before moving onto the next sentence.
The underlined words can be replaced with different words to teach vocabulary. The vocabulary words DO NOT need to be spelled correctly to move on.
Spend more or less time on each sentence based on the child's progress and ability.

Additional Common Core State Standards that these activities can address are CCSS.L.K.1.B, L.K.2.A, L.K.2.C, RF.K.2.C, RF.K.2.D, RF.1.2.C and RF.1.3.A.

SENTENCES LIST 1		
Sentence	Spelling Pattern	Vocabulary
1. I AM (NAME).	_AM	NAMES
2. I AM SAD.	_AD	FEELINGS
3. I AM A CAT.	_AT	ANIMALS
4. I SEE A DOG.	_OG	ANIMALS
5. THE WIG IS RED.	_IG and _ED	COLORS
6. I CAN RUN.	_AN and _UN	VERBS
7. I LIKE TO PLAY.	_IKE	VERBS
8. I LIKE TO PLAY AND HOP.	_AY and _OP	VERBS
9. LOOK AT ME JUMP.	_AT and _OOK	VERBS
10. THIS IS MY BOOK.	TH and _OOK	NOUNS-THINGS
11. THIS IS MY FISH.	TH and SH	NOUNS-THINGS
12. IT IS NOT IN THE BOX.	_IT and _OT	NOUNS-THINGS-PLACES
13. WE CAN GO UP.	_AN and _UP	DIRECTIONAL WORDS
14. I HAVE A PEN.	_EN	NOUN-THINGS

WORDS LIST 1: These are new words that the child has learned from these sentences.							
a	at	have	is	look	not	the	up
am	can	I	it	me	play	this	we
and	go	in	like	my	see	to	wig

ASSESS WORDS LIST 1:
As soon as the child has completed all 14 sentences, take time to make sure he/she knows how to spell each sight word before moving on to the next list of sentences. Look at WORDS LIST 1 (above). Say each word, one at a time. Have the child write or verbally spell the word. Highlight each word on the list that the child spells correctly. Have the child continue to practice any misspelled words from LIST 1. As soon as the child can spell all of the words in WORDS LIST 1 correctly, CELEBRATE! Then, move on to SENTENCES LIST 2 found on the next page.

An Easy and On-Going Spelling Strategy

Remember, once a child has learned how to spell and write the sight words in LIST 1, he or she can begin writing and reading these sentences in LIST 2.
The suggested time for each sentence is 1–2 weeks. Students learn how to spell the sight words, a spelling pattern and new vocabulary.
The child should know how to spell *all* of the sight words in one sentence before moving onto the next sentence.
The underlined words can be replaced with different words to teach vocabulary. The vocabulary words DO NOT need to be spelled correctly to move on.
Spend more or less time on each sentence based on the child's progress and ability.

Additional Common Core State Standards that these activities can address are CCSS.L.K.1.B, L.K.1.C, L.K.1.D, L.K.1.F, L.K.2.A, L.1.1.F, L.1.2.A, L.2.1.D, L.3.2.C, L.4.2.B and RF.1.3.A.

SENTENCES LIST 2

	Sentence	Spelling Pattern	Vocabulary
1.	You are my <u>friend</u>.	Focus on the word FRI-END and the word family _END	Nouns-People
2.	Come with me, <u>Tom</u>.	Focus on the words COME, WITH and ME.	Capitalize Names
3.	"Come here," <u>Deb</u> said.	Focus on the words COME, HERE and SAID	Quotation Punctuation
4.	He ate his <u>chips</u>.	_ATE and CH_	Nouns-Food
5.	She ate her <u>meat</u>.	__ATE and _EAT	Nouns-Food
6.	We went to the <u>fair</u>.	_ENT and _AIR	Nouns-Places
7.	Then, they came to the <u>fair</u> too.	_AME and _AIR	Nouns-Places
8.	We took our <u>coats</u>.	_OOK and _OAT	Plural Nouns-Things
9.	We saw two <u>slides</u>.	Focus on the # Words: ONE ,TWO, SIX, TEN (p. 78)	Plural Nouns-Things
10.	There were four <u>rides</u>.	Focus on the # Words: FOUR, FIVE, NINE (79)	Plural Nouns-Things
11.	There were eight <u>sheep</u>.	Focus on the # Words: THREE, SEVEN, EIGHT (p.80–81	Plural Nouns-Animals
12.	One <u>red</u> car was for my friend.	_AR_ and _OR_	Adjectives-Colors
13.	<u>Three</u> birds were hurt.	_ER_, _IR_ and _UR_	Adjectives-Numbers
14.	All of the balls were too <u>small</u>.	_ALL	Adjectives

WORDS LIST 2: These are new words that the child has learned from these sentences.

all	came	for	here	one	she	three	was
are	car	four	his	our	six	they	went
ate	come	friend	hurt	said	ten	too	were
balls	eight	he	nine	saw	then	took	with
birds	five	her	of	seven	there	two	you

ASSESS WORDS LIST 2:
As soon as the child has completed all 14 sentences, take time to make sure he/she knows how to spell each sight word before moving on to the next list of sentences. Look at WORDS LIST 2 (above). Say each word, one at a time. Have the child write or verbally spell the word. Highlight each word on the list that the child spells *correctly*. Have the child continue to practice any misspelled words from LIST 2. As soon as the child can spell *all* of the words in WORDS LIST 2 correctly, CELEBRATE! Then, move on to SENTENCES LIST 3 found on the next page.

Kids Win at Writing!

Remember, once a child has learned how to spell and write the sight words in LIST 2, he or she can begin writing and reading these sentences in LIST 3.
The suggested time for each sentence is 1–2 weeks. Students learn how to spell the sight words, a spelling pattern and new vocabulary.
The child should know how to spell _all_ of the sight words in one sentence before moving onto the next sentence.
The underlined words can be replaced with different words to teach vocabulary. The vocabulary words DO NOT need to be spelled correctly to move on.
Spend more or less time on each sentence based on the child's progress and ability.

Additional Common Core State Standards that these activities can address are CCSS.L.K.1.B, L.K.2.B, L.K.1.D, L.K.2.A, L.1.1.B, L.1.1.F, L.2.1.D and RF.1.3.A.

SENTENCES LIST 3

Sentence	Spelling Pattern	Vocabulary
1. What is that? That is a black hat.	_ACK	Adjectives-Colors
2. Who has the gray rock?	_OCK	Adjectives-Colors
3. Where is the sick duck?	_ICK and _UCK	Adjectives
4. Where are you from? I am from Spain.	_AIN	Proper Nouns-Countries and States
5. When did you eat at Subway?	_ID and _EAT	Proper Nouns-Restaurants
6. Why does she want to fry pie?	Focus on the Y=LONG I as in by, cry, dry, fly, fry, shy, try	Nouns-Foods
7. Which pie do you want?	Go to pg. 89. Continue to practice all 6 question words.	Nouns-Foods
8. We saw one cow fly away.	_AW and _OW	Nouns-Animals
9. How many cows flew away?	_OW and _EW	Nouns-Animals
10. Are there any new cows?	_OW and _EW	Nouns-Animals
11. Do cows know how to mow?	Focus on _OW as is how VS. _OW in know (LONG O)	Verbs
12. We saw a little mouse in our house.	Focus on the words LITTLE, MOUSE and HOUSE.	Pronouns: I, You, He, She, It, They, We
13. We put the mouse out.	_OU_ as in mouse and out	Pronouns: I, You, He, She, It, They, We
14. That was funny!	Focus on the Y=a LONG E as in bunny, funny, runny, sunny	Adjectives

WORDS LIST 3: These are new words that the child has learned from these sentences.

any	do	flew	has	know	new	that	where
away	does	fly	hat	little	out	want	which
cows	duck	from	house	many	put	what	who
did	eat	fry	how	mouse	rock	when	why

ASSESS WORDS LIST 3:
As soon as the child has completed all 14 sentences, take time to make sure he/she knows how to spell each sight word before moving on to the next list of sentences. Look at WORDS LIST 3 (above). Say each word, one at a time. Have the child write or verbally spell the word. Highlight each word on the list that the child spells _correctly_. Have the child continue to practice any misspelled words from LIST 3. As soon as the child can spell _all_ of the words in WORDS LIST 3 correctly, CELEBRATE! Then, move on to SENTENCES LIST 4 found on the page after next.

LET'S PRACTICE SPELLING QUESTION WORDS THAT BEGIN WITH
WH _____?

1. Teach or review these tips and tricks to remembering how to spell the 6 question words:

   WHO-WHAT-WHEN-WHERE-WHY-WHICH

   - They all begin with WH.
   - WHO has the word HO in it, as in, "Who said, 'HO! HO! HO!?'"
   - WHAT has the word HAT in it, as in, "WHAT is that? That is a HAT!"
   - WHEN has the word HEN in it, as in, "WHEN will the HEN wake up?"
   - WHERE has the word HERE in it, as in, "WHERE? HERE or THERE?"
   - The word WHY has the letter Y in it, "Why does WHY have a Y?"
   - The word WHICH begins with WH like all the others. It's not spelled the same as the scary green WITCH. Students can practice the sentence, "Which witch ate the sandwich?"

2. Get a pen, lined paper and old <u>calendar pictures</u>, magazine pictures or stickers for the students to use.

3. Students choose a <u>calendar picture</u>, magazine picture or sticker to write about.

4. Students write 6 serious or silly questions about the picture or sticker using the 6 different question words.

 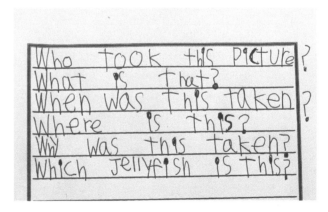

Younger or struggling students can write one question each day. Older or advanced writers can write a couple questions each day, or all 6 questions in one sitting. Be sure and hang the questions next to the pictures!

5. On another day or week, have the student write 6 questions to ask another person. The person can be another student, sibling, parent or teacher. After writing the 6 questions, switch papers. Each person can read the questions and write answers to them!

Kids Win at Writing!

Remember, once a child has learned how to spell and write the sight words in LIST 3, he or she can begin writing and reading these sentences in LIST 4.
The suggested time for each sentence is 1–2 weeks. Students learn how to spell the sight words, a spelling pattern and new vocabulary.
The child should know how to spell _all_ of the sight words in one sentence before moving onto the next sentence.
The underlined words can be replaced with different words to teach vocabulary. The vocabulary words DO NOT need to be spelled correctly to move on.
Spend more or less time on each sentence based on the child's progress and ability.

Additional Common Core State Standards that these activities can address are CCSS.L.K.1.B, L.K.2.A, L.1.1.B, L.1.1.F, L.1.1.G, L.2.2.C, L.3.1.E and RF.1.3.A.

SENTENCES LIST 4

Sentence	Spelling Pattern	Vocabulary
1. That <u>yummy</u> cake was for my mother.	_AKE and _OTHER	Adjectives
2. I'm <u>happy</u>.	Teach the contractions: I'M, YOU'RE, SHE'S, HE'S, IT'S, THEY'RE, WE'RE	Adjectives
3. I'm happy because I have <u>friends</u>.	Review the contractions: I'M, YOU'RE, SHE'S, HE'S, IT'S, THEY'RE, WE'RE	Nouns
4. <u>We're</u> going to the park now.	_ARK	Contractions
5. I want to go, but I'm very <u>tired</u>.	Focus on the word VERY (not vary ☺)	Adjectives
6. It's very <u>cold</u>.	_OLD	Adjectives
7. Let's go after school.	Focus on the words LET'S, AFTER and SCHOOL	Verbs
8. The king will be <u>running</u> around.	_ING and _OUND	Verbs-____ing
9. We will give him some good <u>food</u>.	Focus on the "OO" as in good and wood VS. "OO" in food, roof, room, pool	Nouns
10. Could we go there again soon?	_OON	Verbs
11. Would your grandma like some <u>water</u>?	W vs. WH was, with, want, went, will, would vs. who, what, when, where, why, which	Nouns
12. It's <u>wet</u>, so we can't go over there.	Focus on the contraction CAN'T =cannot	Adjectives
13. I couldn't go under it.	Focus on the contraction COULDN'T=could not	Verbs
14. <u>Sharks</u> don't live on land.	Focus on the contraction DON'T=do not	Nouns-Sea Creatures

WORDS LIST 4: These are new words that the child has learned from these sentences.

after	but	give	him	live	park	under
again	cake	good	I'm	mother	school	very
around	could	going	it's	now	so	will
be	couldn't	grandma	land	on	some	would
because	don't	happy	let's	over	soon	your

ASSESS WORDS LIST 4:
As soon as the child has completed all 14 sentences, take time to make sure he/she knows how to spell each sight word before moving on to the next list of sentences. Look at WORDS LIST 4 (above). Say each word, one at a time. Have the child write or verbally spell the word. Highlight each word on the list that the child spells _correctly_. Have the child continue to practice any misspelled words from LIST 4. As soon as the child can spell _all_ of the words in WORDS LIST 4 correctly, CELEBRATE! Then, move on to SENTENCES LIST 5 found on the next page.

An Easy and On-Going Spelling Strategy

Remember, once a child has learned how to spell and write the sight words in LIST 4, he or she can begin writing and reading these sentences in LIST 5. The suggested time for each sentence is 1–2 weeks. Students learn how to spell the sight words, a spelling pattern and new vocabulary. The child should know how to spell *all* of the sight words in one sentence before moving onto the next sentence. The underlined words can be replaced with different words to teach vocabulary. The vocabulary words DO NOT need to be spelled correctly to move on. Spend more or less time on each sentence based on the child's progress and ability.

Additional Common Core State Standards that these activities can address are CCSS.L.K.1.B, L.K.2.A, L.1.1.F, L.1.1.C, L.2.1.D, L.2.2.C and L.3.1.G

SENTENCES LIST 5

Sentence	Spelling Pattern	Vocabulary
1. Try to pull the <u>sled</u> for them.	Focus on Y=LONG I as in by, cry, dry, fry, try, fly, shy, why	Nouns-Things
2. The story is about a <u>pirate</u>.	Focus on Y=LONG E as in story, army, berry, carry, daisy, etc.	Nouns-People
3. Once upon a time, there was a little <u>dinosaur</u>.	Focus on the words ONCE UPON A TIME	Nouns-Animals
4. You can <u>draw</u> when you're done.	Review the contraction YOU'RE=you are	Verbs
5. The <u>boy</u> isn't ready	Teach, practice and review the negative contractions:	Nouns-People
6. The <u>girl</u> wasn't well on Friday.	ISN'T, AREN'T, WASN'T, WEREN'T, DIDN'T, DOESN'T, HASN'T, HAVEN'T	Nouns-People
7. The <u>horses</u> aren't out right now.	_IGHT	Plural Nouns-Animals
8. There weren't any <u>sheep</u> yesterday.	_EEP	Plural Nouns-Animals
9. The <u>chickens</u> didn't really like the pool.	Focus on the word REALLY and the word family _OOL	Plural Nouns-Animals
10. The farmer doesn't use all of the <u>tools</u>.	Review and focus on the word DOESN'T	Plural Nouns-Things
11. We haven't been to the <u>shore</u> before.	_ORE	Nouns-Places
12. The chicken <u>goes</u> into the barn every day.	Focus on the word EVERY	Add S, ES and IES to Verbs
13. The woman <u>bakes</u> bread every afternoon.	Focus on the _EA_=SHORT E as in bread, head, read, ready, etc.	Add S, ES and IES to Verbs
14. Today, that goat is <u>better</u> than mine.	Focus on the word THAN	Comparative Adjectives __ER

WORDS LIST 5: These are new words that the child has learned from these sentences.

about	before	doesn't	goat	once	right	today	well
afternoon	bread	done	haven't	pool	story	try	weren't
aren't	chicken	every	into	pull	than	upon	woman
barn	day	farmer	isn't	ready	them	use	yesterday
been	didn't	Friday	mine	really	time	wasn't	you're

ASSESS WORDS LIST 5:

As soon as the child has completed all 14 sentences, take time to make sure he/she knows how to spell each sight word before moving on to the next list of sentences. Look at WORDS LIST 5 (above). Say each word, one at a time. Have the child write or verbally spell the word. Highlight each word on the list that the child spells *correctly*. Have the child continue to practice any misspelled words from LIST 5. As soon as the child can spell *all* of the words in WORDS LIST 5 correctly, CELEBRATE! Then, move on to SENTENCES LIST 6 found on the next page.

Remember, once a child has learned how to spell and write the sight words in LIST 5, he or she can begin writing and reading these sentences in LIST 6.
The suggested time for each sentence is 1–2 weeks. Students learn how to spell the sight words, a spelling pattern and new vocabulary.
The child should know how to spell *all* of the sight words in one sentence before moving onto the next sentence.
The underlined words can be replaced with different words to teach vocabulary. The vocabulary words DO NOT need to be spelled correctly to move on.
Spend more or less time on each sentence based on the child's progress and ability.

Additional Common Core State Standards that these activities can address are CCSS.L.K.1.B, L.K.1.C, L.K.2.A, L.1.1.B, L.1.1.D, L.1.1.F L.2.1.D, L.3.1.E, L.3.1.G and RF.1.3.A.

SENTENCES LIST 6

Sentence	Spelling Pattern	Vocabulary
1. My friend's field is the biggest	Focus on the 'S and the IE in FRIEND and FIELD	Superlative Adjectives __EST
2. Quiet people aren't always shy.	Focus on the words PEOPLE and ALWAYS	Adjectives
3. Only the eggs fell off the table.	_ELL and _ABLE	Plural Nouns-Foods
4. Should I bring apples or bananas?	Focus on the word SHOULD and review __ING	Plural Nouns-Foods
5. These bowls shouldn't be full of water.	Focus on the words THESE, BOWLS, FULL and SHOULDN'T	Plural Nouns-Foods
6. The children ate food together.	Focus on the words CHILDREN and TO-GET-HER	Plural Nouns-Foods
7. Those windows are clean and pretty.	_OSE and _EAN	Plural Nouns-Things
8. I want to buy toys for my brother.	Focus on the words WANT, BUY and BROTHER	Plural Nouns-Toys
9. First, I need to earn money by mowing.	Teach, practice and review that: "EAR" sometime sounds like	Verbs-ing
10. It was early when we heard the monkeys.	"ER" as in earn, Earth, early, heard, learn, pearl, search	Plural Nouns-Animals
11. The squirrels played for a long time.	_ONG and _IME	Plural Nouns-Animals
12. The clowns made us laugh so hard!	Focus on the word LAUGH and the word family _ADE	Plural Nouns-People
13. The bears work hard scratch their backs.	_EARS=LONG A and _ATCH=SHORT A	Possessive Pronoun: THEIR + A Noun
14. The bunny found its mom.	_UNNY and __OUND	Possessive Pronoun: ITS + A Noun

WORDS LIST 6: These are new words that the child has learned from these sentences.

always	bunny	earn	full	long	only	quiet	their
bears	buy	fell	hard	made	or	scratch	these
bowls	children	field	heard	money	people	should	those
bring	clean	first	its	need	played	shouldn't	together
brother	early	found	laugh	off	pretty	table	work

ASSESS WORDS LIST 6:
As soon as the child has completed all 14 sentences, take time to make sure he/she knows how to spell each sight word before moving on to the next list of sentences. Look at WORDS LIST 6 (above). Say each word, one at a time. Have the child write or verbally spell the word. Highlight each word that the child spells *correctly*. Have the child continue to practice any misspelled words from LIST 6. As soon as the child can spell *all* of the words in WORDS LIST 6 correctly, CELEBRATE!

STOP!

A general expectation for students completing these sight word sentences is:

Kindergarten: Lists 1 and 2

1st Grade: Lists 3 and 4

2nd Grade: Lists 5 and 6

3rd Grade: Lists 7 and 8

4th Grade: Lists 9 and 10

5th Grade: Lists 11 and 12

After completing Lists 5 and 6 and before moving on to Sentences List 7, I suggest going to www.k12reader.com. Click on the Second Grade Spelling List. Download it and print it. Each week follow these steps:

1. Monday: Have your child verbally spell each word from Week 1 and Week 2.

2. Make note of the words he or she misspells.

3. Combine those misspelled words to create 2–3 sight words sentences for your child to practice the rest of the week.

4. On Monday of the following week, have your child verbally spell the words from Week 3 and 4.

5. Make note of the words he or she misspells.

6. Combine those misspelled words to create 2–3 sight word sentences for him or her to practice throughout the week.

7. Continue this way, week after week, until she or he has learned all the words through Week 36.

After working through the K12 Reader's 2nd Grade List, move on to SENTENCES LIST 7 found on the next page.

Kids Win at Writing!

Remember, once a child has learned how to spell and write the sight words in LIST 6, he/she can begin writing and reading these sentences in LIST 7.
The suggested time for each sentence is 1–2 weeks. Students learn how to spell the sight words, a spelling pattern and new vocabulary.
The child should know how to spell _all_ of the sight words in one sentence before moving onto the next sentence.
The underlined words can be replaced with different words to teach vocabulary. The vocabulary words DO NOT need to be spelled correctly to move on.
Spend more or less time on each sentence based on the child's progress and ability.

Additional Common Core State Standards that these activities can address are CCSS.L.K.1.B, L.K.2.A, L.1.1.B, L.1.1.H, L.3.1.E and L.3.2.E.

SENTENCES LIST 7

Sentence	Spelling Pattern	Vocabulary
1. My aunt bought an <u>egg</u>.	_OUGHT	Nouns that begin with a vowel: apple, egg, elephant, umbrella, etc.
2. Can I please read by myself <u>now</u>?	_EA_=LONG E	Time: now, later, today, tomorrow, etc.
3. My family and I watch the <u>planes</u> fly by.	Y=LONG E family VS. Y=LONG I in fly and by	Nouns-Flying Animals-Objects
4. My <u>aunt's</u> brown horse is my favorite.	Focus on the word FA+VOR+ITE Focus on _ROWN as in brown drown, crown, frown	Singular and Plural Possessive-Nouns
5. Squirrels sleep behind my <u>cousins'</u> house.	SQUI__	Singular and Plural Possessive-Nouns
6. They will tell us what to <u>write</u>.	_ILL and _ELL	Verbs
7. Ask <u>him</u> what happened.	Focus on the word HAPPENED and the word family _ASK	Object Pronouns: me, her, him, it, them, us
8. How far did you <u>walk</u> last night?	_AST and _IGHT	Verbs
9. I have never gotten hurt while <u>camping</u>.	Focus on the words NEVER, GOTTEN and WHILE	_ ING Verbs
10. Each person must carry their own <u>bag</u>.	_EACH=LONG E and _OWN=LONG O	Nouns-Things
11. Use both hands to hold the <u>chicken</u>.	_OLD	Nouns-Things
12. How much does the <u>robot</u> cost?	_OST=SHORT O vs. _OST=LONG O cost, lost VS. host, most, post	Nouns-Things
13. Just open the door and take out the <u>pizza</u>.	_OOR as in door, floor, poor	Nouns-Foods
14. They gave us cold <u>water</u> to drink.	_AVE and _INK	Nouns-Drinks

WORDS LIST 7: These are new words that the child has learned from these sentences.

an	bought	cost	favorite	hold	must	own	squirrels
ask	brown	door	gave	horse	myself	person	take
aunt	by	drink	gotten	just	never	please	tell
behind	carry	each	hands	last	night	read	watch
both	cold	family	happened	much	open	sleep	while

ASSESS WORDS LIST 7:
As soon as the child has completed all 14 sentences, take time to make sure he/she knows how to spell each sight word before moving on to the next list of sentences. Look at WORDS LIST 7 (above). Say each word, one at a time. Have the child write or verbally spell the word. Highlight each word on the list that the child spells _correctly_. Have the child continue to practice any misspelled words from LIST 7. As soon as the child can spell _all_ of the words in WORDS LIST 7 correctly, CELEBRATE! Then, move on to SENTENCES LIST 8 found on the next page.

An Easy and On-Going Spelling Strategy

Remember, once a child has learned how to spell and write the sight words in LIST 7, he or she can begin writing and reading these sentences in LIST 8.
The suggested time for each sentence is 1–2 weeks. Students learn how to spell the sight words, a spelling pattern and new vocabulary.
The child should know how to spell *all* of the sight words in one sentence before moving onto the next sentence.
The underlined words can be replaced with different words to teach vocabulary. The vocabulary words DO NOT need to be spelled correctly to move on.
Spend more or less time on each sentence based on the child's progress and ability.

Additional Common Core State Standards that these activities can address are CCSS.L.K.1.B, L.K.2.A, L.1.1.B, L.1.1.D, L.1.1.F, L.2.1.E and L.2.6.

SENTENCES LIST 8		
Sentence	Spelling Pattern	Vocabulary
1. The drive was <u>hilly</u>.	_IVE=LONG I	Adjectives
2. My uncle's dog is <u>silly</u>.	Focus on the word UNCLE'S and the word family _ILLY	Adjectives
3. What kind of <u>dog</u> does he have?	_IND=LONG I	Nouns-Animals
4. The <u>dogs'</u> owner thought the stadium was beautiful.	Focus on the words THOUGHT and STADIUM Teach: "BE-A-U-TIFUL person" to spell BEAUTIFUL	Singular and Plural Possessive Nouns
5. Which witch lived there for <u>twenty</u> years?	_ITCH and _EARS=LONG E	Number Words to 100
6. For vacation, we went to <u>Florida</u>.	_TION=SH	Capitalize State Names
7. The weather by the ocean was <u>cloudy</u>.	_EATHER=SHORT E	Adjectives: Weather
8. We had a great time even though it was <u>cold</u>.	Focus on the words GREAT and THOUGH	Adjectives: Weather
9. We had to wear our <u>jackets</u>.	_EAR=LONG A as in bear, pear, tear, wear	Nouns: Clothing
10. It rained on the <u>third</u> day we were there.	Focus on the spelling and meaning of ordinal numbers:	
11. That's the <u>eighth</u> house that they have built.	FIRST, SECOND, THIRD, FOURTH, FIFTH, SIXTH, SEVENTH, EIGHTH, NINTH and TENTH	
12. Can you help <u>me</u> draw a round circle?	C = the "S" as in: cell, cent, center, cement, cereal, cider, circus	Object Pronouns: me, him, her, it, them, us
13. We're going to walk through another <u>tunnel</u>.	Focus on the words: THROUGH and ANOTHER	Nouns-Things
14. The <u>cabbage</u> will start to grow in about eight weeks.	_ART, _EEK and _OW=LONG O	Nouns-Vegetables

WORDS LIST 8: These are new words that the child has learned from these sentences.							
another	drive	great	ninth	second	tenth	through	weather
beautiful	eighth	grow	ocean	seventh	that's	uncle's	weeks
built	even	help	owner	sixth	third	vacation	we're
circle	fifth	kind	rained	stadium	though	walk	witch
draw	fourth	lived	round	start	thought	wear	years

ASSESS WORDS LIST 8:
As soon as the child has completed all 14 sentences, take time to make sure he/she knows how to spell each sight word before moving on to the next list of sentences. Look at WORDS LIST 8 (above). Say each word, one at a time. Have the child write or verbally spell the word. Highlight each word on the list that the child spells *correctly*. Have the child continue to practice any misspelled words from LIST 8. As soon as the child can spell *all* of the words in WORDS LIST 8 correctly, CELEBRATE!

STOP!

Remember, a general expectation for students completing these sight word sentences is:

Kindergarten: Lists 1 and 2

1st Grade: Lists 3 and 4

2nd Grade: Lists 5 and 6

3rd Grade: Lists 7 and 8

4th Grade: Lists 9 and 10

5th Grade: Lists 11 and 12

After completing Lists 7 and 8 and before moving on to Sentences List 9, I suggest going to www.k12reader.com. Click on the Third Grade Spelling List. Download it and print it. Each week follow these steps:

1. Monday: Have your child verbally spell each word from Week 1 and Week 2.

2. Make note of the words he or she misspells.

3. Combine those misspelled words to create 2–3 sight words sentences for your child to practice the rest of the week.

4. On Monday of the following week, have your child verbally spell the words from Week 3 and 4.

5. Make note of the words he or she misspells.

6. Combine those misspelled words to create 2–3 sight word sentences for him or her to practice throughout the week.

7. Continue this way, week after week, until she or he has learned all the words through Week 36.

After working through the K12 Reader's 3rd Grade List, move on to SENTENCES LIST 9 found on the next page.

An Easy and On-Going Spelling Strategy

Remember, once a child has learned how to spell and write the sight words in LIST 8, he or she can begin writing and reading these sentences in LIST 9.
At this point, many children can work on 2–3 sentences per week. You can use one sentence that is listed here, plus two sentences that you create using words that the child misspells in his/her free writing. The child should know how to spell *all* of the sight words in one sentence before moving onto the next sentence.
The underlined words can be replaced with different words to teach vocabulary. The vocabulary words DO NOT need to be spelled correctly to move on.
Spend more or less time on each sentence based on the child's progress and ability.

Additional Common Core State Standards that these activities can address are CCSS.L.K.1.B, L.K.2.A, L.1.1.B, L.1.1.F, L.2.1.E, L.2.6, L.3.1.E, L.3.2.C, L.3.2.E and L.4.2.A,

SENTENCES LIST 9		
Sentence	Spelling Pattern	Vocabulary
1. Mr. Hedgehog and I travel to different cities each year.	Focus on the correct order of words: MY FAMILY AND I…	Proper Nouns Abbreviations + Names
2. Mrs. Fancy and I visit the museum on Wednesday mornings.	Focus on spelling the days of the week: Sun+day, Mon+day, Tues+day, Wed+nes+day, Thurs+day, Fri+day, Sa+tur+day	
3. Dr. Dolphin and I go to the aquarium every January.	Focus on spelling the months of the year.	
4. My cousins often ask me to go to their house in August.	Focus on spelling the months of the year.	Nouns-Places-Events
5. Mike's family seldom travels during the month of February.	Focus on the apostrophe 's' in possession: Mike's	Proper Nouns-Names of People
6. Are you sure Jake's cake has sugar in it?	Focus on SU=SH as in sure, surely, sugar, assure, ensure, insure and pressure	Nouns-Foods
7. At the beginning, they were hopping, running and swimming	Short vowels + double consonants as in beginning, dripping, flipping, jabbing, mopping, nodding, stopping, trimming, winning	Verbs-__ING
8. We'll search for the missing kitten tomorrow.	Review short vowels + double consonants as in, apple, add, bigger, copper, digger, fiddle, gobble, hidden, kitten, little, middle	Pronouns-Contractions I'll, He'll, She'll, It'll, They'll, We'll
9. She couldn't believe how many piers there were!	Teach "I BEFORE E" as in achieve, believe, brief, chief, field, etc. See page 112 to write a silly story using words that have IE.	Nouns-Things
10. Has your neighbor ever received a special gift?	Teach "I BEFORE E EXCEPT AFTER C" as in receive and deceive See page 112 to write a silly story using other words that have EI.	Nouns-Things
11. The jet landed safely in Japan.	Focus on past verbs that end in ED. Root verbs that end in T or D will sound like "ED" when you add ED, as in departed, handed, landed, listed, started	Proper Nouns-Countries
12. The kids listened to the sounds of the machines.	Focus on past verbs that end in ED. Root verbs that end in B, G, H, L, M, N, R, S, TH, V, W, Y or Z will sound like "D" when you add ED, as in combed	Nouns-Things
13. They hurried, but still carried the bags slowly.	Focus on verbs that end in Y. Change the Y to I and add ED. These verbs sound like "D" when you add ED, as in carried, cried, hurried, tried, etc.	Nouns-Things
14. Their grandparents watched them often last year.	Focus on verbs that end in ED. Verbs that end in C, CH, CK, F, GH, K, P, SH, SS and X will sound like "T" when you add ED, as in faced, watched, quacked, puffed, coughed, biked, clapped, wiped, etc.	Nouns-Days-Months-Seasons
WORDS LIST 9: These are new words that the child has learned from these sentences.		

April	cities	grandparents	listened	neighbor	safely	sounds	tomorrow
aquarium	cousins	hurried	March/May	November	Saturday	special	travel
August	December	January	missing	October	search	sugar	Tuesday
beginning	different	June/July	Monday	often	seldom	sure	visit
believe	during	kitten	month	received	September	swimming	watched
carried	February	landed	museum	running	slowly	Thursday	Wednesday

ASSESS WORDS LIST 9:
As soon as the child has completed all 14 sentences, take time to make sure he/she knows how to spell each sight word before moving on to the next list of sentences. Look at WORDS LIST 9 (above). Say each word, one at a time. Have the child write or verbally spell the word. Highlight each word on the list that the child spells *correctly*. Have the child continue to practice any misspelled words from LIST 9. As soon as the child can spell *all* of the words in WORDS LIST 9 correctly, CELEBRATE! Then, move on to SENTENCES LIST 10 found on the next page.

STOP!

REVIEW REGULAR PAST VERBS THAT END IN --ED

NOTE: This activity can address the following Common Core Standards:
CCSS.ELA-LITERACY.L.1.1.E, L.1.4.C, L.3.1.D, L.3.1.E

Regular past verbs end in ED. For example:

Landed

Played

Jumped

However, the ED letters don't make the same sound. Listen to these ED sounds.

The --ED in land<u>ed</u> sounds like ED.

The --ED in play<u>ed</u> sounds like D.

The --ED in jump<u>ed</u> sounds like T.

For this activity, try to complete the chart on the next two pages by by writing one past ED verb in each box. For each letter of the alphabet, write an ED verb that sounds like ED, D and T. Letter A and Z have been done for you. There are clues at the top of each column to help you as well.

NOTE: For the letter X, you can write verbs that begin with the letters EX, such as exclaimed.

REGULAR PAST VERBS THAT END IN --ED

ED (root verbs that end in d or t)	D (root verbs that end in the letters b, g, h, l, m, n, r, s, th, v, w, y, z)	T (root verbs that end in the letters c, ch, ck, f, k, p, sh, ss, x)
A acted	arrived	asked
B		
C		
D		
E		
F		
G		
H		
I		
J		
K		
L		

	ED (root verbs that end in d or t)	D (root verbs that end in the letters b, g, h, l, m, n, r, s, th, v, w, y, z)	T (root verbs that end in the letters c, ch, ck, f, k, p, sh, ss, x)
M			
N			
O			
P			
Q			
R			
S			
T			
U			
V			
W			
X			
Y			
Z	zested	zoomed	zapped

This is no easy task. Once you fill in all of the blanks, give yourself a big, "GOOD JOB!!"

An Easy and On-Going Spelling Strategy

Remember, once a child has learned how to spell and write the sight words in LIST 9, he/she can begin writing and reading these sentences in LIST 10.
At this point, many children can work on 2–3 sentences per week. You can use one sentence that is listed here, plus two sentences that you create using words the child misspells in his/her free writing. The child should know how to spell *all* of the sight words in one sentence before moving onto the next sentence.
The underlined words can be replaced with different words to teach vocabulary. The vocabulary words DO NOT need to be spelled correctly to move on.
Spend more or less time on each sentence based on the child's progress and ability.

Additional Common Core State Standards that these activities can address are CCSS.L.K.1.B, L.K.2.A, L.1.1.B, L.1.1.E, L.1.1.F, L.2.1.E, L.2.6, L.3.1.A, L.3.2.C and L.3.2.E

SENTENCES LIST 10

	Sentence	Spelling Pattern	Vocabulary
1.	"Tomorrow evening, we will celebrate Joy's birthday," he <u>reminded</u>.	Focus on the words CELEBRATE, CELEBRATING, CELEBRATION	Instead of Said Verbs
2.	"Remember to bring a dessert to share with everyone," she <u>added</u>.	Focus on the difference between DESSERT and DESERT	Instead of Said Verbs
3.	Let's go straight there instead of stopping by <u>Walmart</u>.	Focus on the differences between BYE, BY and BUY	Proper Nouns-Stores
4.	Having a bad cough was really rough on <u>Mrs. Smith</u>.	OUGH=off vs. OUGH=uf cough, trough vs. enough, rough and tough	Proper Nouns Abbreviations+Names
5.	Although it was tough to go through, <u>Mr. Orr</u> didn't quit.	_OUGH=LONG O sound vs. _OUGH= LONG U sound Although, though and dough vs. through	Proper Nouns Abbreviations+Names
6.	<u>Dr. Ace</u> stated that students rarely drink enough water.	Review _OUGH="uf" as in enough, rough and tough Focus on the words RARELY, WATER and the word family _ink	Proper Nouns Abbreviations+Names
7.	The servers inside the restaurant were respectful and <u>wonderful</u>.	Adjectives that end in __FUL	Adjectives that end in FUL
8.	The temperature outside was comfortable and <u>enjoyable</u>.	Adjectives that end in __ABLE	Adjectives that end in ABLE
9.	The careless team brought the <u>useless</u> signs.	Adjectives that end in __LESS	Adjectives that end in LESS
10.	Soldiers are <u>courageous</u> and enter dangerous situations.	Adjectives that end in __OUS	Adjectives that end in OUS
11.	My friend, <u>Amy</u>, is responsible, patient and encouraging.	Focus on the words RESPONSIBLE, PATIENT and ENCOURAGING	Proper Nouns-Names
12.	Students ask questions that lead to actions and <u>solutions</u>.	Nouns that end in __TION	Nouns-_TION
13.	In your opinion, does a business need <u>cooperation</u> to succeed?	Nouns that end in __TION	Nouns-_TION
14.	Everyone got <u>sick</u> during the exercises, except me.	Focus on words the words EXERCISES and EXCEPT	Adjectives

WORDS LIST 10: These are new words that the child has learned from these sentences.

actions	celebrate	enough	having	patient	responsible	situations	students
although	comfortable	enter	inside	questions	restaurant	soldiers	succeed
birthday	cough	evening	instead	quit	rough	solutions	team
brought	dangerous	everyone	lead	rarely	servers	stated	temperature
business	dessert	except	opinion	remember	share	stopping	tough
careless	encouraging	exercises	outside	respectful	signs	straight	water

ASSESS WORDS LIST 10:
As soon as the child has completed all 14 sentences, take time to make sure he/she knows how to spell each sight word before moving on to the next list of sentences. Look at WORDS LIST 10 (above). Say each word, one at a time. Have the child write or verbally spell the word. Highlight each word on the list that the child spells *correctly*. Have the child continue to practice any misspelled words from LIST 10. As soon as the child can spell *all* of the words in WORDS LIST 10 correctly, CELEBRATE!

STOP!

A general expectation for students completing these sight word sentences is:

Kindergarten: Lists 1 and 2

1st Grade: Lists 3 and 4

2nd Grade: Lists 5 and 6

3rd Grade: Lists 7 and 8

4th Grade: Lists 9 and 10

5th Grade: Lists 11 and 12

After completing Lists 9 and 10 and before moving on to Sentences List 11, I suggest going to www.k12reader.com. Click on the 4th Grade Spelling List. Download it and print it. Each week follow these steps:

1. Monday: Have your child verbally spell each word from Week 1 and Week 2.

2. Make note of the words he or she misspells.

3. Combine those misspelled words to create 2–3 sight words sentences for your child to practice the rest of the week.

4. On Monday of the following week, have your child verbally spell the words from Week 3 and 4.

5. Make note of the words he or she misspells.

6. Combine those misspelled words to create 2–3 sight word sentences for him or her to practice throughout the week.

7. Continue this way, week after week, until she or he has learned all the words through Week 36.

After working through the K12 Reader's 4th Grade List, move on to SENTENCES LIST 11 found on the next page.

An Easy and On-Going Spelling Strategy

Once a child has learned how to spell and write the sight words in LIST 10, he/she can begin writing and reading these sentences in LIST 11.
This list focuses on changing ADJECTIVES to ADVERBS. Page 100-103 explains these exercises in greater detail.

Additional Common Core State Standards that these activities can address are CCSS.L.K.2.A, L.1.1.B, L.1.1.E, L.2.1.E, L.2.2.C, L.2.6, L.3.2.D, L.3.2.C, L.3.2.E, RF.2.3.D and RF.3.3.A.

SENTENCES LIST 11

Sentence	Spelling Pattern	Vocabulary
1. "The guards are pacing <u>frantically</u> around the castle!" she whispered dramatically.	ADVERBS that have TWO "L"s. Change adjectives that **end in C** to adverbs by **adding ALLY** as in artistically, basic+ally, dramatic+ally, energetic+ally, enthusiastic+ally, optimistic+ally	Adverbs that have TWO "L"s and end in _____CAL-LY
2. "The athletes <u>basically</u> train every night," he answered enthusiastically.		
3. "The gymnasts <u>usually</u> compete on Fridays," she replied casually.	ADVERBS that have TWO "L"s. Change adjectives that **end in AL** to adverbs by **adding LY** as in accidental+ly, annual+ly, continual+ly, final+ly, gradual+ly, normal+ly, occasional+ly	Adverbs that have TWO "L"s and end in __ALLY
4. The dog was <u>actually</u> losing weight because of the pain in his mouth.		
5. Hopefully, the veterinarian will <u>carefully</u> remove the infected tooth.	ADVERBS that have TWO "L"s. Change adjectives that **end in ul** to adverbs by **adding LY** as is Beautifully, cheerful+ly, graceful+ly, painful+ly, playful+ly, powerful+ly, respectful+ly,	Adverbs that have TWO "L"s and end in _ULLY
6. Thankfully, the veterinarian completed the surgery <u>successfully</u>.		
7. You'll probably sleep more <u>comfortably</u> over there.	ADVERBS that have ONE "L" Change adjectives that **end in LE** to adverbs by **changing the E to Y** as in gently, horribly, irritably, miserably, questionably, terribly, uncomfortably, unbearably	Adverbs that have ONE "L" and end in __BLY or _TLY
8. The ranger responsibly reported the <u>fire</u>.		
9. The dragons danced <u>happily</u> around the moat.	ADVERBS that have ONE "L" Change adjectives that **end in Y** to adverbs by **changing the Y to I and adding LY**, as in angrily, busily, crazily, dreamily, eerily, fancily, greedily, grumpily, hungrily, lazily, merrily, necessarily, noisily, primarily, quirkily, sleepily, speedily, wearily	Adverbs that have ONE "L" and end in __ILY
10. The queen worried <u>unnecessarily</u>.		
11. Unfortunately, the weather made it extremely difficult to sail <u>safely</u>.	ADVERBS that have ONE "L" Change adjectives that **end in E** to adverbs by **adding LY** as in accurately, actively, approximately, barely, creatively, compassionately, delicately, immediately, rarely, nicely, politely, privately, safely, sincerely, surely, ultimately, wisely	Adverbs that have ONE "L" and end in __ELY
12. The ship stopped <u>immediately</u> and waited approximately forty minutes.		
13. The embarrassed team calmly and <u>courageously</u> entered the field.	ADVERBS that have ONE "L" Change adjectives that **end in everything else** to adverbs by **adding LY** as in awkwardly, briefly, calmly, deeply, evenly, fondly, gladly, hardly, innocently, keenly, lightly, madly, neatly, openly, proudly, quickly, rapidly, slowly, tightly, urgently, wrongly	Adverbs that have ONE "L" and end in _LY
14. The students consistently and <u>consciously</u> display good character.		

WORDS LIST 11: These are new words that the child has learned from these sentences.

answered	character	display	extremely	losing	queen	stopped	veterinarian
approximately	compete	dragons	forty	minutes	ranger	surgery	waited
athletes	completed	dramatically	guards	mouth	remove	thankfully	weight
calmly	consistently	embarrassed	gymnasts	pacing	replied	tooth	whispered
castle	danced	entered	hopefully	pain	reported	train	worried
casually	difficult	enthusiastically	infected	probably	responsibly	unfortunately	you'll

ASSESS WORDS LIST 11:
As soon as the child has completed all 14 sentences, take time to make sure he/she knows how to spell each sight word before moving on to the next list of sentences. Look at WORDS LIST 11 (above). Say each word, one at a time. Have the child write or verbally spell the word. Highlight each word on the list that the child spells _correctly_. Have the child continue to practice any misspelled words from LIST 11. As soon as the child can spell _all_ of the words in WORDS LIST 11 correctly, CELEBRATE! Then, move on to SENTENCES LIST 12 found on the next page.

STOP!

REVIEW HOW TO CHANGE ADJECTIVES TO ADVERBS

NOTE: This activity can address the following Common Core Standards: CCSS.ELA-LITERACY.L.2.1.E and L.2.6

The BIG QUESTION!

Does the adverb have ONE or TWO "L"S at the end?

Follow these tips and tricks:

In tips 1, 2 and 3, the adverbs have TWO Ls. Here, the adjectives already have ONE L. So, when you add LY to change the adjective to an adverb, you are writing the SECOND L.

1. If the adjective ends in _____C, like BASIC, you will add __ALLY to make the adverb BASICALLY=TWO "L"s.

2. If the adjective ends in _____AL, like FINAL, you will add __LY to make the adverb FINALLY=TWO "L"s.

3. If the adjective ends in _____UL, like BEAUTIFUL, you will add __LY to make the adverb BEAUTIFULLY=TWO "L"s.

In tips 4, 5 and 6, the adverbs will only have ONE L.

4. If the adjective ends in _____LE like SIMPLE, you change the E to Y to make the adverb SIMPLY=ONE "L".

5. If the adjective ends in _____Y like, HAPPY, you change the Y to I and add LY to make the adverb HAPPILY=ONE "L".

6. If the adjective ends in _____E like, SAFE, you keep the E and add LY to make the adverb SAFELY=ONE "L".

7. If the adjective ends in anything else, like CALM, you simply add LY to make the adverb CALMLY=ONE "L".

For this activity, try to complete the chart below by writing ten adverbs for each tip. The adverbs under the numbers 1, 2 and 3 will have TWO "L"s. The adverbs under the numbers 4, 5, 6 and 7 will have ONE "L".

Adjectives **to** Adverbs

TWO "L"s		
1	2	3
___c+ally	___al+ly	___ul+ly
basically	finally	beautifully

ONE "L"			
4	5	6	7
___le	___y	___e+ly	___+ly
Change the e to y	Change the y to i+ly	Keep the e+ly	Add ly
simply	happily	safely	calmly

This is no easy task. Once you fill in all of the blanks, give yourself a big, "GOOD JOB!!"

An Easy and On-Going Spelling Strategy

Once a child has learned how to spell and write the sight words in LIST 11, he/she can begin writing and reading these sentences in LIST 12.

At this point, many children can work on 2–3 sentences per week. You can use one sentence that is listed here, plus two sentences that you create using words the child misspells in his/her free writing. The underlined words can be replaced with different words to teach vocabulary. The vocabulary words DO NOT need to be spelled correctly to move on. Spend more or less time on each sentence based on the child's progress and ability.

Additional Common Core State Standards that these activities can address are CCSS.L.K.2.A, L.K.1.B, L.1.1.E, L.1.1.F, L.2.1.E, L.2.6, L.3.2.E, RF.2.3.D and RF.3.3.A

SENTENCES LIST 12

Sentence	Spelling Pattern	Vocabulary
1. "My cousins and I especially like <u>Dunkin Donuts</u>," Ryan mentioned cheerfully.	Focus on SPECIAL and ESPECIALLY	Adverbs
2. "Being safe is most important," Mr. Odom reminded us <u>politely</u>.	Focus on the spelling and meaning of verbs that begin with the prefix RE__ as in recycle, redo, refresh, remind, remove, replay, rerun, return, reuse, review, revisit, etc.	Adverbs / Adverbs
3. The <u>German Shepherd</u> energetically buried a bone, then disappeared.	Focus on the spelling and meaning of verbs that begin with the prefix DIS___ as in disable, disappear, disconnect, discourage, discover, etc.	Proper Nouns Names of Dog Breeds
4. We predict that it will be quite hot in <u>Tampa, Florida</u>.	Focus on the spelling and meaning of verbs that begin with the prefix PRE__ as in predict, prepare, present, pretend, prevent, preview,	Proper Nouns Cities, States
5. The <u>Taj Mahal</u> is <u>India</u> is unlike any other place.	Focus on the spelling and meaning of adjectives that being with the prefix UN__ as in unable, unclear, unending, unfair, unhappy, unknown, unlucky, unsafe	Proper Nouns Landmarks + Countries
6. We accidentally arrived in <u>Barcelona</u>, <u>Spain</u>, and immediately unpacked.	Focus on the spelling and meaning of verbs that being with the prefix UN__ as in uncover, undo, unfold, unlock, unpack, unplug, untie, unwrap,	Proper Nouns Cities, Countries
7. The <u>responsible</u> student government didn't need any equipment.	Focus on the spelling and meaning of nouns that end with the suffix ___MENT as in advertisement, agreement, assessment, basement, department, equipment, management, movement, pavement, retirement, settlement	Adjectives / Adjectives
8. Students <u>work</u> regularly to gain experience and show their independence.	Focus on the spelling and meaning of nouns that end with the suffix ___ENCE as in conference, confidence, difference, experience, independence, preference	Verbs
9. The organized coach advised his <u>players</u> to memorize the opponent's plays.	Focus on the spelling and meaning of the verbs that end with the suffix __IZED as in apologize, memorize, realize, recognize, stabilize, summarize, utilize	Nouns-People
10. The surprised teacher finally advised the group to improvise for their <u>project</u>.	Focus on the spelling and meaning of the verbs that end with the suffix _ISED as in advised, compromised, disguised, exercised, improvised revised, surprised, televised,	Nouns-Events
11. Practice safety whenever you go <u>swimming</u>.	Focus on the spelling and meaning of verbs that end with the suffix _ICE as in office, justice, notice, office, practice, prejudice, service	Verbs-_ing
12. We realize how necessary it is to apologize when we're <u>wrong</u>.	Focus on the spelling and meanings of the words NECESSITY, NECESSARY, UNNECESSARY, NECESSARILY and UNNECESSARILY	Adjectives

WORDS LIST 12: These are new words that the child has learned from these sentences.

accidentally	cheerfully	equipment	friendly	independence	opponent	realize	surprised
advised	coach	especially	government	memorize	organized	regularly	unlike
apologize	disappeared	eventually	group	mentioned	place	reminded	unpacked
arrive	doctor's	experience	immediately	musician	practice	repeat	usually
being	energetically	explained	important	necessary	predict	rhythm	whenever
buried	environment	finally	improvise	office	quite	safety	wrong

ASSESS WORDS LIST 12:
As soon as the child has completed all 12 sentences, take time to make sure he/she knows how to spell each sight word before moving on to a new list. Look at WORDS LIST 12 (above). Say each word, one at a time. Have the child write or verbally spell the word. Highlight each word on the list that the child spells _correctly_. Have the child continue to practice any misspelled words from LIST 12. As soon as the child can spell _all_ of the words in WORDS LIST 12 correctly, CELEBRATE!

STOP!

A general expectation for students completing these sight word sentences is:

Kindergarten: Lists 1 and 2

1st Grade: Lists 3 and 4

2nd Grade: Lists 5 and 6

3rd Grade: Lists 7 and 8

4th Grade: Lists 9 and 10

5th Grade: Lists 11 and 12

After completing Lists 11 and 12, I suggest going to www.k12reader.com. Click on the 5th Grade Spelling List. Download it and print it. Each week follow these steps:

1. Monday: Have your child verbally spell each word from Week 1 and Week 2.

2. Make note of the words he or she misspells.

3. Combine those misspelled words to create 2–3 sight words sentences for your child to practice the rest of the week.

4. On Monday of the following week, have your child verbally spell the words from Week 3 and 4.

5. Make note of the words he or she misspells.

6. Combine those misspelled words to create 2–3 sight word sentences for him or her to practice throughout the week.

7. Continue this way, week after week, until he or she has learned all the words through Week 36.

After working through the K12 Reader's 5th Grade List, continue to make sight word sentences using words the child misspells in his or her free writing.

ADDED SUPPORT

If you notice that the child is not learning or remembering how to write these words simply by copying the sentences each week, you can try any or all of these 8 activities for additional support.

1. Practice spelling the individual words using letter tiles or cut up pieces of paper.

2. Unscramble and write out each word.

3. Write out the sentence using index cards.

4. Unscramble and write out the sentence.

5. Write silly sentences!

Use two magnetic spinners on two circles. Or, make two boxes full of words. In one circle, or box, have sight words that your child is learning. In the 2nd circle, or 2nd box, write **whatever** words the child chooses and tells you to write.

The child spins both spinners, or draws a paper from each box, to find out which two words to use. He or she writes a complete sentence using both words (a sight word and a fun word). A sample sentence might be: *Look at the Pokémon.* In this case, "LOOK, AT and THE" are the sight words and Pokémon is the fun word.

Enjoy the child's laughs at his or her silly sentences!

6. Create more silly sentences!

Have a child choose a calendar picture, magazine picture, printed image or sticker to write about. Then, give the student 2–3 words that they are still misspelling. Have the child write ONE sentence about the picture or sticker using all THREE words.

Take it a step further and have the child place a sticker or glue an image of a favorite movie character onto the calendar or magazine picture. Again, give the student 2–3 words that they are still misspelling. Have the child write ONE sentence about the character and picture using all THREE words.

Look at the two examples below. Here, the students had to write a sentence using the words AGAIN, AROUND and BECAUSE. The first student had a sticker of a kitten. The second student pasted an image of Sonic onto a calendar picture of a golf course. Students love how funny these sentences turn out! This activity is an excellent way to help students tackle those tricky spelling words.

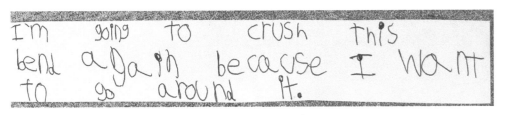

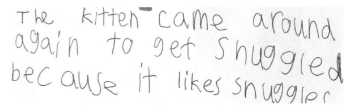

This sentence went along with an image of Sonic pasted to a calendar picture of a golf course.

This sentence went with a sticker of a kitten.

7. Expand Sentences!

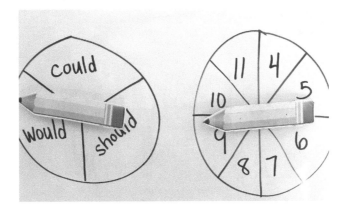

Use two magnetic spinners on two circles. Or, make two boxes. In one circle, or box, write sight words that the child is learning. In the 2nd circle, or 2nd box, write the numbers 4–11. The numbers represent how many words should be in the sentence. For example, if the child spins the word WOULD and the number 9, he or she could write:

Would you like to go to the beach today?

Students often get tangled up and laughing trying to create a sentence with the correct number of words!

8. Write silly stories!

Group words that have the same spelling pattern. Then, have students use as many of the words as they can to write a silly story. ANYTHING can happen in their story as long as they are using the words that they're practicing. Check out these story ideas!

THE GOAT on the BOAT: Words that have "OAT": Boat, Coat, Float, Goat, Moat and Oats

THE BRIGHT NIGHT: Words that have "IGHT":

Bright	Knight	Might	Plight	Slight
Fight	Light	Night	Sight	Tight

THE SEARCH FOR A PEARL: Words that have "EAR" and sound like "ER":

Yearn	Earn	
Search	Learn	Pearl
Earth	Heard	Early

THE CHIEF AND THE THIEF: Words that have "IE" in them:

Characters:	Adjectives:	Settings:	Props:	Reactions/Actions
Chief	Patient	Pier	Pie	Pierce
Thief	Ancient	Field	Piece of pie	Believe/Relieve
Friend	Fierce	Glacier	Shield	Belief/Relief
Scientist	Mischievous			

THEIR WEIRD (or FEISTY) NEIGHBOR: Words that have "EI" in them:

beige	deceive	forfeit	inconceivable	perceive	seize
caffeine	eight	heir	leisure	protein	veil
ceiling	either	height	leisurely	reign	vein
counterfeit	feisty	heist	neither	receive	

Guide students to complete a fictional story using the outline below. The story can be science fiction, fantasy, or a fairy tale.

Introduction: Characters/Setting
Normal Activity
All of a sudden,
Reactions/Actions
Conclusion: Final events and thoughts for the future

Informally Assessing a Student's Progress

Here are 5 ways to informally assess how students are doing.

1. Once a week or twice a month, have the students write as many sight words as they can in five minutes. If an individual child has written correctly at least one more word than the time before, CELEBRATE by giving him or her a sticker or whatever reward you choose!

2. Once or twice a month, say each word that the students have learned and practiced. Have the students write them down to make sure that they can indeed remember how to spell the words learned so far. Continue to practice any forgotten words.

3. Once a month, say complete sight word sentences that the students have learned and practiced. Have the students write them down. Continue to practice any forgotten words.

1. Sample from List 1   2. Sample from List 2   3. Sample from List 2

4. Give students 30 minutes to write about a topic of their choice. It can be a fictional story, non-fiction facts, or a free write about any topic. When the students are done, have them read what they wrote. Praise them for their work and hang it up! Then, later when you read their work, you can see which sight words they are spelling correctly and how they're phonetically spelling new words they don't know yet.

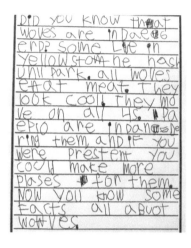

5. Lastly, you can assess the children's ability to **READ** the sight words. Print out the list of words that they've completed most recently. These lists are found on the bottom of pages 86–107. Have each child highlight all of the words that they can read easily and confidently.

Continue practicing any unknown words. Be sure and CELEBRATE when the students can read and write all of the words on their list!

SECTION 4

Complete Guided Writing Lessons for Grades K–5

This section focuses on how to guide children ages 5–11 to write complete stories and compositions. Differentiation at best, it shows teachers and parents how to use the **same** writing lesson at the **same** time with a group of multi-leveled students, or a group of multi-aged children in Grades K–5.

These guided writing lessons were specifically designed to help students think creatively, organize their ideas and finish their work in a short amount of time.

The goal is to get kids to write often and to be able to complete a short story or essay within a 30–60 minute time period. This way, they can regularly feel the satisfaction of finishing and can celebrate their work by adding <u>easy art accents</u>, which are explained in Section 6 of this book.

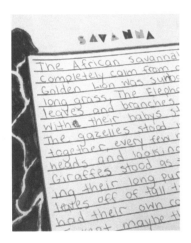

There is definitely a time to focus on the complete writing process, drafting, writing, revising and editing. It's also very important to allow children time to free write without any guidance or structure, but neither of these is the focus here.

This method of teaching writing guides children to complete compositions step by step. The focus for these lessons is to finish with an organized beginning, middle and end. The steps provided in each lesson support children from start to finish until, over time, they are able to complete a composition or story on their own. This method helps eliminate the statement, "I don't know what to write."

If you Google search "writing prompts" you will find hundreds of topics to write about. But, they are just topics. Children can easily, and will often still say, "I don't know what to write." This book outlines actual <u>guided writing lessons</u> that help children figure out what they want to write from beginning to end.

In summary, the goal for each writing lesson is to:

1. Stimulate creative thinking
2. Teach children the skill and habit of organizing their ideas
3. Provide a fun platform for the students to regularly practice simple sentence structure, spelling and vocabulary

Now let's look at the key elements to these lessons.

PENS

First, when I teach students to write, we write with pen. For these guided writing lessons, their first draft is their final draft. I teach the children ahead of time that if they write something they don't like, to "simply cross it off with one line and keep going."

PAPER

Second, we used lined paper with a border around it. When students are done writing, they add an easy art accent to the border of their writing. The pens, coupled with the art accents, presents a final story that has color and charm.

Younger children in Grades K–2 typically use wider lines while advanced writers in Grades 2–5 use narrow lines. The bordered paper for Pre-K–K students doesn't have any lines and is good for very early writers who may only write one or two words or sentences. You can find each of these on pages 125–127 of this book.

DIFFERENTIATION AT BEST

Thirdly, these lessons can be taught to a group of students who vary in age and ability. When I teach year round writing classes and camps, children ages 5–11 are in the **same group**. So, I create writing lessons with differentiation in mind. These guided writing lessons can easily be applied to a regular classroom setting because in most cases, not all students are exactly on grade level with their writing. In a 3rd Grade classroom, some students might be writing at a 1st, 2nd, 3rd, 4th, or 5th Grade level. These lessons were designed with the heart for EVERY child to feel successful in writing their own story or essay.

In Section 1 of this book, on page 4, I shared one 5th Grader's story and will briefly share it again here. One school year, I had the absolute privilege of working with a 5th Grade boy who struggled terribly with writing. I only worked with him for one hour each week. At the beginning of the school year, he wasn't able to write a single word on his paper by himself. In fact, the only way I could get him to write was to stand next to him, ask him what he wanted to write and then verbally spell out each word for him. There were many times when I also had to speak out <u>proper letter strokes</u> to help him move along.

The general expectation that I have for 5th Graders is to write about 25 total sentences for each guided writing lesson. (You'll learn how this works below.) So, at the beginning of the school year, this student couldn't write one sentence independently. However, by the end of the year, he was able to write 2–3 sentences per section, or 10-15 sentences total, on his own! That's after only working with him one hour per week from September-March. He is proof that the strategy behind these guided writing lessons can work for even our most struggling writers.

HOMESCHOOL FAMILIES

Additionally, these writing lessons are ideal for parents who are homeschooling students in Grades K–5. A parent can conduct the **same** writing lesson with a 1st, 3rd and 5th grader at the **same** time.

For example, below there are three samples of students' writing from the <u>Candy Corn-Opinion writing lesson</u> which is found on page 138 of this book. These three students were in Grades K, 1st and 5th and attended my after school writing class. They were in the **same** class at the **same** time.

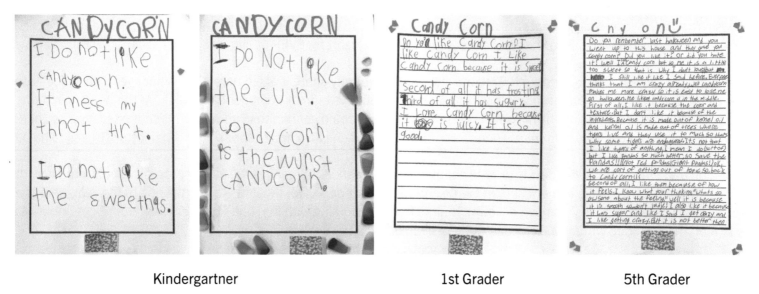

| Kindergartner | | 1st Grader | 5th Grader |

NOTE: The Kindergartner mixed his knowledge of simple sight words and phonetic spelling. It reads, "I do not like candy corn. It makes my throat hurt. I do not like the sweetness. I do not like the color. Candy corn is the worst candy corn."

HOW GUIDED WRITING LESSONS WORK

Each guided writing lesson has 5 steps:

1. Tell the story line.
2. Brainstorm.
3. Show the 5 sections.
4. Show the expectations.
5. Write.

These 5 steps are specified in each guided writing lesson that I create. In the next section, beginning on page 129, you will find 46 lessons to get you started. That's more than one guided writing lesson per week for a 180-day school year. If you want to find complete guided writing lessons regularly, go to my website, <u>www.funwritingideas.com</u>. There you can also subscribe to my monthly newsletter where I will be sending out new lessons as I post them.

Here are the 5 steps explained in detail.

TELL THE STORY LINE

1. First, begin each lesson by telling the genre and story line. If there is specific vocabulary or a certain spelling pattern that you and your students are focusing on, introduce it at this time.

BRAINSTORM

2. Second, brainstorm ideas with the students. Brainstorming can include settings, characters, problems, solutions, opinions, reasons, facts, etc.

SHOW THE 5 SECTIONS

3. Next, show the 5 sections of the writing prompt. These 5 sections are crucial to helping children organize their ideas. For example, a creative story will have an introduction, beginning, middle, end and conclusion. A persuasive piece will have an introduction, reason 1, reason 2, reason 3 and conclusion. Regardless of the genre (except for poetry), I always divide the writing prompt into 5 sections. Then, I write them out on the top left corner of a classroom whiteboard, or on a piece of paper for 1–2 students.

   Teaching children to anticipate and prepare to write 5 sections regularly sets them up for writing essays in middle school and high school. Older students are simply elaborating and writing more details, using more words and sentences.

SHOW THE EXPECTATION

4. Fourth, show students how many sentences they should try to write for **each section**. On the left side of the white board, under the 5 sections, you can write:

   K–1st–1 Sentence for each section

   2nd Grade–2 Sentences

   3rd Grade–3 Sentences

   4th Grade–4 Sentences

   5th Grade–5 Sentences

This is a very important step. Showing the five sections and a **general** idea of how many sentences each age group should write helps the students anticipate their entire story and keep their ideas organized. Ironically, I will often have a child speak out and say, "Is that all? Can I write more?" While I say they **can**, I remind them that their goal is to finish **ALL 5** sections in the allotted time.

If I skip this step, students will tend to write too little leaving out interesting and important details, or write way too much creating a run on story that doesn't have a clear beginning, middle and end.

Again, if your child is older and struggles with writing or is just getting started, have him or her start off by writing 1–2 sentences per section. As time goes on, work up to 3 sentences per section, and so on.

If you are homeschooling students in grades K–5 and use these lessons, over time, your children will catch on to the pattern. Your 1st Grader will get used to writing 5 sentences per story, your 3rd Grader about 15 sentences, and your 5th Grader about 25 sentences.

TIME TO WRITE!

5. Last, students begin writing. When it comes time to write, I explain the general content of the **first** section. Then I give the students time to write their own words. We continue through each of the 5 sections this way.

YOUNG OR STRUGGLING WRITERS

For the youngest writers or those with specific needs, I will ask them their ideas, then **simplify** their ideas into sentences that they can write and read. I write these sentences on the board for them to copy while the older children are writing independently.

Some instructors argue against copying. They want students to freely and phonetically write whatever they want to say. I understand that and agree that children should definitely be given time to free write without any guidance or structure. At the same time, I'm not a fan of children copying just **any** text for the sake of copying. There is little to no benefit for students to copy content without knowing what it says.

If children are going to copy a sentence, it should be a sentence that they are learning to read, such as sight word sentences outlined in Section 3 of this book, or a sentence that they have spoken and want to write. This exercise is strategic and useful to the child because it enables them to finish a piece of writing that they can **read**. You should see how proud and excited the small children are to read their simple stories to their parents!

OLDER OR ADVANCED WRITERS

For independent writers, I offer my help continuously. My students will often hear me say, "How's everyone doing? Does anyone need anything? I'm here to help." I tell them that if they want to know how to spell something to just ask. Then, I write it on the right side of the board for them, and others, to see.

Above all, I want the students to enjoy getting their ideas on paper. I don't want them to stumble over spelling or get stuck on "writer's block." I stand and walk around the room, quick to help and serve as a resource anytime they ask for it.

By supporting students often and regularly, they gradually move towards independent and confident writing.

CONDUCTING THESE LESSONS AT HOME

If you are homeschooling students in Grades K–5, you can conduct the same lessons at your kitchen table. Imagine sitting with your children next to, or across from, you. Each child has an extra piece of paper in front of them. If they ask you how to spell a word, you can write it down on their piece of paper. Or, if you have a large whiteboard nearby, you can write the 5 sections and any words that they want you to spell there.

SAVING TIME!

Sitting with your children while they complete the writing prompt will save you so much time! First of all, the 30–60 minutes you take to sit **with** them will ensure they feel supported. As a result, they will be able to finish and feel more confident in their ability to start and finish a story.

Second, when homeschooling students in Grades K–5 and conducting these lessons, you can check "writing" off your list for **all** of your children. Each child will have completed their writing lesson in the same 30–60 minutes.

Lastly, instead of spending a day begging and pleading for a child to finish a vague writing prompt on his or her own, you can create this rhythm of completing writing prompts in 30–60 minutes, 1–3 times per week. Your children will feel excited about their story and you will be spared the stress of nagging all day long and ending the day with unfinished work.

Eventually, there will come a time when you can give older children the 5 sections to a writing prompt and they will be able to write their 15–25 sentences independently. Ultimately, this sets them up for comfortable and confident writing that ideally will carry over into middle school, high school, college, and even into the workplace.

RECAP

So, to recap, a 30–60+ minute writing lesson will look something like this:

1. Introduce the genre, story line and any spelling pattern or vocabulary that you want to focus on.

2. The children brainstorm their ideas. Write their responses on the board.

3. Show the 5 sections on the board. Briefly, explain each section.

4. Write out how many sentences each grade level should generally write.

5. Hand out <u>lined writing paper</u> and pens.

6. Explain section one. Give the children time to write.

7. Set aside one section of the board to write a model story for small children, or struggling writers, to copy if need be.

8. Explain section two. Give the children time to write.

9. Explain section three. Give the children time to write.

10. Explain section four. Give the children time to write.

11. Explain section five. Give the children time to write.

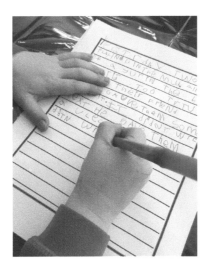

LESSON OUTLINES

On the next page, I show the 5 sections that I typically use for each genre listed. Each section represents a paragraph.

INTRODUCTIONS and CONCLUSIONS:

For fictional stories, the introduction will state the characters and settings. This can include naming and describing the characters. The setting tells where the story takes place. This can include ANY place big or small, such as under a slide or in a country like France. The setting can also include the season, weather, month, day, or time of day.

The conclusion in fictional stories is used to write any final events and can include the characters' reflections and thoughts for the future.

For non-fiction pieces, the introduction will state the main idea. Older students who need to elaborate and write more than one sentence can use the introduction to engage the reader by writing questions, exclamations, famous quotes, facts, or even dialogue.

For non-fiction pieces, the conclusion will usually restate the main idea. It can also be used to encourage the reader to learn more, to try something new, or to consider a thought or question that the writer has written about.

You can use the following outlines for ANY theme that you and your students are working on! Outlines can be tailored for specific writing prompts as you will see in the guided writing lessons found in Section 5.

Non-Fiction Main Idea/Details
Introduction: Engage the reader
First of all,
Second of all,
Third of all,
Conclusion

Opinion/Persuasive Writing
Introduction: Engage the reader
Reason/Example 1
Reason/Example 2
Reason/Example 3
Conclusion: Encourage the reader

Descriptive
Introduction
Aspect 1
Aspect 2
Aspect 3
Conclusion

Instructions
Introduction: Engage the reader
Materials
Steps 1–2
Steps 3–4
Conclusion: Encourage the Reader

Summary
Title/Characters
Setting
Problem
Solution
Ending

Personal Narrative (sequence of events)
Introduction: (Time/People/Place/Weather/Feelings)
First,
Next,
Then,
Last,

Personal Narrative (surprising, silly or scary moment)
Introduction: (Time/People/Place/Weather/Feelings)
Normal Activity: (Before the moment)
All of a sudden, (The surprising, silly or scary moment)
Reactions/Actions: (After the moment)
Solution/Conclusion: (Final events and thoughts for the future)

Fiction/Science Fiction/Fantasy/Fairy Tale (same as above)
Introduction:
Normal Activity
All of a sudden,
Reactions/Actions
Solution/Conclusion

Compare/Contrast
Introduction: Engage the reader
Similarities
Differences: Item 1
Differences: Item 2
Conclusion

Letter
Date/Greeting/Introduction/Main Idea
Detail 1
Detail 2
Detail 3
Conclusion/Salutation

Below, you can find links to print lined **portrait paper** for your students to use. The pages below are vertical and ones that we use the most. For some writing prompts, like The Never Ending Syrup Sundae found on page 176 and The Q-U-QUEEN Fairy Tale on page 154, we use the lined landscape paper just shown on pages 125–127.

I give wider lines for younger writers (Grades K–2) and narrow lines for more advanced writers (Grades 2–7) The Pre K-K page doesn't have any lines and is good for very early writers who may only write one or two words or sentences.

Click below to view and print each page:

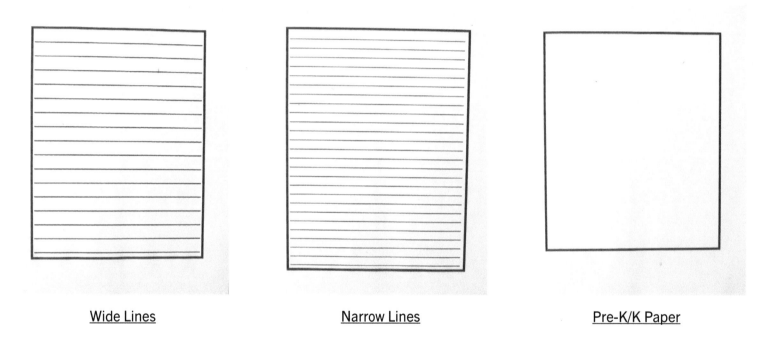

Wide Lines   Narrow Lines   Pre-K/K Paper

Notice the wide border around the lines. When students are done writing their story or essay, they can add an easy art accent around their writing. These art accents add color and charm to their stories and are addressed in Section 6.

SECTION 5

A Year's Worth of Guided Writing Lessons To Get You Started!

1. All About Me—Non-Fiction
2. Apples—Non-fiction
3. African Savanna—Science Fiction
4. A Serval's Personal Narrative
5. You've Got to Visit!—Persuasive
6. I'm Not Mean!—The Giant gives a Persuasive Speech
7. 3 Little Lemurs and the Big Bad Fossa—Fairy Tale
8. A Gnome in a Pumpkin Patch—Fantasy
9. Candy Corn—Opinion
10. Exhausted Electronics—Science Fiction
11. I'm Thankful—A List Poem
12. Our Thanksgiving Turkey—An A to Z Poem
13. Ring Toss—Instructions
14. Lost Something—Personal Narrative
15. Sweet Dreams—Fantasy
16. Reindeer Sandwiches—Instructions
17. Birthday Bash—Science Fiction
18. Snow—Journal
19. Snow, Cows and a Barn—Science Fiction
20. Acknowledge These People—Letter Writing
21. Haiku
22. Relational Conflict—Personal Narrative
23. The Q-U-Queen—Fairy Tale

24. A Popping President-Fantasy
25. Aliens in the Arctic-Science Fiction
26. Hot Tamales!—Journal
27. Concrete Poems
28. Green Attack!—Science Fiction
29. Green Attack!—Reaction Letter
30. Puddle Jumping—Fantasy
31. Mud Mites—News Article
32. Fairy Tale Character Siting—News Article
33. Got Hurt—Personal Narrative
34. A Living Creature—Non-Fiction
35. Popcorn—Non-fiction
36. Magical Seed—Fairy Tale
37. Favorite Park—Suggestion Letter
38. Diamond Poem
39. Beach—Journal
40. Solar Seeds—Science Fiction
41. Strawberry Soup-Instructions
42. A Slinky on Stairs—Descriptive
43. The State Fair—Descriptive
44. The Never-Ending-Syrup-Sundae—Instructions
45. Camping—Opinion
46. End of Summer—Letter Writing

You can find more guided writing lessons at www.funwritingideas.com.

1. ALL ABOUT ME—NON-FICTION

This is the best lesson to use to introduce the 5 sections for the first time. In a classroom setting, students can write all about themselves WITHOUT writing their name. At the end of the lesson, the teacher can read each child's writing while the classmates try to guess WHO wrote it!

Now for the lesson!

1. Tell the story line: *"Today, you're going to write all about yourself."*

2. Brainstorm. Have the students think about the following:

   - Their hobbies
   - Books they like to read
   - Movies they like to watch
   - Sports they like to play or watch
   - Teams they like to follow
   - Foods they love or hate
   - Things they would like to do one day

3. Show the 5 sections:

   > Hobbies
   > Books/Movies/TV
   > Sports/Teams
   > Foods
   > One day, I'd like to…

4. Show the expectations:

   K—1st Graders are encouraged to write 1 sentence for each section, 2nd Graders-2 sentences, 3rd Graders-3 sentences, 4th Graders-4 sentences, 5th Graders-5 sentences

Now to write: Pass out pens and paper to the students. Guide the students through the following steps so their writing is organized and complete. For this first lesson, K—1st Graders can write their name and use the following sentence starters for their 5 sentences:

> I am _____.
> I can _____.
> I like _____.
> I have _____.
> I want to _____.

Students in Grades 2—5 can follow these steps:

1. Write 2—5 sentences about your hobbies.
2. Write 2—5 sentences about books and movies that you like.
3. Write 2—5 sentences about sports and teams. If you don't like sports, say so and tell why!
4. Write 2—5 sentences about foods that you love or hate.
5. Write 2—5 sentences about things that you would like to do in the future. Tell why you want to do them.
6. Remember to read their writing. Have the classmates guess who wrote it! Hang the students' writing next to their picture.

2. APPLES—NON-FICTION

This lesson focuses on facts about apples. Whenever you teach children to write non-fiction, remind them not to use the words I or MY. This will prevent them from including opinions in their non-fiction writing. The main idea for this lesson is, "Apples are used in many ways." It's a great lesson to use to teach children how to spell the words USE, USED and USES.

NOTE: This lesson can address the following Common Core State Standards: CCSS.ELA.LITERACY.W.K.2, W.1.2, W.2.2, W.3.2, W.3.2.A, W.3.2.B, W.3.2.C, W.3.2.D, W.4.2, W.4.2.A, W.4.2.B, W.4.2.C, W.4.2.D, W.4.2.E, W.5.2, W.5.2.A, W.5.2.B, W.5.2.C, W.5.2.D and W.5.2.E

Now for the lesson!

1. Tell the story line: *"Today, you're going to write and explain the many ways that apples are used. This is a non-fiction piece so you will only write information and not your own opinion. You won't write I or my."*

   Next, teach the words USE, USED and USES. Make sure students know how to spell these words to use in their writing.

2. Brainstorm ways that apples are used:

FOODS/DRINKS	DESSERTS	ACTIVITIES
Apple juice	Apple pie	Picking apples
Apple cider	Apple muffins	Bobbing for apples
Apple jam	Apple cake	Apple volcanoes
Apple butter	Apple ice cream	

   If possible, allow the children to try to bob for an apple in their own bowl of water. They will laugh trying and understand better what bobbing for apples is if they decide to write about it. You can also show them an apple volcano by cutting out the center, putting some baking soda in it and adding vinegar. Watch the suds flow out of the apple!

3. Show the 5 sections:

   > Introduction: Engage the reader and state the main idea.
   > Foods/Drinks
   > Desserts
   > Activities
   > Conclusion

4. Show the expectations:
   K—1st Graders are encouraged to write 1 sentence for each section, 2nd Graders-2 sentences, 3rd Graders-3 sentences, 4th Graders-4 sentences, 5th Graders-5 sentences

Now to write: Guide the students through the following steps so their writing is organized and complete. They are free to write these ideas in their own words. Remind the students not to use I or MY so that they just write facts and not opinions. There is a 2nd Grade example in italics for your own guidance.

1. For the introduction, engage the reader by asking questions. Then, state the main idea: *Do you eat apples? Apples are used in many ways.*
2. Write how apples are used to make foods and drinks: *First of all, people drink apple juice and apple cider. Many children eat applesauce as a snack.*
3. Write how apples are used to make desserts: Second of all, *people make apple pie. There is even apple bread, ice cream and cake.*
4. Write how apples are used for activities: *Third of all, there are many apple activities. You can even do a volcano experiment in an apple!*
5. Write a conclusion: *There are many ways to use apples. How do you like to use apples?*
6. Add an easy art accent: Students can draw and color one big apple or many small apples around the border of their writing.

3. AFRICAN SAVANNA—SCIENCE FICTION

This is a great lesson for addressing the African savanna and writing Science Fiction. NOTE: This lesson can address the following Common Core State Standards: CCSS.ELA-Literacy.W.K.3, W.1.3, W.2.3, W.3.3, W.3.3.A, W.3.3.B, W.3.3.C, W.3.3.D, W.4.3, W.4.3.A, W.4.3.B, W.4.3.C, W.4.3.D, W.4.3.E, W.5.3, W.5.3.A, W.5.3.B, W.5.3.C, W.5.3.D and W.5.3.E

Now for the lesson!

1. Tell the story line to your writers: *"It's a normal day in the savanna. All of a sudden, something shocking, surprising or silly happens. The animals develop super powers to solve the problem."*

2. Brainstorm savanna animals and what they might be doing on a normal day. Examples include:

Antelope—running	Giraffes—eating leaves	Rhinoceroses—fighting
Cheetahs—hunting	Lions—napping	Servals—hiding
Elephants—drinking water	Leopards—sleeping	Wildebeests—grazing
Gazelles—running	Meerkats—playing	Zebras—grazing

Brainstorm shocking, surprising or silly things that could happen. Examples include:

- A UFO lands in the savanna
- Cheetahs shoot lasers from their spots
- It starts snowing

- Robots approach the animals
- The zebras' stripes turn blinding yellow
- The lions start squeaking.

3. Show the 5 sections:

Introduction: Setting/Characters
Normal Activity
All of a sudden,
Reactions/Actions
Solution/Conclusion

4. Show the expectations:
K—1st Graders are encouraged to write 1 sentence for each section, 2nd Graders-2 sentences, 3rd Graders-3 sentences, 4th Graders-4 sentences, 5th Graders-5 sentences

Now to write: Guide the students through the following steps. They are free to use their own words. Remind them that ANYTHING can happen in their story as long as they follow the steps to keep their story organized. There is a 2nd Grade example in italics for your own guidance.

1. Introduce the savanna and the animals there. *The savanna was quiet. The animals were getting along.*
2. Write what the animals were doing. *The giraffes were eating leaves from the trees. The zebras were grazing.*
3. Write about the shocking, surprising or silly moment. *All of a sudden, a UFO landed. Aliens ran out of it.*
4. Write about the reactions and actions of the animals. *The zebras stopped grazing. Their stripes turned bright and blazing hot.*
5. Write about the solution to the problem or ending to the event. *The aliens started burning up. They ran back to their ship and took off.*
6. Add an easy art accent: Students can draw and color zebra stripes, giraffe patterns, hyena spots, etc. around the border of their writing. (See page 185.)

4. A SERVAL'S PERSONAL NARRATIVE

This is a very fun piece! The serval "writes" a personal narrative about its time as a pet and then later as a wild cat at a rescue location, such as the Carolina Tiger Rescue. This prompt can be used for any animal that is meant for the wild but is often taken in as a pet. NOTE: This lesson can address the following Common Core State Standards: CCSS.ELA-LITERACY.W.K.3, W.1.3, W.2.3, W.3.3, W.3.3.B, W.3.3.C, W.3.3.D, W.4.3, W4.3.A, W.4.3.B, W.4.3.C, W.4.3.D, W.4.3.E, W.5.3, W.5.3.A, W.5.3.B, W.5.3.C, W.5.3.D and W.5.3.E. Plus, all the information about servals was gathered from in person tours at the Carolina Tiger Rescue (www.carolinatigerrescue.org).

Now for the lesson!

1. Tell the story line: *"Explain to the students that they are going to write a personal narrative from the serval's perspective. The serval is going to complain about its care as a pet, make fun of human behavior, end up at the rescue location and commend its new care there."*

2. Discuss facts about servals:

They are native to Africa and live south of the Sahara Desert.
They love tall grass, streams, rivers and lakes.
They are solitary and nocturnal.

They have long legs, short tails, larges ears and spotted coats.
There are white spots on the back of their black ears.
They eat rodents and small mammals.

Brainstorm bad care, silly human behavior and quality care at the rescue location:

Care:	**Human Habits:**		**Quality Care:**
Small crate	Mowing the grass	Watching TV	Tall grass and trees
No trees	Walking on 2 legs	Playing loud music	Space and friends
Cat food	Using silverware	Running a vacuum	Real meat
		Disappearing for days	

3. Show the 5 sections:

Introduction
Complains about the care
Makes fun of human behavior
Goes to the rescue location
Conclusion

4. Show the expectations:
K—1st Graders are encouraged to write 1 sentence for each section, 2nd Graders-2 sentences, 3rd Graders-3 sentences, 4th Graders-4 sentences, 5th Graders-5 sentences

Now to write: Guide the students through the following steps so their story is organized and complete. They are free to write these ideas in their own words. There is a 2nd Grade example in italics for your own guidance.

1. Write the introduction. *I'm a serval. I used to be a pet and hated it!*
2. Complain about the care: *First of all, the care was horrible! I had to eat cat food.*
3. Make fun of human habits: *Second of all, my owners were so strange. They kept cutting the grass!*
4. Write about the transition to the rescue location: *One day, I tore up all of their curtains and couches. My owners brought me to the Carolina Tiger Rescue.*
5. State the good things at the rescue location. *I love it here! They give me real meat and tall grass. I never want to be a pet again!*
6. Add an easy art accent: Use green tempera paint to brush vertical strokes on one side of a plastic page protector. Spray it with Mod Podge and let it dry. Place a picture of a serval inside the plastic page protector. The green paint represents tall grass. (See page 189.)

5. YOU'VE GOT TO VISIT—PERSUASIVE

Kids like to talk about places they have been to and like. This lesson takes it a step further and asks students to try to persuade readers to visit a place that they like.

NOTE: This lesson can address the following Common Core State Standards: CCSS.ELA.LITERACY.W.K.1, W.1.1, W.2.1, W.3.1, W.3.1.A, W.3.1.B, W.3.1.C, W.3.1.D, W.4.1, W.4.1.A, W.4.1.B, W.4.1.C, W.4.1.D, W.5.1, W.5.1.A, W.5.1.B, W.5.1.C and W.5.1.D.

Now for the lesson!

1. Tell the students the story line: *"You're going to try to persuade a reader to visit a place that you really like."*

2. Brainstorm names of places that the students like, such as a local aquarium, zoo, museum, carnival, water park, etc.

    Brainstorm reasons that they like that place: rides, activities, food, people, music, events, nature, etc.

3. Show the 5 sections:

    > Introduction: Engage the reader and state the main idea.
    > Reason 1
    > Reason 2
    > Reason 3
    > Conclusion: Encourage the reader.

4. Show the expectations:
    K–1st Graders are encouraged to write 1 sentence for each section, 2nd Graders-2 sentences, 3rd Graders-3 sentences, 4th Graders-4 sentences, 5th Graders-5 sentences

Now to write: Guide the students through the following steps so their essay is organized and complete. They are free to write these ideas in their own words. There is a 2nd Grade example in italics for your own guidance.

1. Engage the reader by writing questions about places the reader has been to or likes to go. *Have you ever been to an aquarium?*
2. Finish the introduction by telling the reader where to go. *You've got to visit Ripley's Believe It or Not Aquarium!*
3. Write and explain the first reason in detail. *First of all, you get to walk through a hallway surrounded by water. Sharks swim over you!*
4. Write and explain the second reason in detail. *Second of all, you get to pet the stingrays. You lay down and touch them when they swim by.*
5. Write and explain the third reason in detail. *Lastly, you can stand in a glass tube. Penguins walk around you!*
6. Write a conclusion that encourages the reader to go to that place one more time. *You should go to the Ripley's aquarium. You will love it!*
7. Add an easy art accent: Students can print, cut and paste the logo of their location. If you have a picture of the place that they write about, hang their work next to it.

6. I'M NOT MEAN—THE GIANT FROM JACK AND THE BEANSTALK GIVES A PERSUASIVE SPEECH

Kids enjoy a twist on a familiar story. For this prompt, the students write as if they are the giant from *Jack and the Beanstalk*. They try to convince the reader that the giant is nice and not mean.
NOTE: This lesson can address the following Common Core State Standards: CCSS.ELA-LITERACY.RL.K.3, RL.K.9, RL.1.3, RL.1.9, RL2.3, RL.2.6, RL.3.6, RL.4.3, RL.4.6, RL.5.3 and RL.5.6

Now for the lesson!

1. First, read *Jack and the Beanstalk* to the children. Then, tell the story line: *"You're going to use the words "I" and "my" to write in 1st person as if you are the giant from Jack and the Beanstalk. You're going to try and convince the reader that you are nice and not mean."*

2. Have the students brainstorm thoughts that the giant could have had:

   - Jack came to me and entered MY house without permission
   - He HID in MY house
   - Jack stole from me 3 times!
   - I was tired because…

   - I was grumpy because… (describe a bad day that doesn't involve Jack)
   - I was counting my money because I'm saving for…(a good cause)

   - I actually say, "Fee Fi Fo Fum…" Create a rhyme! Words that rhyme with fum are: gum, thumb, numb, come, some, hum, bum, tum…)

   Have the students brainstorm kind gestures that the giant could offer:

   Invite Jack and his mom to dinner
   Buy a new cow for Jack and his mom

   Provide another animal, machine or tool that can generate income
   Hire Jack and his mom to work for him and his good cause

3. Show the 5 sections:

   Introduction/Main Point
   First of all,
   Second of all,
   Third of all,
   Conclusion/Kind Gesture

4. Show the expectations:

   K−1st Graders are encouraged to write 1 sentence for each section, 2nd Graders-2 sentences, 3rd Graders-3 sentences, 4th Graders-4 sentences, 5th Graders-5 sentences

Now to Write: Guide the students through the following steps. Remind your students to use 1st person, "I" and "my" throughout their writing. Encourage them to refer to the list of thoughts that the giant could have and include them in their writing. Their words can be serious or super silly! There is a 2nd Grade example in italics for your own guidance.

1. Write an introduction and state your main point. *Hello! I am the giant from Jack and the Beanstalk. I just want you to know that I am not mean!*
2. Write and explain reason #1: *First of all*, Jack came into MY house. I was just trying to eat breakfast.
3. Write and explain reason #2: *Second of all, he HID in my house. That is so scary!*
4. Write and explain reason #3: *Third of all, he stole from me three times. I was saving my gold to build houses for families who need one.*
5. Write a conclusion that offers a kind gesture. *Truly, I'm not mean. Maybe, I will buy every family a cow right now.*
6. Add an easy art accent: Students can color their border green. Then, they can add googly eyes and glue on gold glitter (See pages 186 and 187.)

7. THREE LITTLE LEMURS AND THE BIG BAD FOSSA—FAIRY TALE

The fossa is the lemurs' main predator. They look like a mix between a mountain lion and a weasel. Many kids have never heard of the fossa and they find it fascinating. A fairy tale titled, *The Three Little Lemurs and the Big Bad Fossa* helps solidify their new knowledge of it. NOTE: All facts for this writing prompt have been gathered at the Duke Lemur Center in Durham, NC. Also, this prompt addresses the following Common Core State Standards: CCSS.ELA-LITERACY.W.K.3, W.1.3, W.2.3, W.3.3, W.3.3.B, W.3.3.C, W.3.3.D, W.4.3, W4.3.A, W.4.3.B, W.4.3.C, W.4.3.D, W.4.3.E, W.5.3, W.5.3.A, W.5.3.B, W.5.3.C, W.5.3.D and W.5.3.E. Plus, all the information about lemurs was gathered from in person tours at the Duke Lemur Center (www.lemur.duke.edu).

Now for the lesson!

1. Tell the story line: "*You're going to write your own version of The Three Little Pigs using lemurs and a fossa.*"
2. Discuss a series of facts about lemurs and write the list on the board:

They live in Madagascar.
Some lemurs live low to the ground.
Some live half way up the trees.
Others live in the top canopy of the forest.
Most are diurnal (awake during the day).
Some are nocturnal (awake at night).
They stay in groups called 'troops'.
They love to eat fruit.

They forage for food. Forage means to look for food.
They have an opposable thumb, so their hands work like a mitten.
They are great climbers.
Their long tail gives them balance.
They can't hang from their tail but can hang from their hands and feet.
They communicate through smell.
Their scents give other lemurs information.

Encourage the students to incorporate at least 2–3 facts in their fairy tale.
Discuss materials available to the lemurs in the forest: *leaves of all sizes, fruit, sticks, bamboo, etc.*
Make sure the students know how to spell LEMURS. ☺

3. Show the 5 sections:

Characters/Setting
Problem
Lemurs Build
The Fossa
Solution/Conclusion

4. Show the expectations:
K–1st Graders are encouraged to write 1 sentence for each section, 2nd Graders-2 sentences, 3rd Graders-3 sentences, 4th Graders-4 sentences, 5th Graders-5 sentences

Now to write: Guide the students through the following steps. They are free to use their own words. Remind them that ANYTHING can happen in their story as long as they follow the steps to keep their story organized. There is a 2nd Grade example in italics for your own guidance.

1. Begin by naming the time, location and characters: *Once upon a time, there was a troop of baby lemurs. They lived in Madagascar.*
2. Write what their mom said to them. Name the problem: *One day, their mom said, "You are big now. You need to build a house to keep you safe from the fossa."*
3. Write what each lemur builds. *The first lemur used leaves to build a house. The second lemur used sticks and the third lemur used bamboo shoots.*
4. Write what the fossa does to each lemur. *The fossa tore through the leaves and sticks. But, the bamboo shoots were too strong.*
5. Write the ending of the story. Tell what happens to the fossa and the three lemurs. *The three lemurs were safe in the bamboo house. The fossa got tired and left.*
6. Add an easy art accent: Students can draw and color ring-tailed lemur tails around their border, or draw leaves sticks and bamboo to complement their story.

8. A GNOME IN A PUMPKIN PATCH—FANTASY

This lesson is great for the fall. Students like this fictional lesson because ANYTHING can happen in their stories! NOTE: This lesson can address the following Common Core State Standards: CCSS.ELA-LITERACY.W.K.3, W.1.3, W.2.3, W.3.3, W.3.3.B, W.3.3.C, W.3.3.D, W.4.3, W4.3.A, W.4.3.B, W.4.3.C, W.4.3.D, W.4.3.E, W.5.3, W.5.3.A, W.5.3.B, W.5.3.C, W.5.3.D, W.5.3.E. L.K.2, L.1.2, L.2.2, L.3.2, L.3.2.C, L.4.2, L.4.2.B and L.5.2.

Now for the lesson!

1. Tell the story line. *"A gnome lives in a pumpkin patch and is in charge of taking care of the pumpkins through the night. The gnome experiences an unusual event in the pumpkin patch. It can be a problematic or silly event. You're going to start your story with the gnome saying something."*

2. To get the kids thinking, have them imagine the gnome in the pumpkin patch at night. Have them brainstorm unusual things that might occur. Here are just a few examples:

    —there's a crow attack

    —the pumpkins come alive and have a huge party

    —the pumpkins turn mean

    —the pumpkins battle each other

Think of ways the problem is solved or the fun ends:

    —the pumpkins defeat the crows

    —the pumpkins celebrate the gnome's birthday

    —the pumpkins get tired and stop fighting

3. Show the 5 sections:

    > Dialogue/Characters/Setting
    > Normal Activity
    > All of a sudden,
    > Reactions/Actions
    > Solution/Conclusion

4. Show the expectations:

    K—1st Graders are encouraged to write 1 sentence for each section, 2nd Graders-2 sentences, 3rd Graders-3 sentences, 4th Graders-4 sentences, 5th Graders-5 sentences

Now to write: Guide the students through the following steps. They are free to use their own words. Remind them that ANYTHING can happen in their story as long as they follow the steps to keep their story organized. There is a 2nd Grade example in italics for your own guidance.

1. Start the story with the gnome saying something routine to the pumpkins: *"Good night, pumpkins! Tomorrow there will be lots of kids here," said the gnome.*

    NOTE: If you want your student(s) to practice dialogue punctuation, start off slow. Verbalize the following steps for your writers:
    a. Write the opening quotation marks.
    b. Write what the character is saying. Begin the sentence with a capital letter.
    c. Finish the sentence(s) with a ?, !, or, comma.
    d. Write the closing quotation marks.
    e. Write who said it and end with a period:

2. Describe the gnome completing his or her daily tasks in detail. *The gnome walked up and down each aisle. He made sure the vines weren't tangled.*

3. Describe the scary, surprising or silly moment. *All of a sudden, the pumpkins started singing Happy Birthday! The pumpkins danced and sang around the gnome.*

4. Describe the characters' reactions and actions. *The gnome cried and laughed. No one ever celebrated his birthday.*

5. Write the solution and conclusion. *The gnome and pumpkins sang, danced and played games all night long. Then, they slept all day while the kids came.*

6. Add an easy art accent: Students can draw and color pumpkins around the border of their writing. They can also add googly eyes to the pumpkins.

9. CANDY CORN—OPINION

To start off the lesson, hang images of candy corn. Show the candy bag and hand out pieces of candy corn for each student to try. Expect rants and raves, questions and complaints! NOTE: This lesson can address the following Common Core State Standards: CCSS.ELA.LITERACY.W.K.1, W.1.1, W.2.1, W.3.1, W.3.1.A, W.3.1.B, W.3.1.C, W.3.1.D, W.4.1, W.4.1.A, W.4.1.B, W.4.1.C, W.4.1.D, W.5.1, W.5.1.A, W.5.1.B, W.5.1.C and W.5.1.D.

Now for the lesson!

1. Tell the story line: *"You're going to write your opinion about candy corn and explain why you do or don't like them."*

2. Discuss the candy's color, texture, taste, use and ingredients. List ideas on the board.

COLOR	TEXTURE	TASTE	USES	INGREDIENTS	
Orange	Hard	Sugary	Top Cupcakes	Tons of sugar	titanium, dioxide color
White	Sticky	Sweet	Top Cakes	honey, corn syrup	yellow 6, red 3
Brown	Crystalized	Chewy	Dessert Design	confectioner's glaze	blue 1
Yellow	Squishy	Gummy	Candy jar	dextrose, salt	*some have cocoa powder
		Buttery	Trail mix	soy protein, gelatin	and hydrogenated oils
		Like hard frosting		artificial flavor	

3. Show the 5 sections:

> Introduction: Engage the reader and state your opinion.
> Reason 1 (Color/Texture/Taste)
> Reason 2 (Ingredients/Nutrition)
> Reason 3 (Uses)
> Conclusion

4. Show the expectations:

> K–1st Graders are encouraged to write 1 sentence for each section, 2nd Graders-2 sentences, 3rd Graders-3 sentences, 4th Graders-4 sentences, 5th Graders-5 sentences

Now to write: Guide the students through the following steps so their writing is organized and complete. They are free to write these ideas in their own words. There is a 2nd Grade example in italics for your own guidance.

1. Engage the reader by writing questions or exclamations. State your opinion about candy corn: *Halloween is coming and that means candy corn. I love candy corn!*
2. Write and explain the first reason (color, texture and taste): *First of all, they are squishy and chewy. They taste like frosting.*
3. Write and explain the second reason (ingredients and nutrition): *Second of all, some candy corn have honey. I really like the ones with cocoa powder!*
4. Write and explain the third reason (uses): *Lastly, my mom makes cupcakes every Halloween. She lets me put candy corn on top of them.*
5. Write a final sentence restating your opinion using different words. *We also mix candy corn with peanuts, raisins and popcorn. Candy corn is the best!*
6. Add an easy art accent: Students can draw and color candy corn, place candy corn stickers or past an images of candy corn around the border of their writing.

10. EXHAUSTED ELECTRONICS—SCIENCE FICTION

Our electronics are wiped out, tired and bored. They want a vacation! This is a great lesson for addressing electronics, practicing dialogue and writing Science Fiction. NOTE: This lesson can address the following Common Core State Standards: CCSS.ELA-Literacy.W.K.3, W.1.3, W.2.3, W.3.3, W.3.3.A, W.3.3.B, W.3.3.C, W.3.3.D, W.4.3, W.4.3.A, W.4.3.B, W.4.3.C, W.4.3.D, W.4.3.E, W.5.3, W.5.3.A, W.5.3.B, W.5.3.C, W.5.3.D, W.5.3.E, L.K.2, L.1.2, L.2.2, L.3.2, L.3.2.C, L.4.2, L.4.2.B and L.5.2.

Now for the lesson!

1. Tell the story line to your writers: *"An electronic in your home comes to life and starts talking about its problem. You have to help solve its problem or battle it."*
    Tip: Use scenic <u>calendar pictures</u>. Have your student(s) choose a picture, then incorporate the calendar scene into the story. For example. The electronic might beg to visit the mountains. After writing the story, the child can draw the electronic and glue it onto the <u>calendar picture</u> with the mountains.

2. Brainstorm electronics and what they could say:
    A TV says, "I'm tired of just sitting here, day after day."   An iPad says, "I miss my family."
    A phone speaks from a purse, "Someone, get me out of here!"   A toaster says, "I'm bored."

    Brainstorm electronic super powers:
    Electronics talk   An iPhone shoots electric shocks   A TV turns invisible
    A toaster shoots painful bread   An iPad teleports to another location   A refrigerator opens and throws food

3. Show the 5 sections:
    Dialogue (An electronic speaks.)
    Characters/Setting
    The Problem
    Reactions/Actions
    Solution/Conclusion

4. Show the expectations:
    K—1st Graders are encouraged to write 1 sentence for each section, 2nd Graders-2 sentences, 3rd Graders-3 sentences, 4th Graders-4 sentences, 5th Graders-5 sentences

Now to write: Guide the students through the following steps. They are free to use their own words. Remind them that ANYTHING can happen in their story as long as they follow the steps to keep their story organized. There is a 2nd Grade example in italics for your own guidance.

1. Begin the story with a conversation: *"I'm bored," the toaster said. "Where is everyone?"*
    NOTE: If you want your student(s) to practice punctuating dialogue, start off slow. Verbalize the following steps for your writers:
    a.   Write the opening quotation marks.
    b.   Write what the character is saying. Begin the sentence with a capital letter.
    c.   Finish the sentence(s) with a ?, !, or comma.
    d.   Write the closing quotation marks.
    e.   Write who said it and end the sentence with a period.
2. Second, name the main characters and write about the conversation: *"Toaster? Is that you?" Jack asked. "Did you just say something?"*
3. Write about the electronic and its problem: *All of a sudden, the toaster jumped off the counter and shouted, "I want to go to a horse farm!"*
4. Write the characters reactions and actions: *Jack was shocked. "Okay," he said.*
    NOTE: If you are working with older students, this is a good time to encourage them to SHOW the reactions and feelings by describing in detail the character's actions. For example, if a character is shocked, a student can write: *Jack froze. He didn't say anything. His eyes were wide open.*
5. Write about how the problem gets solved and any thoughts for the future: *Jack and the toaster went to a horse farm once a month after that. The toaster loved it!*
6. Add an easy art accent. Draw a picture of the electronic. Cut it out and paste it to the top of the story or on a scenic calendar picture.

11. "I'M THANKFUL FOR"—A LIST POEM

My mom, mud and marshmallows!

This is a fun lesson that gets kids to write things that they are thankful for. You can also use it to write a silly list of things that they might pack for a trip. It actually has 4 levels of difficulty. The 4th level, and original idea for this lesson, guides students in completing a long list of words that <u>alternate between rhyme and alliteration</u>. Choose the level that best fits your students. As the students write the poem, they can add words that may be silly or odd, but that fit the pattern of rhyme or alliteration. This adds humor to their poem!

NOTE: This lesson can address the following Common Core State Standards, CCSS.ELA-LITERACY.RF.K.2.A. L.K.2.C and L.K.2.D.

4 LEVELS OF SKILLS

Level 1: Students write a list of things that they are thankful for by writing **the sounds that they hear for each word** (phonetic spelling).

Level 2: Students write a list of things that they are thankful for by writing **groups of words that begin with the same sound** (alliteration).

Level 3: Students write a list of things that they are thankful for by writing **groups of words that rhyme**.

Level 4: Students write a list of things that they are thankful for by writing alternate groups of words containing rhyme, alliteration, rhyme, alliteration, etc.

Here are the steps to complete LEVEL 4:

Have your students:

1. Brainstorm a long list of things that they are actually thankful for.
2. Group words that begin with the same sound (alliteration).
3. Group words that rhyme.
4. Add words to each set of rhyme and alliteration so that there are 2 or more words in each group. These added words can be ANYTHING! They don't have to make sense and can be silly.
5. Draw a **square** around each group of words that begin with the same sound (alliteration).
6. Draw a **circle** around each group of words that rhyme.

Now to write:

1. First, write the title "I'm Thankful For" at the top of the page.
2. Then, to write the list, alternate by writing
   —one group of words that rhyme (circled group)
   —one group of words that begin with the same sound (squared group)
   —another group of words that rhyme (circled group)
   —another group of words that begin with the same sound and so on, until they've written all the groups of words that have circles and squares.
3. Remind the students to consider rhythm so that the poem has a bit of a beat. To create this, they might need to add the word "and" here and there.
4. Add an easy art accent: Students can place a cornucopia sticker at the top of their poem, place stickers of items they've written or draw pictures of them.

12. OUR THANKSGIVING TURKEY—AN A TO Z POEM

This humorous poem can be written about any food for any occasion and is not limited to Thanksgiving. NOTE: This lesson can address the following Common Core State Standards: CCSS. ELA-LITERACY.L.1.1.E, L.2.1.D and L.5.1.C

Now for the steps!

1. Show your students the ABC template (found on the next page).

2. Tell them that they're going to write an ABC poem about a specific Thanksgiving food, or any other food.

3. Give them time to rattle off their favorite foods!

4. Now, explain to them that in this ABC poem, each letter of the alphabet is a little person. Each letter is going to *DO* something to the Thanksgiving food. The action has to begin with that letter. For example, the easiest way to start is to write *A ate it. B bit it., etc.*

5. Stop and make sure the students understand step #4.

6. Tell the students that the letters can do *ANY VERB* to the food. (i.e. Bought it, Broke it, Begged for it, etc.)

Now to write:

1. Leave the top line blank. Explain to the children that they're going to title their poem "OUR _____". The name of their food will go in the blank. Some examples are, *OUR THANKSGIVING TURKEY, OUR MASHED POTATOES, OUR SWEET POTATO PIE,* etc. They can write the title with ABC stickers or markers once they're done with the poem.

2. Remind the children that each letter is a little person. Each letter is the subject or noun in the short sentence. Make sure they leave a space between the letter and the actual verb like this:

   A ate it.
   B bit it.

3. For younger writers, talk about the verb ideas with them and write an example for them on the board. They can copy the sample or write independently.
   For older writers, let them fill out the ABC poem independently.

4. Once a student is done writing, he or she can complete the title with ABC stickers or markers.

5. The students can also draw their food somewhere on their poem or paste an image of it.

6. Be sure and give your students time to share their poems. They will enjoy making their classmates laugh!

OUR _____

A	N
B	O
C	P
D	Q
E	R
F	S
G	T
H	U
I	V
J	W
K	X
L	Y
M	Z

13. THANKSGIVING RING TOSS—INSTRUCTIONS

Kids love this lesson because they get to make their own ring toss and play it later! Note: This lesson can address the following Common Core State Standards: CCSS.ELA.LITERACY.W.K.2, W.1.2, W.2.2, W.3.2, W.3.2.A, W.3.2.C, W.3.2.D, W.4.2, W.4.2.D, W.4.2.E, W.5.2, W.5.2.D and W.5.2.E.

Making the Ring Toss:

Materials: 1 ft. long strong and skinny stick, a pipe cleaner and a 24" piece of yarn. (A thick popsicle stick can be used in place of a stick, but it isn't quite as fun.)

Steps:
1. Cut the pipe cleaner in half. Use one half.
2. Form the pipe cleaner into a circle and twist the ends tightly.
3. Tie one end of the yarn to the circle.
4. Tie the other end of the yarn to the stick.
5. To play, the child holds the stick. Then, he or she tries to catch the ring onto the end of the stick.

The Writing Lesson:
1. Tell the story line: *"You just finished making your own ring toss. Now, you're going to write out the instructions so someone else can make it."*
2. Brainstorm: Give the students time to recall the materials they used and the steps they took. Have them speak these items out loud. Write them on the board.
3. Show the 5 sections:

   Introduction (Engage the reader.)
   Materials
   Steps 1 and 2
   Steps 3 and 4
   Conclusion (Encourage the reader.)

4. Show the expectations:
   K—1st Graders are encouraged to write 1 sentence for each section, 2nd Graders-2 sentences, 3rd Graders-3 sentences, 4th Graders-4 sentences, 5th Graders-5 sentences

Now to Write: Guide the students through the following steps so their instructions are organized and complete. They are free to write these ideas in their own words. There's a 2nd Grade example in italics for your own guidance.

1. Write the title, **_RING TOSS_**, on the first line in the center.
2. Write questions or exclamations about Thanksgiving fun and children. What's your favorite toy?
3. Introduce the ring toss: This ring toss is easy to make and fun!
4. Write the word MATERIALS on the next line, left side and list them: a stick, yarn and a pipe cleaner
5. Skip a line. On the next line, left side, write INSTRUCTIONS or STEPS.
6. Write steps one and two using the words First and Next: First, get a stick. Next, make a circle.
7. Write steps three and four using the words Then and Last: Then, tie the yarn. Last, you can play!
8. Encourage older writers to elaborate their instructions for each material. They can also use the words, *First, Next, Then, Last*. Here's a detailed example:
   First, go outside and find a small, sturdy stick. The stick should be about a foot long. Next, cut a pipe cleaner into two equal parts. Form one half into a circle. Tightly twist the ends of the pipe cleaner together and into the circle. Then, cut a piece a yarn so that it's 24 inches long. Tie one end of the yarn to the circle. Tie the other end of the yarn to the stick. Last, hold the stick in one hand. Swing the ring up into the air and try to catch it onto the end of your stick.
9. Write a conclusion that encourages readers to make their own and play it! Count how many times you catch it! This game is so fun, so I hope you make one soon!
10. The ring toss is the child's easy art accent. Give the children time to play with their ring toss!

14. LOST SOMETHING—PERSONAL NARRATIVE

This guided writing lesson helps students write out their own story about a time that they lost something. Many kids love telling about a time that they lost a tooth. If they can't remember the time they lost a tooth, they can usually remember a time that they lost something else. NOTE: This lesson can address the following Common Core State Standards: CCSS.ELA-LITERACY.W.K.3, W.1.3, W.2.3, W.3.3, W.3.3.B, W.3.3.C, W.3.3.D, W.4.3, W4.3.A, W.4.3.B, W.4.3.C, W.4.3.D, W.4.3.E, W.5.3, W.5.3.A, W.5.3.B, W.5.3.C, W.5.3.D and W.5.3.E

Now for the lesson!

1. Tell the story line: *"You're going to write a personal narrative about a time that you lost a tooth, or lost something important to you."*

2. Brainstorm things that children lost:

A tooth	A favorite toy	Their mom's keys
A favorite stuffy	Jewelry	Their soccer cleats

Give the students 5–10 minutes to think about an item that they lost.

Encourage the students to think about actions and dialogue that occurred when they lost the item or found it asking the following questions:

   "What did you say? What did you do? How did you act? What did other say or do?"

Encourage them to think about sensory details by answering the following questions in their writing: *Did you see, hear, smell, feel or taste anything specific?*

3. Show the 5 sections:

   Time/People/Place
   Normal Activity
   All of a sudden,
   Reactions/Actions
   Solution/Conclusion

4. Show the expectations:
   K–1st Graders are encouraged to write 1 sentence for each section, 2nd Graders-2 sentences, 3rd Graders-3 sentences, 4th Graders-4 sentences, 5th Graders-5 sentences

Now to write: Guide the students through the following steps so their story is organized and complete. They are free to write these ideas in their own words. There's a 2nd Grade example in italics for your own guidance.

1. Begin by introducing the time, people and place: *It was summer time. My little brother and I were sitting on the floor in the living room.*
2. Describe what you were doing before you lost the tooth or item. *We were getting ready for Jiu Jitsu. I said, "My tooth hurts."*
3. Write about the moment you lost your tooth, or the moment you realized that you lost the item. *All of a sudden, my brother reached in my mouth. He pulled out my tooth!*
4. Write each person's reactions and actions: *"Ouch!" I yelled. I hit him in the arm.*
5. Write the ending to the story and any thoughts for the future. *Then, we laughed. We couldn't believe my little brother pulled out my tooth!*
6. Add an easy art accent: Students can write their title with ABC stickers or markers. Then, they can draw the item that they lost in the border of their writing.

15. SWEET DREAMS—FANTASY

This lesson can be taught anytime of the year using any candy or sweet treat. For the Christmas season, you can use candy canes!

NOTE: This lesson can address the following Common Core State Standards: CCSS.ELA-LITERACY.W.K.3, W.1.3, W.2.3, W.3.3, W.3.3.B, W.3.3.C, W.3.3.D, W.4.3, W4.3.A, W.4.3.B, W.4.3.C, W.4.3.D, W.4.3.E, W.5.3, W.5.3.A, W.5.3.B, W.5.3.C, W.5.3.D and W.5.3.E.

Now for the lesson!

1. Tell the story line: *"The title of this story is going to be <u>SWEET DREAMS</u>. You're going to write about a dream that has candy canes (or any other candy) in it. Anything can happen in your dream! You just have to incorporate candy canes (or candy in general) in some way."*

2. Have your students tell a dream that they remember.

    Brainstorm characteristics of dreams:

    A familiar place that is different
    Famous people
    Flying

    Trying to do something but can't, see, hear or talk
    Falling
    Etc.

3. Show the 5 sections:

    > Introduction
    > Actions
    > Problem
    > Attempt
    > Ending

4. Show the expectations:
    K–1st Graders are encouraged to write 1 sentence for each section, 2nd Graders-2 sentences, 3rd Graders-3 sentences, 4th Graders-4 sentences, 5th Graders-5 sentences

Now to write: Guide the students through the following steps. They are free to use their own words. Remind them that ANYTHING can happen in their story as long as they follow the steps to keep their story organized. There is a 2nd Grade example in italics for your own guidance.

1. Write the introduction and describe the place: *Last night, I had the _____ est dream.* (strangest, best, scariest, craziest, silliest, funniest…)
    Last night, I had the strangest dream. I was at my cousin's house. The floor was water.
2. Describe your actions. *We were floating on candy canes. My sister was swimming around us.*
3. Show the problem. *All of a sudden, all of the water turned into fudge. Then, a shark swam through the door.*
4. Show your attempt. *I tried to fight the shark with a candy cane. The shark bit it.*
5. Write the ending. *The shark was about to eat me. Then, I woke up!*
6. Add an easy art accent: Students can draw and color candy canes around the border of their writing. Or, they can place candy cane stickers.

16. REINDEER SANDWICHES—INSTRUCTIONS

This is a super easy and charming lesson. It works best with smaller groups but can be used for larger groups if an assembly line for making the sandwiches is strategically set up. The recipe was found on www.aspottedpony.com (Bond, K. 2012). It's simple and highly motivating to writers! NOTE: This lesson can address the following Common Core State Standards: CCSS.ELA.LITERACY.W.K.2, W.1.2, W.2.2, W.3.2, W.3.2.A, W.3.2.C, W.3.2.D, W.4.2, W.4.2.D, W.4.2.E, W.5.2, W.5.2.D and W.5.2.E.

Making the Sandwich:
Ingredients: bread, butter or peanut butter, jam, small twist pretzels and M&Ms,
Materials: Paper plates, two butter knives, a heart-shaped cookie cutter and napkins.
Steps:
1. Make a sandwich.
2. Cut out a heart with a cookie cutter.
3. Place two twist pretzels for the ears.
4. Place two M&Ms for the eyes and one M&M for the nose.

The Writing Lesson
1. Tell the story line: *"You just finished making your own reindeer sandwich. Now you're going to write out the instructions so someone else can make one."*
2. Brainstorm: Give the students time to recall and tell the ingredients and materials that they used, as well as the steps they took. Write them on the board.
3. Show the 5 sections:

    Introduction: Engage the reader.
    Ingredients and Materials
    Steps 1 and 2
    Steps 3 and 4
    Conclusion: Encourage the reader.

4. Show the expectations:
    K—1st Graders are encouraged to write 1 sentence for each section, 2nd Graders-2 sentences, 3rd Graders-3 sentences, 4th Graders-4 sentences, 5th Graders-5 sentences

Now to Write: Guide the students through the following steps so their instructions are organized and complete. They are free to write these ideas in their own words. There's a 2nd Grade example in italics for your own guidance.

1. On the 1st line, center, write the title **<u>REINDEER SANDWICHES</u>** or anything else a writer thinks of.
2. Write questions or exclamations about Christmas foods: *Have you ever seen a reindeer sandwich before?*
3. Then, introduce the reindeer sandwich: *It's easy to make and super yummy!*
4. Write the word INGREDIENTS on the next line, left side, and list them: bread, jam, small pretzels and M&Ms.
5. Skip a line. On the next line, left side, write the word MATERIALS and list them. Skip a line.
6. Write the word STEPS or INSTRUCTIONS on the next line, left side. Skip a line.
7. Write steps one and two using the words, *First* and *Next: First, make a sandwich. Next, add the ears.*
8. Write steps three and four using the words, *Then* and *Last: Then, put two eyes. Last, put one nose.*
9. Encourage older writers to elaborate their instructions and write 2–4 sentences for each step. They can also use the words, *First, Next, Then* and *Last.* For example:
    First, make the sandwich. Take a piece of bread and spread butter and jam on it. Take a second piece of bread and place it on top of the jam and butter. Next, find a cookie cutter that is in the shape of a heart. Center the cookie cutter. Press down and cut a heart out of the sandwich. Then, take two pretzels. Put them between the bread at the top of the heart. Put one on each side to make the ears. Last, take two M&Ms that are the same color. Place them to make the eyes. Use a third M&M to make the nose.
10. Write a concluding statement that encourages readers to make the sandwich and eat it too! *These sandwiches are so fun and yummy. I hope you can make one soon!*

17. BIRTHDAY BASH—SCIENCE FICTION

This is a great lesson for practicing dialogue and writing Science Fiction. This particular lesson focuses on time travel. NOTE: This lesson can address the following Common Core State Standards: CCSS.ELA-Literacy.W.K.3, W.1.3, W.2.3, W.3.3, W.3.3.A, W.3.3.B, W.3.3.C, W.3.3.D, W.4.3, W.4.3.A, W.4.3.B, W.4.3.C, W.4.3.D, W.4.3.E, W.5.3, W.5.3.A, W.5.3.B, W.5.3.C, W.5.3.D, W.5.3.E, L.K.2, L.1.2, L.2.2, L.3.2, L.3.2.C, L.4.2, L.4.2.B and L.5.2.

Now for the lesson!

1. Tell the story line to your writers: *"You are at a birthday party (or New Year's Eve celebration). All of a sudden, a balloon pops. When it pops, everyone at the party time travels. You have to figure out a way to get back."*

2. Brainstorm times and places. Here are a few to get you started:

   - Year 3030
   - Ancient Egypt
   - Dinosaur times
   - 1849 Gold Rush
   - The Ice Age
   - Year 3,000 on Mars

   Brainstorm ways to get back. Examples include:

   - A balloon travels with them and pops
   - The characters discover a code
   - The characters find a secret hole/door/passage way
   - A dust storm carries them back home

3. Show the 5 sections:

   Dialogue
   Characters/Setting
   All of a sudden,
   Reactions/Actions
   Solution/Conclusion

4. Show the expectations:
   K—1st Graders are encouraged to write 1 sentence for each section, 2nd Graders-2 sentences, 3rd Graders-3 sentences, 4th Graders-4 sentences, 5th Graders-5 sentences

Now to write: Guide the students through the following steps. They are free to use their own words. Remind them that ANYTHING can happen in their story as long as they follow the steps to keep their story organized. There is a 2nd Grade example in italics for your own guidance.

1. Begin the story with a conversation: *"Time for cake!" Sara shouted. "Yeah!" All the kids came running.*
   NOTE: If you want your student(s) to practice punctuating dialogue, start off slow. Verbalize the following steps for your writers:
   1. Write the opening quotation marks.
   2. Write what the character is saying. Begin the sentence with a capital letter.
   3. Finish the sentences with a ?, !, or comma.
   4. Write the closing quotation marks.
   5. Write who said it and end the sentence with a period.
2. Describe the characters, setting and birthday party: *It was Sara's 6th birthday. Her house was full of people.*
3. Write about how the balloon popped and the time travel: *Suddenly, a balloon popped. Everyone was on Mars. It was the year 3030.*
4. Write about everyone's reactions and actions: *Sara's friends were shocked. Two kids started to cry.*

   NOTE: If you are working with older students, this is a good time to encourage them to SHOW the reactions and feelings by describing in detail the character's actions. For example, if a character is shocked, a student can write: *Sara froze. She didn't say anything. Her eyes were wide open.*

5. Write about how the problem was solved and any thoughts for the future: *A balloon flew by and popped. Everyone was back home.*
6. Add an easy art accent: Students can place birthday stickers, draw and color balloons, or even write their story on birthday stationary to add color and charm to their story.

18. SNOW—JOURNAL

Whether kids live in an area where there are blizzards year after year, or no snow at all, they most likely have something to say about snow. This lesson gives them a chance to do so!

NOTE: This lesson can address the following Common Core State Standards: CCSS.ELA-LITERACY.W.K.1, W.1.1, W.2.1, W.3.1, W.4.1, W.5.1, W.K.3, W.1.3, W.2.3, W.3.3, W.4.3, W.5.3, L.1.2.A, L.1.2.C and L.2.2.B.

Now for the lesson:

1. *First, tell the story line: "You're going to write your honest thoughts about snow and also tell a short story about a time that you were in snow or what you will do the first time you see snow."*

    Explain to the students that a journal is a great place to jot down your most honest feelings; excitement, frustration, disappointment, angst, fear, anger, humor, etc.

    Explain to the students that they're going to write a journal about SNOW.

2. Discuss how snow can generate many different thoughts and feelings: *Someone may love or hate snow. Snow activities may excite or bore someone. Someone may have never seen snow and wish they had. Another may live in a heavy snow area and wish they didn't.*

3. Show the 5 sections:

    Date/Greeting/Opinion
    Describe Snow
    Snow Activities
    Short Story
    Conclusion/Salutation/Name

4. Show the expectations:
    K—1st Graders are encouraged to write 1 sentence for each section, 2nd Graders-2 sentences, 3rd Graders-3 sentences, 4th Graders-4 sentences, 5th Graders-5 sentences

Now to write: Guide the students through the following steps to keep their writing organized. There is a 2nd Grade example in italics for your own guidance.

1. On the first line, right side, write the date. Make sure the month is capitalized and that there is a comma between the day and year. Skip a line.
2. On the 3rd line, left side, write the greeting, Make sure both words are capitalized and followed by a comma. *Dear Journal,*
3. On the 5th line, left side, write an introduction using 1–2 sentences: *It is snowing again. I hate it!*
4. Describe snow. This section can focus on the positive or negative aspects of snow. *The snow is heavy and cold. It gets my pants wet.*
5. Write about snow activities such as sledding, building a snowman, snowball fights, skiing, shoveling, etc. *Snow brings so much work! We have to shovel the driveway.*
6. Tell a short story about a time you were in snow. OR, what you'll do the first time you see snow: *Last year, we were shoveling. My sister threw snow in my face.*
7. Write a conclusion using 1–2 sentences: *I hope the snow melts fast! Maybe I'll save up for a snow blower.*
8. Under the conclusion and in the center of the paper write the salutation: (*Your Friend,*) **Under** the salutation write your name.
9. Add an easy art accent: Students can add snowflakes to the border of their writing. They can use glitter glue, glitter, marker, paint or stickers. You can find an image of a glitter glue snowflake on page 186.

19. SNOW, COWS AND A BARN—SCIENCE FICTION

This is a great lesson for addressing farm life, practicing dialogue and writing Science Fiction. NOTE: This lesson can address the following Common Core State Standards: CCSS.ELA-Literacy.W.K.3, W.1.3, W.2.3, W.3.3, W.3.3.A, W.3.3.B, W.3.3.C, W.3.3.D, W.4.3, W.4.3.A, W.4.3.B, W.4.3.C, W.4.3.D, W.4.3.E, W.5.3, W.5.3.A, W.5.3.B, W.5.3.C, W.5.3.D, W.5.3.E, L.K.2, L.1.2, L.2.2, L.3.2, L.3.2.C, L.4.2, L.4.2.B and L.5.2.

Now for the lesson!

1. Tell the story line to your writers: *"It's a snowy day. There's a problem on the farm. The cows develop and use a super power to solve the problem."*
2. Brainstorm farm problems. Examples include:

The barn collapses	Illness/Starvation	Dairy cows are tired of being milked
Thieves/Hunters	Bobcat/Snakes	Too much snow and no grass

   Brainstorm cow super powers. Here are a few to get you started:

A cow's spots turn blinding yellow	The cows can shoot corn/kernels	The cows can turn all the corn to popcorn
The cows can fly	The cows can shoot hot water and scald thieves	A cow's spots turn hot and melt the snow

3. Show the 5 sections:
   Dialogue
   Characters/Problem
   All of a sudden, (discover a super power)
   Reactions/Actions
   Solution/Conclusion
4. Show the expectations:
   K–1st Graders are encouraged to write 1 sentence for each section, 2nd Graders-2 sentences, 3rd Graders-3 sentences, 4th Graders-4 sentences, 5th Graders-5 sentences

Now to write: Guide the students through the following steps. They are free to use their own words. Remind them that ANYTHING can happen in their story as long as they follow the steps to keep their story organized. There is a 2nd Grade example in italics for your own guidance.

1. Begin the story with a conversation: *"I'm stuck!" one cow said. "I can't move my feet!"*
   NOTE: If you want your student(s) to practice punctuating dialogue, start off slow. Verbalize the following steps for your writers:
   1. Write the opening quotation marks.
   2. Write what the character is saying. Begin the sentence with a capital letter.
   3. Finish the sentences with a ?, !, or comma.
   4. Write the closing quotation marks.
   5. Write who said it and end the sentence with a period.
2. Introduce the characters and describe the problem: *It snowed all night. The cows were outside.*
3. Write about a cow, or the cows, suddenly having a super power: *WOOSH! All of a sudden, one cow had yellow spots. They were hot.*
4. Write about what the characters reactions and actions. *The spots melted the snow. The cows' feet started to move.*
   NOTE: If you are working with older students, this is a good time to encourage them to SHOW the character's feelings by writing the character's actions. For example, if a cow is brave, a student can write: *The cow didn't hesitate. He confronted the puma. He pointed his blazing spots at the puma until the puma left.*
5. Write about how the problem gets solved and any thoughts for the future: *The cows went back to the barn. They wondered how they could get the same yellow spots!*
6. Add an easy art accent: Students can draw and color large cow spots or a red barn around the border of their writing. They can use a Q-tip to paint white dots for snow.

20. ACKNOWLEDGE THESE PEOPLE—LETTER WRITING

This lesson is meant to honor people who work hard in our communities and demonstrate noble character. Students choose someone that they admire based on that individual's work ethic and/or career choice. It can be someone that the child already knows, or someone new that they learn about. This lesson provides an exciting opportunity for you and your students to research different people from various ethnic groups who work as architects, beauticians, bus drivers, business owners, CEOs, computer programmers, doctors, electricians, engineers, fire fighters, mathematicians, police officers, scientists, soldiers, teachers, veterinarians, web designers, X-ray technicians, etc. Plan to give your students plenty of time to research people who work in their career of interest. The research makes this lesson extra fun!! Lastly, make sure that you can find an address for the person each child wants to write to.

Note: This lesson can address the following Common Core State Standards: CCSS.ELA-LITERACY.L.1.2.A, L.1.2.C, L.2.2.A, L.2.2, and L.3.2.B

Now for the lesson!

1. Tell the students the story line: *"You're going to write a letter to a person working in a profession that you admire."*

2. Explain to them that asking questions is an integral part of letter writing. It expresses interest in the other person and also elicits a response letter for continued dialogue. Have the students think of questions they can ask the person in their letter.

3. Show the 5 sections:

   Date/Greeting/Introduction
   Tell your own interests.
   Tell what you know about the person you're writing to.
   Ask questions.
   Conclusion/Salutation/Name

4. Show the expectations:
   K—1st Graders are encouraged to write 1 sentence for each section, 2nd Graders-2 sentences, 3rd Graders-3 sentences, 4th Graders-4 sentences, 5th Graders-5 sentences

Now to write: Guide the students through the following steps so their letter is organized and complete. They are free to write these ideas in their own words. There is a 2nd Grade example below in italics for your own guidance. The letter is written to Mario Shaw (Fellows Echoing Green n.d.).

1. Begin by writing the date on the first line, right side of the page. Skip a line.
2. Write the greeting on the 3rd line, left side (Dear Capital Letters and a comma): *Dear Mario Shaw,* Skip a line.
3. In your own words, write a greeting and introduce yourself: *Hello! My name is _____. I'm in _____ Grade.*
4. Write about your own interests: *I love playing basketball, drawing and math. I like to draw animals best.*
5. Write what you know about the person you're writing to: *I know you were a teacher in Charlotte, NC. Then, you helped other black men become teachers. Great!*
6. Ask questions. Sample questions could be: *Was teaching hard? What do you like to do when you're not working?*
7. Write a conclusion that is positive: *I think I want to be a teacher when I grow up. I would love to meet you one day!*
8. Write the salutation under the body of the letter. *Respectfully, Kindly, Sincerely...*
9. Write your name UNDER the salutation.
10. If possible, photo copy each child's letter before sending it so they can have their own copy. Complete an envelope. Stick a stamp and send it away!

21. HAIKU

Haikus are simple for the students to do and fun for them because the ideas are endless! They go great with ANY theme! If you are focusing on a particular Science, History, Geography or Math lesson, take a break and let the kids write a haiku poem about the topic! If you have old calendar pictures, have your students choose a picture and write a haiku about it.

Here are the steps I use to teach this prompt:

1. Explain to the children that haiku poems originated in Japan and are typically about nature.
2. Explain that a haiku is a three line poem in which the 1st line has 5 syllables, the 2nd line has 7 syllables and the 3rd line has 5 syllables.
3. Review syllables by clapping 1, 2, 3 and 4 syllable words (i.e. dog, jumpy, excited, energetic)
4. Give each student a piece of paper.
5. In order to remember what a haiku is, have them use markers or ABC stickers to write the word HAIKU at the top of their page.
6. Next, they draw a Japanese flag.

HAIKU

5
7
5

7. Third, they use a marker or number stickers to write a 5, 7, and 5 in a vertical line.
8. Give them a 2nd piece of paper to write their Haiku draft on.

Now to write: Guide the students through the following steps.

1. Choose a noun, topic or theme to write about.
2. On the first line, write a 5 syllable phrase describing the chosen noun/topic/theme.
3. On the second line, write a 7 syllable phrase describing the chosen noun/topic/theme.
4. On the third line, write a 5 syllable phrase describing the chosen noun/topic/theme.
5. Write a final draft on a nice sheet of paper, like the one on the next page.
6. Have students write a title using markers or ABC stickers. They can illustrate their poem or place stickers to add color and charm.
7. Complete as many haiku poems as you want!

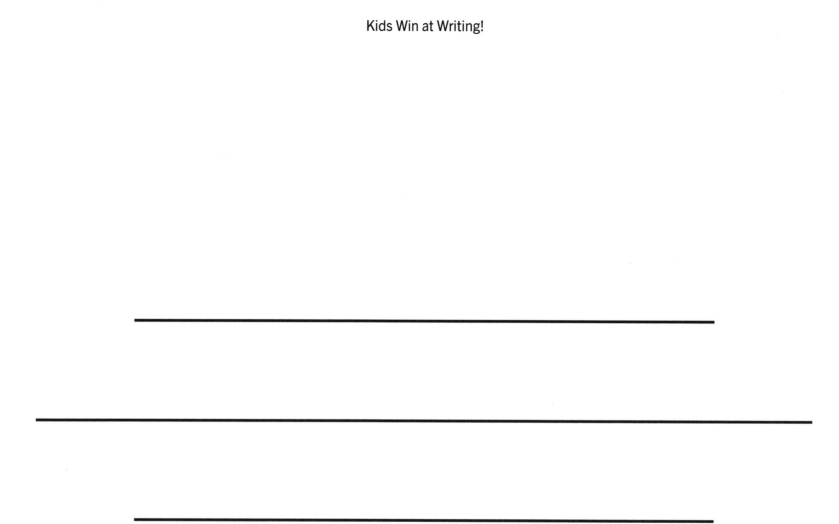

22. RELATIONAL CONFLICT—PERSONAL NARRATIVE

This lesson gets kids laughing as they reminisce their frustrating conflicts. In most cases, hindsight makes the conflict seem trivial and humorous. Secondly, this guided writing prompt helps students write out their own story about a conflict with a person, whether it be a classmate, neighbor, friend, cousin, sibling, etc. NOTE: This lesson can address the following Common Core State Standards: CCSS.ELA-LITERACY.W.K.3, W.1.3, W.2.3, W.3.3, W.3.3.B, W.3.3.C, W.3.3.D, W.4.3, W4.3.A, W.4.3.B, W.4.3.C, W.4.3.D, W.4.3.E, W.5.3, W.5.3.A, W.5.3.B, W.5.3.C, W.5.3.D and W.5.3.E

Now for the lesson!

1. Tell the story line: *"You're going to write a personal narrative about a time you didn't get along with someone and the outcome."*
   Read the book, *My Red Headed Rotten Brother* by Patricia Polacco.

2. Brainstorm sample conflicts:

   Two siblings fight over a toy

   Two classmates compete

   A neighbor gets left out

   Two cousins fight for the last piece of cake

   Give the students 5–10 minutes (or more) to think about a personal conflict to write about.

   Encourage the students to think about actions and dialogue that occurred during the conflict by asking the following questions:

   "What did you say? What did you do? How did you act? What did the other person say or do?"

   Encourage them to think about sensory details by answering the following questions in their writing: *Did you see, hear, smell, feel or taste anything specific?*

3. Show the 5 sections:

   > Time/People/Place
   > Normal Activity
   > The Conflict
   > Reactions/Actions
   > Solution/Conclusion

4. Show the expectations:
   K—1st Graders are encouraged to write 1 sentence for each section, 2nd Graders-2 sentences, 3rd Graders-3 sentences, 4th Graders-4 sentences, 5th Graders-5 sentences

Now to write: Guide the students through the following steps so their story is organized and complete. They are free to write these ideas in their own words. There's a 2nd Grade example in italics for your own guidance.

1. Begin by introducing the two characters: *Mark is my best friend. He lives next to me.*
2. Describe a normal day before the conflict occurred. State the season, time or day: *After Christmas, I went to his house to look at his new things. He got a Zelda sword.*
3. Write about the conflict. Use a transitional or temporal word such as *All of a sudden, or Suddenly. I was playing with it. All of a sudden, it broke!*
4. Write each person's reactions and actions: *Mark started yelling at me! I felt so bad and said sorry.*
5. Write the ending to the conflict and any thoughts for the future. *Later, I told Mark I would buy him another sword, but he said I didn't have to Next time, I'll be more careful.*

23. THE 'Q-U'-QUEEN—FAIRY TALE

This is a great lesson for practicing words that start with 'q-u'. NOTE: This lesson can address the following Common Core State Standards: CCSS.ELA-LITERACY.W.K.3, W.1.3, W.2.3, W.3.3, W.3.3.B, W.3.3.C, W.3.3.D, W.4.3, W4.3.A, W.4.3.B, W.4.3.C, W.4.3.D, W.4.3.E, W.5.3, W.5.3.A, W.5.3.B, W.5.3.C, W.5.3.D and W.5.3.E.

Now for the lesson!

1. Tell the general story line: "*A king is in desperate need of a queen, but he is very picky. Explain that all of the reasons he doesn't like a woman have to begin with "qu." Also, the reasons he DOES like a woman have to start with "qu". Explain that he doesn't like the first two women he meets. Then, he likes a woman that doesn't like him. Finally, he finds a woman he loves. She loves him too.*"

2. Brainstorm a list of words that start with "QU". Write the students' responses on the board:

Quack	Quarter	Question	Quill	Quiver
Quail	Quartz	Quick	Quilt	Quiz
Quality	Queen	Quickly	Quirky	Quote
Quarrel	Queasy	Quiet	Quit	

Brainstorm "q-u" reasons a king may like, or dislike, a woman. She:

Is too quiet.	Is quirky.	Can't pass a quiz
Asks too many questions.	Quacks when she laughs.	Is obsessed with quilts or quilts beautifully.
Talks too quickly.	Refuses to eat quail or has a pet quail.	
Eats too quickly.	Quivers every time she….	

Explain to the students that the story can be normal or really funny. It's funny if a very picky king finally falls in love with a woman who is quirky or quacks when she laughs. The story is also funny if he simply meets these quirky women time after time, but then finally meets a lovely woman whom he falls in love with. The story can go either way!

3. Show the 5 sections:

> Introduce the king.
> Describe the first woman that he doesn't like.
> Describe the 2nd woman that he doesn't like.
> Describe the 3rd woman that he likes but doesn't like him.
> Describe the 4th woman that he marries.

4. Show the expectations:
   K−1st Graders are encouraged to write 1 sentence for each section, 2nd Graders-2 sentences, 3rd Graders-3 sentences, 4th Graders-4 sentences, 5th Graders-5 sentences

Now to write: Guide the students through the following steps. They are free to use their own words. Remind them that ANYTHING can happen in their story as long as they follow the steps to keep their story organized. There's a 2nd Grade sample in italics for your own guidance.

1. Introduce the king and the problem: *Long ago, there lived a king named Quinn. He needed a queen, but he was very picky.*
2. Write about the first woman he met and didn't like: *One woman was too quiet. When she spoke, he couldn't hear what she said!*
3. Write about the 2nd woman he met and didn't like: *Another woman ate too quickly. As soon as she got her food, it was gone in 60 seconds.*
4. Write about the 3rd woman he met and liked but who didn't like him: *Then, he met a woman who was quite nice. He liked her! But, she said he asked too many questions.*
5. Older students can describe the king's feelings at this point: *The king was disappointed. He started to worry that he would never get married.*
6. Write about the 4th woman that he met and liked: *Then, one day, a woman brought him a beautiful quilt. The king quacked and married her!*
7. Add an easy art accent: Students can draw and color a queen's tiara around the border of their writing. They can use glue dots to stick sequins on the tiara (See page 188).

24. A POPPING PRESIDENT—FANTASY

You don't have to serve popcorn for this lesson but it sure motivates and rewards the students! Having an actual popcorn machine where the kids can *watch* the pops fits this lesson perfectly. NOTE: This lesson can address the following Common Core State Standards: CCSS.ELA-LITERACY.W.K.3, W.1.3, W.2.3, W.3.3, W.3.3.B, W.3.3.C, W.3.3.D, W.4.3, W4.3.A, W.4.3.B, W.4.3.C, W.4.3.D, W.4.3.E, W.5.3, W.5.3.A, W.5.3.B, W.5.3.C, W.5.3.D and W.5.3.E.

Now for the lesson!

1. Tell the story line: *"The president of (name the country) sits down to watch a movie and enjoy popcorn. As soon as the president starts eating the popcorn he or she starts to pop, pop, pop up and out of his or her seat and can't stop. Your story has to come up with a solution on how to get the president to stop popping. Your 1st and 2nd ideas won't work. The last idea will."*

2. Brainstorm possible solutions to get the president to stop popping. Write the students' responses on the board. Here are some ideas:

Sprinkling the president with salt   Giving the president soda to drink
Putting the president out in the cold   Catching the president in a net

3. Show the 5 sections:

> Time/People/Place/Event
> Problem
> 1st Attempt
> 2nd Attempt
> 3rd Attempt and Conclusion

4. Show the expectations:
K—1st Graders are encouraged to write 1 sentence for each section, 2nd Graders-2 sentences, 3rd Graders-3 sentences, 4th Graders-4 sentences, 5th Graders-5 sentences

Now to write: Guide the students through the following steps. They are free to use their own words. Remind them that ANYTHING can happen in their story as long as they follow the steps to keep their story organized. There's a 2nd Grade sample in italics for your own guidance.

1. Begin by writing when, where, who and what event: *Last night, Mr. President was in the White House. He sat down to watch a movie and eat popcorn.*
2. Tell the problem: *As soon as Mr. President began eating the popcorn, he started to pop, pop, pop, up and out of his seat. He couldn't stop.*
3. Write about the 1st attempt to stop the popping. *The First Lady, called 911 and tried to catch Mr. President. It didn't work.*
4. Describe the 2nd attempt to get him to stop popping: *Then, the First Lady thought to sprinkle salt on him. It didn't work.*
5. Describe the 3rd attempt that worked and a conclusion:
   > *Finally, a fire fighter grabbed his feet and gave him soda. The president took a sip and fell to the floor.*
6. Remember, older students can elaborate and add something like:
   > *No one knows what caused the popping. FBI agents are investigating the popcorn company that made the popcorn.*
7. Add an easy art accent: Students can use a pen to draw popcorn around the border of their story. (See the top of page 163.)

25. ALIENS IN THE ARCTIC—SCIENCE FICTION

This is a great lesson for addressing arctic animals, practicing dialogue and writing Science Fiction. NOTE: This lesson can address the following Common Core State Standards: CCSS.ELA-Literacy.W.K.3, W.1.3, W.2.3, W.3.3, W.3.3.A, W.3.3.B, W.3.3.C, W.3.3.D, W.4.3, W.4.3.A, W.4.3.B, W.4.3.C, W.4.3.D, W.4.3.E, W.5.3, W.5.3.A, W.5.3.B, W.5.3.C, W.5.3.D, W.5.3.E, L.K.2, L.1.2, L.2.2, L.3.2, L.3.2.C, L.4.2, L.4.2.B and L.5.2.

Now for the lesson!

1. Tell the story line: *"Arctic animals are playing. Friendly and lost aliens land in the Arctic OR aliens attack the Arctic. The Arctic animals have to help or get rid of the aliens."*

2. Brainstorm arctic animal super powers. Examples include:

   Arctic foxes have claws that extend far   Polar bear lasers freeze or melt objects   Snowshoe hares blind others with their whiteness
   A Musk Ox's horns extend and crush   Reindeer horns shoot webs that trap objects   Seals super whack with their tails

   Brainstorm alien super powers or problems. Here are a few to get you started:

   Aliens shoot toxic slime   Aliens blow bubbles that pop a sticky substance   Aliens communicate back to their mother ship
   Aliens melt the ice around them   Aliens change the weather   Aliens have an innocent super strength

3. Show the 5 sections:

   Dialogue
   Characters/Setting/Activity
   All of a sudden,
   Reactions/Actions
   Solution/Conclusion

4. Show the expectations:
   K–1st Graders are encouraged to write 1 sentence for each section, 2nd Graders-2 sentences, 3rd Graders-3 sentences, 4th Graders-4 sentences, 5th Graders-5 sentences

   Now to write: Guide the students through the following steps. They are free to use their own words. Remind them that ANYTHING can happen in their story as long as they follow the steps to keep their story organized. There's a 2nd Grade sample in italics for your own guidance.

1. Begin the story with a conversation: *"Goal!" polar bear yelled. "We won!"*
   NOTE: If you want your student(s) to practice punctuating dialogue, start off slow. Verbalize the following steps for your writers.
   1. Write the opening quotation marks.
   2. Write what the character is saying. Begin the sentence with a capital letter.
   3. Finish the sentences with a ?, !, or comma.
   4. Write the closing quotation marks.
   5. Write who said it and end the sentence with a period.
2. Second, name the main characters and write about them playing: *Polar bear was playing fish soccer with his friends. The penguins were watching.*
3. Write about the arctic animals suddenly noticing the aliens and the problem: *BOOM! All of a sudden, aliens crash-landed. They started pouring out of their ship.*
4. Write about the animals' or aliens' reactions and actions: *Polar bear ran to the ship. He saw that their ship was broken.*
   NOTE: If you are working with older students, encourage them to SHOW the reactions and feelings by describing in detail the character's actions.
   For example, if a character is brave, a student can write: *Polar bear didn't hesitate. He ran straight for the ship. He confronted the aliens.*
5. Write about how the problem gets solved and any thoughts for the future: *Polar bear used his eye lasers to fix it. The aliens were thankful and went home.*
6. Add an easy art accent: Students can use marker to draw and color aliens around the border of their writing. Then, they can glue googly eyes onto the aliens (p.187).

26. HOT TAMALES—JOURNAL

For this lesson you'll need one set of chopsticks for each student and 1–2 boxes of Hot Tamales candy. Students try to eat the hot tamales candy with their chopsticks. Then, they write about the experience! NOTE: This lesson can address the following Common Core State Standards: CCSS.ELA-LITERACY.W.K.1, W.1.1, W.2.1, W.3.1, W.4.1, W.5.1, W.K.3, W.1.3, W.2.3, W.3.3, W.4.3, W.5.3, L.1.2.A, L.1.2.C and L.2.2.B.

Now for the lesson!

1. Tell the story line: "You're going to try to eat Hot Tamales candy using a pair of chopsticks. Then, you're going to write about the experience."

2. Explain to the students that a journal is a great place to jot down your most honest feelings; excitement, frustration, disappointment, angst, fear, anger, humor, etc.
   Explain to the students that eating HOT TAMALES (the candy) using CHOPSTICKS can generate so many different thoughts and feelings:
   "Someone may love chewy candy but hate the spicy cinnamon. Or, another may love the spicy cinnamon and hate the chewy candy stuck in their teeth. People may be completely discouraged having to use the chopsticks or laugh trying to do so."

   Give students time to eat the Hot Tamales with chopsticks. Listen to the raves and complaints. Give them time to share their thoughts verbally!

3. Show the 5 sections:

   > Date/Greeting/Opinion
   > The Experience
   > Hot Tamales Opinion
   > Chopsticks Opinion
   > Conclusion/Salutation/Name

4. Show the expectations:
   K–1st Graders are encouraged to write 1 sentence for each section, 2nd Graders-2 sentences, 3rd Graders-3 sentences, 4th Graders-4 sentences, 5th Graders-5 sentences

Now to write: Guide the students through the following steps. There's a 2nd Grade sample in italics for your own guidance.

1. On the first line, right side, write the date. Make sure the month is capitalized and that there is a comma between the day and year. Skip a line.
2. On the 3rd line, left side, write the greeting, Make sure both words are capitalized and followed by a comma. *Dear Journal,*
3. Skip a line.
4. On the 5th line, left side, write an introduction using 1–2 sentences: *You won't believe what I had to do today! I had to eat Hot Tamales using chopsticks!*
5. Write about the whole experience: *It was hard. My hand started to cramp!*
6. Write your opinion about the Hot Tamales candy: *The candy was great! I liked the spicy cinnamon!*
7. Write about using chopsticks: *Chopsticks are tricky. The candy kept falling.*
8. Write a conclusion using 1–2 sentences: *Finally, I got one piece of candy in my mouth! It was a difficult and delicious day!*
9. Under the conclusion and in the center of the paper write the salutation: *(Your Friend,)*
10. **Under** the salutation write your name.
11. Add an easy art accent. Students can glue their chopsticks to the border of their story. Or, they can print and glue the Hot Tamales logo at the top.

27. CONCRETE POEMS

Concrete poems form a picture using words. Children enjoy concrete poems because of their outcome and also because they can write about ANYTHING. In addition, they don't have to worry about complete sentences or punctuation.

 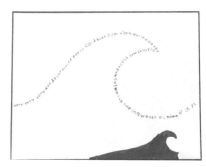 

Here's the lesson!

1. First, children choose a simple image. Then, they draw an outline of their simple image on a clean piece of white paper. They can use a black marker to make wide lines. For K–1st Graders, you will need to help them draw their simple image. Look at these examples:

 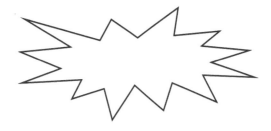 

2. Next, place the image under a second piece of white copy paper.

3. Then, the child writes words where the black lines show through. Wherever there is a line, children should write words, phrases or sentences about the image.

4. For example, over the outline of the fireworks, children might write any, or all, of the following:

5. Loud, colorful, huge, bright, July 4th, 1776, crowds of people watching, oohs and ahhs, blue, red, white. Fireworks celebrate Independence Day in the United States of America. Families sit on blankets outside. Picnics, music, friends.

6. Finally, children can add stickers, use markers to draw, or even paint around the concrete poem to add color and charm.

28. LEPRECHAUN ATTACK—SCIENCE FICTION

For St. Patrick's Day, students write a Science Fiction story in which leprechauns attack planet Earth. Or, the leprechauns can be friendly, but terribly lost and need help getting back to their home. Science Fiction, like fantasy, is fun because students can make ANYTHING happen in their story. NOTE: This lesson can address the following Common Core State Standards: CCSS.ELA-LITERACY.W.K.3, W.1.3, W.2.3, W.3.3, W.3.3.B, W.3.3.C, W.3.3.D, W.4.3, W4.3.A, W.4.3.B, W.4.3.C, W.4.3.D, W.4.3.E, W.5.3, W.5.3.A, W.5.3.B, W.5.3.C, W.5.3.D and W.5.3.E.

Now for the lesson!

1. Tell the story line: "*A boy or girl is in a futuristic setting doing an ordinary activity. He or she notices unusual green in various places and encounters one or more leprechauns. The encounter can be problematic or friendly. The ending can be anything.*"

2. Brainstorm characters and everyday superpowers: *Ability to fly, supernatural strength, telekinesis (lift/move something using the mind), etc.*

   Brainstorm things found in a futuristic setting: *Flying cars and skateboards, family robots, hologram calls, etc.*

   Brainstorm unusual places and ways to find green: *faucet water is green, stoplights shine green only, increase in grass, broccoli multiplies in the fridge, etc.*

   Brainstorm problems: *Leprechauns are mean and attacking with green, tying people's shoes together and tripping them, tricking people with false images of gold, etc. OR, the leprechauns are friendly and lost, begging for help to get back home.*

   Brainstorm solutions for your problem: *Leprechauns grant 3 wishes to be freed, leprechauns promise to tell where gold is if freed, OR humans defeat the leprechauns by...*

3. Show the 5 Sections:

   > Character's ordinary day in a futuristic setting
   > Notices unusual green
   > Encounters leprechauns/Problem
   > Reactions/Actions
   > Solution/Conclusion

4. 4. Show the expectations:
   K—1st Graders are encouraged to write 1 sentence for each section, 2nd Graders-2 sentences, 3rd Graders-3 sentences, 4th Graders-4 sentences, 5th Graders-5 sentences

Now to write: Guide the students through the following steps. They are free to use their own words. Remind them that ANYTHING can happen in their story as long as they follow the steps to keep their story organized. There's a 2nd Grade sample in italics for your own guidance.

1. Name the character and describe what the character is doing in his or her ordinary day. *It was an ordinary day. Joshua plugged in his flying hover-board to charge.*
2. Describe when and where the character notices green in an unusual place. *He got dressed and brushed his teeth. The water was green!*
3. Describe the encounter with the leprechaun(s). *All of a sudden, Joshua felt something tug at his laces. He looked down and there was a tiny LEPRECHAUN!*
4. Write the character's reaction and action. *"Ah!" Joshua shouted. Using his telekinesis Joshua stared at the leprechaun and suspended him in midair.*
5. Write about the solution and ending to the story: *The leprechaun got scared and said, "I think I'm in the wrong place." Then, it disappeared!*
6. Add an easy art accent: Students can color the border of their writing green. They can use ABC stickers or paint to write a title.

29. GREEN ATTACK—REACTION LETTER

Leprechauns attack the classroom or house! Then, students write a reaction letter to the leprechauns. NOTE: This lesson can address the following Common Core State Standards: CCSS.ELA-LITERACY.L.1.2.A, L.1.2.C, L.2.2.A, L.2.2.B, and L.3.2.B

Setting up for the lesson:

Very early in the morning at school (or after the kids have gone to bed if doing this at home), start making a mess with everything GREEN.
In a Kindergarten or 1st Grade Classroom it could include pulling the following items out and onto the floor in front of where they're stored:

GREEN markers and crayons	GREEN socks, underwear, shirts, pants, shoes
GREEN pattern, connecting and/or play blocks	GREEN blocks, toys or stuffed animals
GREEN construction paper	GREEN markers, crayons, colored pencils
GREEN ANYTHING	GREEN construction paper
Add GREEN food coloring to the classroom toilet, HA!	GREEN foods from the pantry and/or fridge
At home, it could include pulling the following items out and onto the floor, kitchen counter, etc.	Add GREEN food coloring to any/all toilets

Upon entering the classroom or waking up at home, give the students plenty of time to react and discover all of the leprechaun's mischief. React with them to play along!!
Once they settle down, walk them through the following writing lesson.

1. Tell the story line: *"Leprechauns just attacked our classroom/house! You're going to write a letter to the leprechauns telling them what you saw and think."*

2. Have students brainstorm the many things that they saw. Write their responses on the board.

3. Show the 5 sections:

    Date/Greeting/Introduction
    1–2 Things you saw
    1–2 Things you saw
    1–2 Things you saw
    Conclusion/Salutation/Name

4. Show the expectations:
    K–1st Graders are encouraged to write 1 sentence for each section, 2nd Graders-2 sentences, 3rd Graders-3 sentences, 4th Graders-4 sentences, 5th Graders-5 sentences

Now to write: Guide the students through the following steps so their story is organized and complete. They are free to write these ideas in their own words. There's a 2nd Grade sample in italics for your own guidance.

1. Write the date on the first line right side. Skip a line.
2. Write the greeting on the 3rd line left side: *Dear Leprechaun,* Then, skip a line.
3. On the next line, write an exclamatory question or statement: *What were you thinking?! Do you see this mess we have to clean up?! OR Ha! Ha! You are funny!*
4. Write about one thing that you saw: *There are green markers on the floor. There are green crayons on the table.*
5. Write about another thing that you saw or found: *Only green books fell off the book shelf. Green construction paper is sticking out of the pile.*
6. Write about another thing that you saw or found: *My green Legos are out of the bin. You even found my green Beyblades.*
7. Write a conclusion: *I'm going to get you! Watch out! We will find you!*
8. Write the salutation on the next line, under the body of the letter and in the center: *Your Friend, Your Enemy, etc.*
9. Write your name **under** the salutation.
10. Add an easy art accent: Students can color the border of their writing green.

30. PUDDLE JUMPING—FANTASY

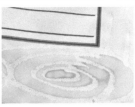

Kids like this prompt for two reasons. One, ANYTHING can happen in their story and two, they get to add a charming rainy art accent to their border. The art accent came from http://www. blackfootartcenter.blogspot.com (Weston, H. 2015). This prompt was created with fantasy in mind, but if students want to use Science Fiction, by all means let them! NOTE: This lesson can address the following Common Core State Standards: CCSS.ELA-LITERACY.W.K.3, W.1.3, W.2.3, W.3.3, W.3.3.B, W.3.3.C, W.3.3.D, W.4.3, W4.3.A, W.4.3.B, W.4.3.C, W.4.3.D, W.4.3.E, W.5.3, W.5.3.A, W.5.3.B, W.5.3.C, W.5.3.D and W.5.3.E.

Now for the lesson!

1. Tell the story line: *"A character is having a bad, takes a walk and steps into a magic puddle. Something happens in the puddle that helps the character solve the problem or gain a new perspective of the problem. The character feels better at the end."*

2. Brainstorm reasons the character is having a bad day. Write them on the board. He or She:

—lost a dog   —couldn't go to a party   —broke a toy
—couldn't have a play date   —got a bad grade   — just moved

3. Show the 5 sections:

> Character/Problem
> Walking Outside
> Magic Puddle
> Inside the Puddle
> Solution/Lesson

4. Show the expectations:
K—1st Graders are encouraged to write 1 sentence for each section, 2nd Graders-2 sentences, 3rd Graders-3 sentences, 4th Graders-4 sentences, 5th Graders-5 sentences

Now to write: Guide the students through the following steps. They are free to use their own words. Remind them that ANYTHING can happen in their story as long as they follow the steps to keep their story organized. There's a 2nd Grade sample in italics for your own guidance.

1. Introduce the character and problem: *Gia liked to play soccer and chase her dog, Ace. One day, Ace got out of the house and Gia couldn't find him.*
2. Describe walking outside: *So, Gia went outside to look for him. It was raining and the streets were wet and empty.*
3. Describe the magic puddle and entering it: *There were so many puddles. One was big and shiny, so Gia decided to step in it.*
4. Describe what happens in the magic puddle: *Suddenly, Gia started spinning and landed in a sparkling park. The rain drops had faces and were talking.*
5. Tell how the problem is solved and what the character thinks and feels: *The next thing Gia knew, she was home on her porch. Ace was there too! Gia was so happy!*
6. Add an easy art accent: Students can use white crayon to draw rain drops and puddles around the border of their writing. Then, they use blue watercolor to paint the border. The white crayon will show through so you can see the rain drops and puddles. (See page 190.)

31. MUD MITES—FICTIONAL NEWS ARTICLE

There's an outbreak of mud mites. Students write a new article about it. NOTE: This lesson can address the following Common Core State Standards: CCSS.ELA-LITERACY.W.K.3, W.1.3, W.2.3, W.3.3, W.3.3.B, W.3.3.C, W.3.3.D, W.4.3, W4.3.A, W.4.3.B, W.4.3.C, W.4.3.D, W.4.3.E, W.5.3, W.5.3.A, W.5.3.B, W.5.3.C, W.5.3.D and W.5.3.E.

This lesson is a big hit if you show the students the mud mites art accent. It is an easy TWO steps:

1. Color the border with brown marker.
2. Use a glue stick to glue 5–10 pairs of tiny googly eyes. Note: The eyes stick best if you put the glue on the *paper*. Then, place the eyes on the glue.

Now for the lesson!

1. Tell the story line: *"You're going to write a news article about an outbreak of mud mites. The mud mites can be anywhere and can create ANY reaction. Your story will include a cure for the reaction **and/or** a way to get rid of the mud mites."*
2. Brainstorm possible reactions to the mud mite bites:

Itchy rash	Ears swelling	Shrinking/growing
Purple spots	Can't stop giggling	Feet becoming gigantic

   Brainstorm possible cures for the breakout and ways to get rid of the mud mites:

Spraying fruit punch on your skin	Wearing a suit for 24 hours	Drying the mud with hot lamps
Bathing in lime juice	Flooding the area with Dr. Pepper	Mixing vinegar into the mud

3. Show the 5 sections:

   Time/People/Place/Event
   Attempt 1 Who/What
   Attempt 2 Who/What
   Attempt 3 Who/What
   Conclusion (Prevention/Warning)

4. Show the expectations:
   K–1st Graders are encouraged to write 1 sentence for each section, 2nd Graders-2 sentences, 3rd Graders-3 sentences, 4th Graders-4 sentences, 5th Graders-5 sentences

Now to write: Guide the students through the following steps. They are free to use their own words. Remind them that ANYTHING can happen in their story as long as they follow the steps to keep their story organized. There's a 2nd Grade sample in italics for your own guidance.

1. Write a title using an eye catching exclamation: *News Flash! Breaking News! Mud Mites Mess in North Dakota!*
2. Write when, where and to whom the outbreak occurred:
   Last night, in Bismark, North Dakota, two children were playing in the mud. Suddenly, they had purple spots all over their arms and legs.
3. Write the first attempt to help them: *Their mom sprayed them with the hose. Nothing happened.*
4. Write the second attempt to help them: *Paramedics rubbed chocolate all over the spots. That didn't work.*
5. Write the third attempt to help them: *Two friends gave them a spoonful of lemon juice. That worked and the spots went away!*
6. Write the conclusion that includes a prevention or warning: *No one knows what caused the outbreak. Be careful around mud until scientists can figure it out!*
7. Add an easy art accent: Students can color the border brown, then glue tiny googly eyes to represent the mud mites.

32. FAIRY TALE CHARACTER SITING—FICTIONAL NEWS ARTICLE

A fairy tale character is spotted at a famous landmark. Students write a news article about it. NOTE: This lesson can address the following Common Core State Standards: CCSS.ELA-LITERACY.W.K.3, W.1.3, W.2.3, W.3.3, W.3.3.B, W.3.3.C, W.3.3.D, W.4.3, W4.3.A, W.4.3.B, W.4.3.C, W.4.3.D, W.4.3.E, W.5.3, W.5.3.A, W.5.3.B, W.5.3.C, W.5.3.D and W.5.3.E.

This lesson is a big hit if you show the students the Fairy Tale Siting Art Accent. The art accent is an easy TWO steps:

1. Choose a <u>calendar picture</u> of a famous landmark or park.
2. Choose a fairy tale character. Print, cut and paste an image of it to the calendar picture.

Now for the lesson!

1. Tell the story line: *"You're going to write a news article about a fairy tale character that shows up at a famous landmark or park. You will write about what the fairy tale character does and how other people react."*

2. Brainstorm fairy tale characters:

The Three Little Pigs	Goldilocks	Snow White	Little Red Riding Hood
The Three Little Bears	The Gingerbread Man	The Seven Dwarfs	The Little Red Hen

Review landmarks and famous parks:

The Statue of Liberty	Taj Mahal	The Colosseum
Mt. Rushmore	The Great Wall of China	The Leaning Tower of Pisa
The White House	The Eiffel Tower	Big Ben

3. Show the 5 sections:

Time/People/Place
Normal Activity
The Siting
Reactions/Actions
Solution/Conclusion

4. Show the expectations:
K–1st Graders are encouraged to write 1 sentence for each section, 2nd Graders-2 sentences, 3rd Graders-3 sentences, 4th Graders-4 sentences, 5th Graders-5 sentences

Now to write: Guide the students through the following steps. They are free to use their own words. Remind them that ANYTHING can happen in their story as long as they follow the steps to keep their story organized. There's a 2nd Grade sample in italics for your own guidance.

1. Write a title using an eye catching exclamation: *Breaking News in Washington D.C.!*
2. Write when and where people were visiting: *This morning, a group of students were in Washington D.C. They were walking past the monuments.*
3. Write what people were doing before the character was sited: *They stopped in front of the White House. Everyone was taking pictures.*
4. Write about the moment the character was sited: *All of a sudden, something in the grass started to move. A child shouted, "Mom, look! It's Sleepy!"*
5. Write about the reactions and actions of the people and the character: *Sleepy slowly started to wake up. People crowded around him.*
6. Write what happened next: *Sleepy cleared his eyes and said, "Where am I?" Security guards came and helped Sleepy find his way home.*
7. Add an easy art accent: Students can cut and paste their fairy tale character to their calendar picture.

33. GOT HURT—PERSONAL NARRATIVE

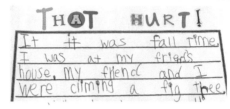

This guided writing lesson gives students an opportunity to write about a time they got hurt. I personally haven't come across a student yet that doesn't have a story about a time he or she got hurt. Kids get hurt and they like retelling their stories! NOTE: This lesson can address the following Common Core State Standards: CCSS.ELA-LITERACY.W.K.3, W.1.3, W.2.3, W.3.3, W.3.3.B, W.3.3.C, W.3.3.D, W.4.3, W4.3.A, W.4.3.B, W.4.3.C, W.4.3.D, W.4.3.E, W.5.3, W.5.3.A, W.5.3.B, W.5.3.C, W.5.3.D and W.5.3.E

Now for the lesson!

1. Tell the story line: *"You're going to write a personal narrative about a time that you got hurt."*
2. Brainstorm ways that children get hurt:

   Riding a bike or scooter   Jumping on a trampoline   Walking down the stairs
   Climbing on monkey bars   Playing a sport   Jumping on their bed.

   Give the students 5–10 minutes to think about a time they got hurt.

   Encourage the students to think about actions and dialogue that occurred during or after the moment they got hurt:
   "What did you say? What did you do? How did you act? What did other people say or do?"

   Encourage them to think about sensory details by answering the following questions in their writing: *Did you see, hear, smell, feel or taste anything specific?*

3. Show the 5 sections:

   Time/People/Place
   Normal Activity
   All of a sudden,
   Reactions/Actions
   Solution/Conclusion

4. Show the expectations:
   K–1st Graders are encouraged to write 1 sentence for each section, 2nd Graders-2 sentences, 3rd Graders-3 sentences, 4th Graders-4 sentences, 5th Graders-5 sentences

Now to write: Guide the students through the following steps so their story is organized and complete. They are free to write these ideas in their own words. There's a 2nd Grade example in italics for your own guidance.

1. Begin by introducing the time, people and place: *It was fall time. I was at my friend's house.*
2. Describe what you were doing before you got hurt. *My friend and I were climbing a tree. I went up to the next branch.*
3. Write about the moment you got hurt. *All of a sudden, the branch broke! I fell to the ground.*
4. Write each person's reactions and actions: *My mom came running. There was blood everywhere, so my mom took me to the hospital.*
5. Write the ending to the story and any thoughts for the future. *I had to get stiches in my back. Even though I have a scar, I still like to climb trees.*
6. Add an easy art accent: Have students write their title with ABC stickers or markers. They can place a Band-Aid to the border of their writing.

34. A LIVING CREATURE—NON-FICTON

For this lesson, a child can choose to write about ANY animal. It's especially fun if you have a <u>calendar picture</u> or printed image of the animal that the child wants to write about.

NOTE: This lesson can address the following Common Core State Standards: CCSS.ELA.LITERACY.W.K.2, W.1.2, W.2.2, W.3.2, W.3.2.A, W.3.2.B, W.3.2.C, W.3.2.D, W.4.2, W.4.2.A, W.4.2.B, W.4.2.C, W.4.2.D, W.4.2.E, W.5.2, W.5.2.A, W.5.2.B, W.5.2.C, W.5.2.D and W.5.2.E.

Now for the lesson!

1. Tell the story line: *"You're going to write facts about an animal. This is non-fiction, so you won't write your opinion. You won't use the words I or my."*

2. Brainstorm facts about the animal. Write the students' responses on the board. Encourage them to think about the following information:

   Where the animal lives and what it eats   What the animal looks like and how it moves   Dangers to the animal and its form of protection

3. Show the 5 sections:

   Introduction: Engage the reader
   Lives/Eats
   Looks/Moves
   Dangers/Protection
   Conclusion: Encourage the reader

4. Show the expectations:
   K—1st Graders are encouraged to write 1 sentence for each section, 2nd Graders-2 sentences, 3rd Graders-3 sentences, 4th Graders-4 sentences, 5th Graders-5 sentences

Now to write: Guide the students through the following steps so their writing is organized and complete. They are free to write these ideas in their own words. Remind the students not to use I or MY so that they just write facts and not opinions. There is a 2nd Grade example in italics for your own guidance.

1. Engage the reader by writing questions or exclamations about the animal. *Have you ever heard of an axolotl? By the way, it's pronounced, "AX-O-LOT-LE!"*
2. Write about where the animal lives and what it eats. *Axolotls live in the lakes of Mexico. They eat worms, insects and small fish.*
3. Write about how the animal looks and moves. *It is an amphibian. It can grow back its tail, legs, eyes, brain, spine and organs.*
4. Write about the dangers the animal experiences and how it protects itself. *They are endangered because of big cities and pollution. People are building shelters to help them.*
5. Write a conclusion. Add fun facts and/or encourage the reader to learn more about the animal. *You can help too! How about you start your own axolotl shelter?!*
6. Add an easy art accent: Students can hang their writing next to the calendar picture or printed image of their animal.

35. POPCORN—NON-FICTION

This lesson is a lot of fun if you're able to provide popcorn for the kids. If you provide popcorn, I strongly suggest bringing different flavors for the kids to sprinkle onto the popcorn that they get to eat. It will go well with the lesson. NOTE: This lesson can address the following Common Core State Standards: CCSS.ELA.LITERACY.W.K.2, W.1.2, W.2.2, W.3.2, W.3.2.A, W.3.2.B, W.3.2.C, W.3.2.D, W.4.2, W.4.2.A, W.4.2.B, W.4.2.C, W.4.2.D, W.4.2.E, W.5.2, W.5.2.A, W.5.2.B, W.5.2.C, W.5.2.D and W.5.2.E

Now for the lesson!

1. Tell the story line: *"You're going to write facts about popcorn. This is a non-fiction piece so you will write information and not your opinion. You won't write I or my."*

2. Brainstorm facts about popcorn with the kids. Ask them what they know about popcorn. Write their responses on the board. Here are some examples:

   Popcorn can be popped in several ways (stove, microwave, popcorn machine).
   Popcorn can be flavored in many ways (butter, salt, sugar, garlic powder, cheese, caramel, chili powder, lime, etc.)
   Popcorn is sold in many places (cinema, sports events, concerts, fairs, carnivals, etc.)
   Popcorn is a healthy snack (low calorie, low fat, low sugar, fiber, some protein)
   Popcorn can be used to decorate (Christmas trees, Halloween faces, etc.)
   Popcorn is inexpensive

   Explain to the students that they are going to hook the reader with a question(s) about popcorn. The question can be almost anything as long as it's about popcorn. Ask them for their ideas. Here are some examples:

   When was the last time you ate popcorn?   *How do you like to flavor your popcorn?*
   Where were you when you ate it?   *Did you know that...(Write an interesting fact about popcorn.)*

   Brainstorm questions for the conclusion. These questions give the reader something to think about. Here are some examples:

   When will you eat popcorn next?   *What new flavors can you think of?*
   What new flavor will you try?   *Does this make you hungry for popcorn?*

3. Show the 5 sections:

   Introduction: Engage the reader
   Fact 1 explained
   Fact 2 explained
   Fact 3 explained
   Conclusion: Encourage the reader.

4. Show the expectations:

   K—1st Graders are encouraged to write 1 sentence for each section, 2nd Graders-2 sentences, 3rd Graders-3 sentences, 4th Graders-4 sentences, 5th Graders-5 sentences

   Encourage writers to use any of the following words in their writing: *First, Second, Third, Another Fact, For Example, Also, and, but, especially*

Now to write: Guide the students through the following steps so their writing is organized and complete. They are free to write these ideas in their own words. Remind the students not to use I or MY so that they just write facts and not opinions. There is a 2nd Grade example in italics for your own guidance.

1. Write a question to grab the reader's attention: *When was the last time you ate popcorn? How did you make it?*
2. Write about the 1st fact and explain it: *Popcorn is a popular snack in America. There are several ways to make it.*
3. Write about the 2nd fact and explain it: *There are many different ways to flavor popcorn. You can add butter and salt, cheese, sugar, or even chili powder!*
4. Write about the 3rd fact and explain it: *Popcorn is a snack that's sold in many places besides movie cinemas. You can get it at almost every sports event.*
5. Write final statements or questions: *Are you hungry for popcorn yet? Where will you get it? How will it taste?*
6. Add an easy art accent: Students can use a black pen to draw popcorn around their border or glue their favorite popcorn seasoning.

36. MAGICAL SEED—FAIRY TALE

This is a fun story that can be used with any fruit or vegetable that has seeds. For the sake of this lesson, I use watermelon. NOTE: This lesson can address the following Common Core State Standards: CCSS.ELA-LITERACY.RL.K.3, RL.1.3, RL.1.7, RL.2.3, RL.3.3, RL.4.3, and RL.5.3.

Now for the lesson!

1. Tell the general story line: "*Today you're going to write a fairy tale that has a legend about a magical watermelon seed. Greedy people try to get it. A poor humble family stumbles upon it and uses it for good.*"

2. Encourage your students to think about the following questions:

What does the legend say?
How do the greedy people behave?
How does the poor family get the seed?

What magical thing does the seed actually do?
How does the poor family respond?

Have the students brainstorm answers to the above questions. (If they can't think of anything on their own, you can share some of the ideas below.)

   a. The legend says that the seed will grow golden watermelons with golden seeds inside.
   b. The greedy people fight over watermelons at the market, steal watermelons, smash watermelons, look continuously for the magical watermelon, etc.
   c. A watermelon rolls into their yard, they pick up a broken watermelon, one just so happens to grow behind their hut, they get the lucky watermelon, etc.
   d. The seed produces golden stalks, golden watermelons, watermelons with seeds of gold, etc.
   e. The poor family quietly leaves town and builds an orphanage, or something charitable. They become wealthy and rule the town in a positive way, or they give golden seeds to people, etc.

3. Show the 5 sections:

   Setting and Legend
   Greedy behavior
   The Poor Family
   The Seed is Found
   The Good Fortune

4. Show the expectations:
   K—1st Graders are encouraged to write 1 sentence for each section, 2nd Graders-2 sentences, 3rd Graders-3 sentences, 4th Graders-4 sentences, 5th Graders-5 sentences

Now to write: Guide the students through the following steps. They are free to use their own words. Remind them that ANYTHING can happen in their story as long as they follow the steps to keep their story organized. There's a 2nd Grade sample in italics for your own guidance.

1. Introduce the setting. Name the town, state or region: *Long ago, in Scotland, there was a legend.*
2. Describe the legend in detail: *The legend said that one day a watermelon would hold a magical seed. The seed would grow small golden watermelons.*
3. Describe how the greedy people behaved. *Every summer the townspeople fought over watermelons at the market. They pushed to get the biggest ones.*
4. Describe the poor family's attitude: *However, the Ainsley's were different. They were quiet and poor and didn't seem to care about the legend.*
5. Write about how the seed was found: *One day, they took home a watermelon and enjoyed every bite. One month later, they saw a golden watermelon in their trash pile!*
6. Write about the good fortune: *The Ainsley's quietly moved to the other side of Scotland. They built a house where they fed and took care of orphans happily ever after.*
7. Remember, older students can elaborate and add something like: *The people in Scotland never knew about the Ainsley's fortune. They are still fighting over watermelons.*
8. Add an easy art accent: Students can draw one large watermelon slice or many small watermelon slices around the border of their writing. They can glue one sequin to represent the magical seed. (You can find an image of this art accent on page 188.)

37. FUN PARK or PLACE—SUGGESTION LETTER

This lesson is engaging because writers get to talk about a favorite fun park or place. It's also thought provoking in that it encourages students to think about their surroundings and changes that can be made. NOTE: This lesson can address the following Common Core State Standards: CCSS.ELA-LITERACY.W.K.1, W.1.1, W.2.1, W.3.1, W.4.1, W.5.1, L.1.2.A, L.1.2.C, L.2.2.A, L.2.2.B and L.3.2.B

Now for the lesson!

1. Tell the story line: *"You're going to write a letter to the staff of a fun park. You're first going to tell them all the things that you like about the park. Then, you're going to offer a suggestion that can improve the park. Your suggestion can be realistic and possible, or imaginative and unlikely."*

2. Start off by asking students to name places that they like to visit:

an amusement park	a local carnival	a stadium
a zoo	a local park	the state fair

   Give them some time to briefly share their positive experiences. Then, ask, "Have you ever noticed anything negative at the place? Have you ever needed something that you couldn't find at that place?" Give them a couple minutes to respond.

   Explain to the students that one way to make a park aware of a need or something negative is to write a polite letter. Give the students some time to think of a fun place that they like to go to and a suggestion that they can make. As a group, brainstorm possible suggestions:

Create more shade	Offer more nutritious food	Create an area for babies to crawl and play
Add more water fountains	Have more snack carts	Add a spray ground

3. Show the 5 sections:

   Date/Greeting/Introduction
   Describe 1st positive
   Describe 2nd positive
   Offer a suggestion
   Conclusion/Salutation/Name

4. Show the expectations:
   K–1st Graders are encouraged to write 1 sentence for each section, 2nd Graders-2 sentences, 3rd Graders-3 sentences, 4th Graders-4 sentences, 5th Graders-5 sentences

Now to write: Guide the students through the following steps so their letter is organized and complete. They are free to write these ideas in their own words. There's a 2nd Grade sample in italics for your own guidance.

1. Write the date on the first line, right side. Make sure the month is capitalized. Make sure there is a comma between the day and the year. Skip a line.
2. Write the greeting on the 3rd line, left side (*Dear Zoo Staff,*). Make sure the names are capitalized and there is a comma. Skip a line.
3. Write the introduction on the next line, left side. *Hi! My name is _____. Last month, I went to your zoo and had so much fun!*
4. Describe the first thing that you liked about the park: *First of all, I loved the elephants. They came so close to us!*
5. Describe the second thing that you liked about the park: *Second of all, there were so many lemurs. They were my favorite.*
6. Offer a suggestion and explain it: *One problem was that we couldn't find shade. My grandma had to go inside a lot to get out of the sun.*
7. Write a positive conclusion: *So many people like visiting your zoo. Adding more shade can help everyone.*
8. Skip a line. Write the salutation on the left side: *Kindly, Respectfully, Sincerely, etc.*
9. Write your name <u>under</u> the salutation.
10. Make a photo copy of the letter. Address an envelope, add a stamp, place the original letter in the envelope and put it in the mail!

38. DIAMOND POEM—AROUND THE WORLD

This lesson is a big hit if you have calendar pictures of different landmarks around the world. Students choose a picture and write a diamond poem about it! Most writers respond well to diamond poems because the expectations are so clear.

NOUN

ADJECTIVE, ADJECTIVE

VERB-ing, VERB-ing, VERB-ing

NOUN, NOUN, NOUN, NOUN

VERB-ing, VERB-ing, VERB-ing

ADJECTIVE, ADJECTIVE

NOUN

Diamond poems also lend the opportunity to teach or review nouns, adjectives and verbs.

Here are the steps I use to teach this lesson:

1. Explain to the students that they're going to write a diamond poem about a famous landmark in the world such as The Great Wall of China, Big Ben, The Eiffel Tower, etc. If you have calendar pictures of landmarks around the world, allow your students to choose a picture to write about.

2. Show the format of a diamond poem (shown above).

3. Take a minute to make sure your writers know that:

> A noun is a person, place or thing.
> An adjective describes a noun.
> A verb is an action word. It tells what the noun does.

Now to write!

1. On the top line, write the name of the landmark.
2. On the second line, write 2 adjectives that describe that place.
3. On the third line, write 3 —ing verbs that you can do in that place.
4. On the fourth line, write 4 nouns of things you can see, hear, taste, smell or feel in that place.
5. On the fifth line, write 3 new —ing verbs that you can do in, on or around the landmark.
6. On the sixth line, write 2 new adjectives that describe the landmark.
7. On the seventh line, write the name of the country or city where the landmark is.
8. When the child is finished writing, he or she can decorate the 4 corners of the border.

_____

_____

_____

_____

_____

_____

_____

39. THE BEACH—JOURNAL

Whether kids live in an area where there are beaches close by or not, they most likely have something to say about the beach. This lesson gives them a chance to do so!

NOTE: This lesson can address the following Common Core State Standards: CCSS.ELA-LITERACY.W.K.1, W.1.1, W.2.1, W.3.1, W.4.1, W.5.1, W.K.3, W.1.3, W.2.3, W.3.3, W.4.3, W.5.3, L.1.2.A, L.1.2.C and L.2.2.B.

Now for the Lesson:

1. First, tell the story line: *You're going to write your honest thoughts about the beach and also write a short story about a time that you were at the beach.*

2. To get the students thinking, have them reminisce and brainstorm any experiences that they've had at a beach.

   Explain to the students that they are going to write a journal entry about the beach. Explain that a journal is a great place to jot down your most honest feelings; excitement, frustration, disappointment, angst, fear, anger, humor, etc.

   Brainstorm with the students how the beach can generate so many different thoughts and feelings. List reasons why people would like or dislike the beach.

LIKES		**DISLIKES**	
Water	Flying kites	The heat	Salty or smelly water
Waves	The sound of the waves	Sunburn	Shells cutting your feet
Surfing	Looking for shells or crabs	Applying sunscreen	
Building sandcastles	Dolphins eating	Sand sticking to you	
	Sunrises/sunsets		

   Give students time to think about reasons why they like or dislike the beach.

3. Show the 5 sections:

   > Date/Greeting/Opinion
   > Reason 1
   > Reason 2
   > A Short Story
   > Conclusion/Salutation/Name

4. Show the expectations:
   K–1st Graders are encouraged to write 1 sentence for each section, 2nd Graders-2 sentences, 3rd Graders-3 sentences, 4th Graders-4 sentences, 5th Graders-5 sentences

Now to write: Guide the students through the following steps to keep their story organized. There is a 2nd Grade example in italics for your own guidance.

1. On the first line, right side, write the date. Make sure the month is capitalized and that there is a comma between the day and year. Skip a line.
2. On the 3rd line, left side, write the greeting, Make sure both words are capitalized and followed by a comma. *Dear Journal,*
3. Skip a line.
4. On the 5th line, left side, write an introduction using 1–2 sentences: *I love the beach! We're going to the beach this summer and I can't wait!*
5. Write and explain a reason why you like or dislike the beach. *My brother and I jump the waves. We also dive through them.*
6. Write a 2nd reason why you like or dislike the beach. *At night, we take a flashlight out to the beach. We watch crabs run across the sand.*
7. Finish with a fun, funny or bad memory that happened to you at the beach. *Last summer, I was diving through a wave. A jellyfish stung me. It hurt so bad!*
8. Write a conclusion using 1–2 sentences: *I still love the beach. I can't wait to go again!*
9. Under the conclusion and in the center of the paper write the salutation: (Your Friend,). Under the salutation write your name.
10. Add an easy art accent: Students can use glue dots to stick sequins and googly eyes to the border of their writing. Then, they can put white glue around the googly eyes and sequins. Lastly, they can drop sand onto the glue. Lift the paper to let the excess sand run off. (See page 192.)

40. SOLAR SEEDS—SCIENCE FICTION

This is a great lesson for practicing dialogue and writing Science Fiction. NOTE: This lesson can address the following Common Core State Standards: CCSS.ELA-Literacy.W.K.3, W.1.3, W.2.3, W.3.3, W.3.3.A, W.3.3.B, W.3.3.C, W.3.3.D, W.4.3, W.4.3.A, W.4.3.B, W.4.3.C, W.4.3.D, W.4.3.E, W.5.3, W.5.3.A, W.5.3.B, W.5.3.C, W.5.3.D, W.5.3.E, L.K.2, L.1.2, L.2.2, L.3.2, L.3.2.C, L.4.2, L.4.2.B and L.5.2.

Now for the lesson!

1. Tell the story line: *"This story is about sunflower seeds that give a character a special super power related to the sun. Anything can happen in your story!"*

2. Brainstorm sun related super powers. Examples include:

    A person gives off extreme heat.   The sunflower seeds blind people.   A person creates electricity as needed.
    A person gives off extreme brightness.   A person's mouth shoots flames.   Things around the person grow exponentially

3. Show the 5 sections on the board:

    > Dialogue
    > Characters/Seeds
    > All of a sudden,
    > Reactions/Actions
    > Solution/Conclusion

4. Show the expectations:
    K–1st Graders are encouraged to write 1 sentence for each section, 2nd Graders-2 sentences, 3rd Graders-3 sentences, 4th Graders-4 sentences, 5th Graders-5 sentences

Now to write: Guide the students through the following steps. They are free to use their own words. Remind them that ANYTHING can happen in their story as long as they follow the steps to keep their story organized. There is a 2nd Grade example in italics for your own guidance.

1. Begin the story with a conversation: *"These seeds are good," Kate said. "Can I try one" her friend said.*
    NOTE: If you want your student(s) to practice punctuating dialogue, start off slow. Verbalize the following steps for your writers:
    a.   Write the opening quotation marks.
    b.   Write what the character is saying. Begin the sentence with a capital letter.
    c.   Finish the sentences with a, ?, !, or comma.
    d.   Write the closing quotation marks.
    e.   Write who said it and end the sentence with a period.
2. Name the main characters and write about the snack. *Kate was eating sunflower seeds. She was having her snack at school.*
3. Write about what happens suddenly. *All of a sudden, her hands got really bright. There was light everywhere.*
4. Write the characters' reactions and actions. *"I can't see!" her friend shouted. "My hands!" shouted Kate.*
    NOTE: If you are working with older students, this is a good time to encourage them to SHOW the reactions and feelings by describing in detail the character's actions.
    For example, if a character is shocked, a student can write: *Kate froze. She didn't say anything. Her eyes were wide open.*
5. Write how the problem is solved and thoughts for the future. *Kate stopped eating the seeds and the light slowly went away. Her friend didn't eat any.*
6. Add an easy art accent: Students can color a sun around the border of their writing, then glue sunflower seeds to the sun. (See page 192.) Let them eat some seeds in the process!

41. STRAWBERRY SOUP—INSTRUCTIONS

Kids like this lesson because they get to make strawberry soup and then eat it! Below are the instructions to make the soup along with the guided writing lesson. NOTE: This lesson can address the following Common Core State Standards: CCSS.ELA.LITERACY.W.K.2, W.1.2, W.2.2, W.3.2, W.3.2.A, W.3.2.C, W.3.2.D, W.4.2, W.4.2.D, W.4.2.E, W.5.2, W.5.2.D and W.5.2.E.

Materials:
Strawberries, a bowl, a masher and a sweet addition (optional)

Steps:
1. Get strawberries and clean them.
2. Put them in a bowl and mash them.
3. Add a little maple syrup, honey or agave (optional)
4. Eat it plain or on your favorite foods!

Now for the writing lesson!
1. Tell the story line: "*You just finished making your own strawberry soup. Now, you're going to write out the instructions so someone else can make it.*"
2. Brainstorm. Give the students time to recall the materials they used and the steps they took. Have them speak these items out loud. Write them on the board.
3. Show the 5 sections:

> Introduction: Engage the reader.
> Materials
> Steps 1 and 2
> Steps 3 and 4
> Conclusion: Encourage the reader.

4. Show the expectations:
K–1st Graders are encouraged to write 1 sentence for each section, 2nd Graders-2 sentences, 3rd Graders-3 sentences. 4th Graders-4 sentences, 5th Graders-5 sentences

Now to Write!
Guide the students through the following steps so that their instructions are organized. There's a second grade example in italics for your own guidance.

1. Write a title on the first line in the center: *STRAWBERRY SOUP*
2. Engage the reader by asking a question about strawberries: *Do you like strawberries? Have you heard of Braddock's famous strawberry soup? It's easy to make.*
3. Write the word MATERIALS on the next line, left side.
4. Write out the materials that the reader will need: *You will need strawberries, a bowl and a masher. If you want it sweetened, you can add agave, syrup or honey.*
5. Skip a line. On the next line, left side, write INSTRUCTIONS or STEPS. Then, skip line.
6. Write steps one and two: *First, you wash the strawberries. Next, you put them in a bowl.*
7. Write steps three and four: *Then, you mash the strawberries and put agave, honey or syrup. Last, you eat it plain or you can spread it on things.*
8. Encourage older writers to elaborate their instructions with details. Here's a detailed example:
> *To start, gather as many strawberries as you can. You can either pick them from a patch or buy them in a store. Rinse them thoroughly.*
> *Next, cut off the tops of the strawberries. Place them in a bowl. Use a potato masher to squish all the strawberries. It should look soupy now.*
> *Third, add a little bit of maple syrup, honey or agave. This step is optional. The strawberries are usually sweet by themselves.*
> *Last, pour the strawberry soup into bowls and eat it plain. Or, you can pour it on pancakes, waffles or bread.*
> *Try putting it in your oatmeal or cereal. It also tastes good on yogurt and in milk!*

Write a conclusion that encourages the reader to make the strawberry soup: *The next time you have strawberries, try making strawberry soup. You'll love it!*

5. Add an easy art accent: Students can draw and color strawberries or strawberry soup dripping around the border of their writing.

42. A SLINKY ON STAIRS—DESCRIPTIVE

This is a great lesson to spur on students' imaginations. If possible, purchase a slinky for each student to motivate them to write and reward them for their work! NOTE: This writing prompt can address the following Common Core State Standards: CCSS.ELA-LITERACY.W.K.3, W.1.3, W.2.3, W.3.3., W.3.3.C, W.3.3.D, W.4.3, W.4.3.A, W.4.3.C, W.4.3.D, W.4.3.D, W.5.3, W.5.3.A, W.5.3.C, W.5.3.D and W.5.3.E.

Now for the lesson:

1. Tell the story line: *"You're playing with a slinky at the top of the stairs. The slinky hits the bottom step and falls through an imaginary hole into a new world of stairs. There are stairs everywhere! The slinky continues to travel down stairs into a 2nd and 3rd world and then finally ends up back at the top of the original stairs. You follow the slinky the entire time. You have to describe each of the 3 worlds. The worlds can be full of ANYTHING!"*

2. Brainstorm possible worlds: bubbles, candy, flying bee bots, Lego people..Write the students' responses on the board.

3. Show the 5 sections:

    Time/People/Place/Playing
    Describe world 1
    Describe world 2
    Describe world 3
    Back home-reaction

4. Show the expectations:
    K—1st Graders are encouraged to write 1 sentence for each section, 2nd Graders-2 sentences, 3rd Graders-3 sentences, 4th Graders-4 sentences, 5th Graders-5 sentences

Now to write: Guide the students through the following steps. They are free to use their own words. Remind them that ANYTHING can happen in their story as long as they follow the steps to keep their story organized. There is a 2nd Grade example in italics for your own guidance.

1. Write about the time, place and playing with the slinky: *Last night, I sent my slinky down my stairs. When the slinky hit the bottom, it spun me into another world!*
2. Describe everything that you see, hear, smell, feel or even taste in the 1st world: *There were stairs and bubbles everywhere! It smelled like soap.*
3. Tell how the slinky travels to the 2nd world. Describe the 2nd world using the 5 senses. *The slinky kept going and took me into a desert of stairs. I started to sweat.*
4. Tell how the slinky arrives to the 3rd world. Describe the 3rd world using the 5 senses. *The slinky turned a corner. There were waterfalls crashing to the ground.*
5. Tell how you and the slinky end up back in the original place. *All of a sudden, I was back on my stairs. "What just happened?!" I said to myself.*
6. Add an easy art accent: Students can write their title with ABC stickers or markers. Then, give them time to play with their Slinkys!

43. THE STATE FAIR—DESCRIPTIVE

You can use this same lesson to describe any amusement part, local carnival or even a big family reunion. This is an especially fun prompt to do around the time of the state or local fair. NOTE: This lesson can address the following Common Core State Standards: CCSS.ELA-LITERACY.W.4.3.D and W.5.3.D.

Now to for the lesson!

1. Tell the story line: *"You are going to describe the state fair by writing about the things that you see, hear, smell, taste and feel there."*

Younger or Struggling Writers: Explain that they are going to describe the fair by writing simple sentences such as:
I see _____. I hear _____. I smell _____. I taste ≈. I feel _____.

Write these starter sentences on the board for them. When it's time to write, they write the sample sentence and then fill in the blanks with phonetic spelling. Phonetic spelling is writing the *sounds* that they hear in the word. Correct spelling is NOT important in phonetic spelling. What's important is that they are writing letters that represent the sounds that they hear. For example, a child might write, *I smell kotin cande* for "I smell cotton candy."

Older or Advanced Writers:

2. Explain to the older students that they are going to describe the fair by writing what they see, hear, smell, taste and feel but are going to try not to use those words.
Write the five senses on the board and brainstorm ideas for each sense:

See	Hear	Smell	Taste	Feel
Crowds of people	Music	Fried Food	Cotton Candy	People pushing
Rides	Screams	Barn Animals	Ice Cream	Hot weather

Give a sample sentence for each sense.

Crowds of people move through the pathways.	Music plays loudly from each ride.	The aroma of fried food fills the air.	Cotton candy is sweet on my tongue.	People push to be first in line.

3. Show the 5 sections:
Introduction/See
Hear
Smell
Taste
Feel/Conclusion

4. Show the expectations:
K–1st Graders are encouraged to write 1 sentence for each section, 2nd Graders-2 sentences, 3rd Graders-3 sentences, 4th Graders-4 sentences, 5th Graders-5 sentences

Now to write: Guide the students through the following steps. They are free to use their own words as long as they follow the steps to keep their description organized. There is a 2nd Grade example in italics for your own guidance.

1. Start off with an introductory statement that describes the fair in one word: *The fair is such a blast!*
2. Write about things that people see. *The Ferris wheel moves around and around*
3. Write about things that people hear. *Bumper cars crash into each other. People scream and laugh.*
4. Write about things that people smell. *The stench of barnyard animals fill the air. The smell of grease and fried foods makes me hungry.*
5. Write about things that people taste. *Sweet cotton candy melts on my tongue. Crispy elephant ears crunch between my teeth.*
6. Write about things that people feel. *My stomach jumps to my throat going down the roller coaster.*
7. Write a concluding sentence about the fair. Include thoughts for the future. *I love the fair and can't wait to go again!*
8. Add an easy art accent: Students can use markers to draw a tent, popcorn, ice cream, rollercoaster, or anything else that represents the fair. (See page 185.).

44. THE NEVER-ENDING SYRUP SUNDAE—INSTRUCTIONAL MANUAL

The "Never-ending Syrup Sundae" is a bowl with compartments at the bottom that hold different syrups for ice cream. Each compartment has a button. The left and right sides of the bowl have straw-like tubes that shoot the syrup up and down onto the bowl of ice cream. That way, you can eat a layer of ice cream with syrup, then push a button to add more syrup! For children who are lactose intolerant or simply don't want to write about ice cream, remind them that they can create the machine using any food/sauce combination, such as gravy and mashed potatoes, ketchup and fries, what have you! Remind your kids that the ideas are endless!

NOTE: This lesson can address the following Common Core State Standards: CCSS.ELA.LITERACY.W.K.2, W.1.2, W.2.2, W.3.2, W.3.2.A, W.3.2.C, W.3.2.D, W.4.2, W.4.2.D, W.4.2.E, W.5.2, W.5.2.D and W.5.2.E.

Now the Lesson!

1. Tell the story line: *"You're going to write an instructions manual for a food machine that squirts syrup, gravy, ketchup or some kind of sauce."*

2. Brainstorm food/sauce ideas. Chocolate syrup on a sundae, gravy on mashed potatoes, ketchup on fries or syrup on a pile of pancakes...what have you!

3. Show the 5 sections:

   Introduction/Parts
   Set Up
   Operation
   Care
   Warnings

4. Show the expectations:
   K—1st Graders are encouraged to write 1 sentence for each section, 2nd Graders-2 sentences, 3rd Graders-3 sentences, 4th Graders-4 sentences, 5th Graders-5 sentences

Now to write: Guide the students through the following steps so that their instructions are organized. There is a 2nd Grade example in italics for your own guidance.

1. Write the title on the first line (not in the border): ***THE NEVER ENDING...***
2. On the 2nd line, write questions or exclamations to engage the reader: *Do you like sundaes? Do you run out of chocolate syrup and still have ice cream left in your bowl?*
3. On the next line, left side, write the word PARTS.
4. Under the word PARTS, list the parts that you will need to put the machine together: *one base, one bowl, two tubes and batteries*
5. On the next line, left side, write the words SET UP.
6. Under the words SET UP, write sentences that tell how to put the machine together: *Snap the tubes and bowl to the bottom of the base. Put two batteries in the base.*
7. On the next line, left side, write the word OPERATION.
8. Under the word OPERATION, write sentences that tell how to use the machine: *Fill the bowl with ice cream. Press a button to squirt syrup.*
9. On the next line, left side, write the word CARE.
10. Under the word CARE, write sentences that tell how to take care of the machine: *After you eat your ice cream, wash the bowl. Fold the tubes down so they don't break.*
11. On the next line, left side, write the word WARNINGS.
12. Under the word WARNINGS, write sentences listing any dangers that the machine could cause: *Do not put the base in water. It will ruin the base and could shock you.*
13. Add an easy art accent: Students color the bowl and food around the border of their writing. Then, they use glue dots or staples to add pipe cleaners from the base to the top of the food. These are the pipes that squirt the sauce.

45. CAMPING—OPINION

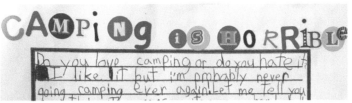

Students usually have something to say about camping. They either love it, hate it, like parts of it, but not all, or have never gone and want to. This guided writing lesson gives students an opportunity to write their honest opinion about camping. NOTE: This lesson can address the following Common Core State Standards: CCSS.ELA.LITERACY.W.K.1, W.1.1, W.2.1, W.3.1, W.3.1.A, W.3.1.B, W.3.1.C, W.3.1.D, W.4.1, W.4.1.A, W.4.1.B, W.4.1.C, W.4.1.D, W.5.1, W.5.1.A, W.5.1.B, W.5.1.C and W.5.1.D.

Now for the lesson!

1. Tell the story line: *"You're going to write your opinion about camping."*

2. Discuss the different aspects of camping that children may like or dislike:

LIKES:		**DISLIKES:**	
Bonfires	Listening to the insects	Building a fire is hard work	Poison ivy
Roasting hotdogs	Hiking	Plain food	No electricity
Roasting marshmallows	Nature	Sticky marshmallows	Too quiet
Sleeping in a tent	Waterfalls	Hard rocky floor to sleep on	Lonely
Looking at the stars	Fishing	Mosquitos	
Looking for animal tracks	Few people	Bee stings	
	Peace and quiet		

3. Show the 5 sections:

> Introduction: Engage the reader and state your opinion.
> Reason 1
> Reason 2
> Reason 3
> Conclusion: Restate your opinion

4. Show the expectations:
   K–1st Graders are encouraged to write 1 sentence for each section, 2nd Graders-2 sentences, 3rd Graders-3 sentences, 4th Graders-4 sentences, 5th Graders-5 sentences

Now to write: Guide the students through the following steps so their writing is organized and complete. They are free to write these ideas in their own words. There is a 2nd Grade example in italics for your own guidance.

1. Engage the reader by writing questions or exclamations. Then, state your opinion about camping: *Do you like camping? I love camping!*
2. Write and explain the first reason. *First of all, I love building a bonfire. Cooking marshmallows and making sticky s'mores is the best!*
3. Write and explain the second reason: *Second of all, sleeping in a tent is so quiet. I like to watch the stars and listen to the crickets.*
4. Write and explain the third reason: *Third of all, I really like hiking. My family and I find trails that take us to big waterfalls.*
5. Write a conclusion that restates your opinion using different words. *Lastly, I like not having electricity. Camping is always an adventure and I love it!*
6. Add an easy art accent: Students can use ABC stickers or markers to write a title. Then, they can draw and color a bonfire, marshmallows, s'mores, a tent, or anything else that represents camping around the border of their writing.

46. END OF SUMMER—LETTER WRITING

At the end of summer students have a lot to say about their summer and perhaps excitement or angst about a new grade, class or teacher. It's a great time to write a letter to a faraway friend or cousin that may be experiencing the same thing. NOTE: This lesson can address the following Common Core State Standards: CCSS.ELA-LITERACY.L.1.2.A, L.1.2.C, L.2.2.A, L.2.2.B, L.3.2.B

Now for the lesson!

1. Tell the students the story line: *"You're going to write a letter to someone telling them about your summer and the start of a new school year."*

2. Explain to them that asking questions is an integral part of letter writing. It expresses interest in the other person and also elicits a response letter for continued dialogue. Have the students think of questions they can ask the person in their letter.

3. Show the 5 sections:

   > Date/Greeting/Questions
   > Describe the summer.
   > Positives about School
   > Concerns or Worries
   > Conclusion/Salutation/Name

4. Show the expectations:
   K—1st Graders are encouraged to write 1 sentence for each section, 2nd Graders-2 sentences, 3rd Graders-3 sentences, 4th Graders-4 sentences, 5th Graders-5 sentences

Now to write: Guide the students through the following steps so their letter is organized and complete. They are free to write these ideas in their own words. There's a 2nd Grade sample in italics for your own guidance.

1. Write the date on the first line and right side of the page. Make sure the month is capitalized and that there is a comma between the day and year.
2. Skip a line. Write the greeting on the 3rd line, left side. Make sure each word is capitalized and the greeting ends with a comma: *Dear Friend,*
3. Skip a line. Write a greeting and questions on the next line, left side: *"Hello! How has your summer been? What have you done?"*
4. Write about your summer, what you've done, where you've gone, people you've seen. *We went to Illinois to visit my grandparents. They took us to Chicago.*
5. Write two positive things that you know about the new school year. *This year I get to study coding. I'm also in the same class as my neighbor.*
6. Write any fears or things that you're nervous about. *I don't know who my teacher is yet. They changed the classrooms, so the school will look different.*
7. Write the conclusion that wishes the friend well, *"I hope you're doing well. I can't wait to see you again!"*
8. Write the salutation centered under the body of the letter. *Your friend, Your cousin, etc.*
9. Write your name UNDER the salutation.
10. Complete an envelope. Stick a stamp and send it away!

SECTION 6

Easy Art Accents That Motivate and Reward Young Writers

I have found in my year round writing classes and camps that even my most timid writers quickly find a reason to write if they know they can add a sticker, paste googly eyes, or paint something small to create a fun border design.

In short, these easy art accents motivate kids to write and reward them for their work! Moreover, they add color and charm to each child's writing. Here's how they work!

Bordered Paper

As mentioned in Section 5, students write on bordered paper. You can find this paper on pages 125–127. The wide border gives students space to decorate their story.

Materials to Have on Hand

Below is a list of materials that my students at camp, or my children at home, always have on hand. We have used each of these materials at least once to complete various art accents.

1. Manila folders to protect a child's work space
2. Glue sticks, Elmer's glue and glue dots.
3. Calendar pictures
4. Stickers
5. Markers
6. Googly Eyes
7. White crayon and watercolor paint
8. Acrylic Paint and paint brushes
9. Pom-Poms (small puff balls from craft stores)
10. Sequins
11. Glitter glue
12. Glitter
13. Sand
14. Salt
15. A flat, rectangular plastic container for catching glitter, sand and salt.
16. Plastic page protectors

An Art Accent Table

If you are a classroom teacher working with a large group of students, I suggest setting up an art accent table in your classroom. This is what I do for my summer camps when I have 12-24 students. My campers write their stories and essays at tables in the front of the room.

Then, if the art accent involves glue, googly eyes, paint, watercolor, sand, glitter or salt, they will go to the art accent table that is set up at the back of the room to complete it. If, however, an art accent only requires markers, a calendar picture or specific stickers, they will complete that art accent at their seat.

Colorful Writing Portfolios

Typically, each art accent only takes no more than 5 minutes to complete. However, the glue, especially the glitter glue, can take time to dry. It's important to have a place in the classroom or at home where the students can put their writing to dry. Then, as soon as the art accent is dry, students place their story in a plastic page protector. Lastly, they put their writing in a 3-prong folder or binder to build a colorful writing portfolio.

Art Accent Ideas to Get You Started

On the following pages, I will share the most popular art accents that my students and children have done. Surely, this list will spur on ideas of your own!

CALENDAR PICTURES

Calendar pictures are by far the most popular art accent that my students use. Kids LOVE to choose a picture! I've had GREAT success motivating children to write using calendar pictures in my year round camps and classes. If you have a large group of students, make sure you have more pictures than students so each child can truly choose.

Calendars, in general, are easy to find and don't have to cost very much. Dollar stores have them and craft stores sell them for a low price also. Most recently, Calendars.com generously donated a box full of outdated calendars to Fun Writing Ideas. I use them in my own lessons and also give them away to teachers and homeschool parents who will use them in their writing lessons. If your students have a specific topic that they would like to write about, definitely check out Calendars.com. They cover any and every theme!

Below are 15 ways that you can use calendar pictures with your writers. The first five ideas are for beginner writers. The last ten ideas are guided writing lessons for students in Grades K–5 that go great with these pictures.

Using Calendar Pictures with Beginner Writers

Here are 5 ways to use calendar pictures with young children. Note, these same 5 activities can be used with single **stickers** just as well. Finally, the Common Core State Standards that can be addressed in each exercise are listed below in parentheses.

1. Beginning Sounds

First, have the child label objects in the picture by writing the beginning sound. (CCSS.ELA-LITERACY.L.K.1.A and RF.K.1.B)

E=Ears, F=Fence, N=Nose, M=Mouth

This is great for beginner writers who are learning their letter strokes and the beginning sounds of words. Students can label the objects that they see several ways: Using ABC stickers, writing the letter on a piece of paper and pasting it like the example above, or writing the letters on white sticky labels and placing them onto the picture.

2. One Word

Second, students can label the objects in the picture with one word. (CCSS.ELA-LITERACY.L.K.2.D)

leaf, red

Here, the children phonetically spell the words that they see. That means that they say the word slowly and write the sounds that they hear. The words most likely will not be spelled correctly. Phonetic spelling is addressed on pages 34–35.

Students can write these words the same 3 ways as idea #1, using ABC stickers, pasting white paper or sticking white labels. Place the calendar picture and writing in the child's binder for reading and review.

3. Sight Word Sentences

Third, students can write sight word sentences to describe the picture. Sight word sentences are discussed in detail in Section 3 of this book. (CCSS.ELA-LITERACY.L.K.2, L.K.2.A, L.K.2.C, L.K.2.D, L.1.2, L.1.2.B, L.1.2.D and L.1.2.E).

Here the child can write 1–3 sight words sentences, depending on age and ability. The sight word sentence above is:

$$I\ AM\ \underline{\hspace{2cm}}.$$

Writers should spell the sight words (in this case, *I AM* _____) correctly because those are the words that they are learning. Next, students choose the word that they want to write in the blank. The blank words are spelled phonetically. That means that the children are writing the letters that they **hear**. The word that they write in the blank may or may not be spelled correctly.

Have the child write one sentence, cut it and paste it to the picture. Or, have the child write 2–3 sentences. Slide the sentences and calendar picture back to back into a plastic page protector. Finally, place each child's writing in a binder for reading and review.

4. A Story or Information

Fourth, students can write a story or information about their calendar picture. (CCSS.ELA-LITERACY.L.K.1, L.K.2, L.K.2.A, L.K.2.C, L.K.2.D, L.1.2, L.1.2.B, L.1.2.D and L.1.2.E)

5 ½ years old: Bears eat salmon. Bears like water. Bears have fur.

When the child is done writing, slide the story and picture back to back into a plastic page protector. Then, place the story in the child's binder. Students LOVE to go back and read what they have written!

5. Questions

Fifth, students can use the words **who**, **what**, **when**, **where**, **why** and **which** to write 6 questions about the picture.

Depending on ability, the child can write all 6 questions in one sitting, or the child can write one question per day or even one question per week. (CCSS. ELA-LITERACY.RF.K.1.C, L.K.1.D, L.K.2, L.K.2.A, L.1.2 and L.1.2.B)

A picture of the Mars rover   6 years old

Using Calendar Pictures with Guided Writing Lessons

Now let's look at 10 guided writing lessons that go well with calendar pictures. Again, I can't state enough that calendar pictures are a winner at my writing camps EVERY TIME! They serve as a most simple art accent and definitely motivate children to write. Make sure you have more pictures than students so each child can truly choose.

SCENIC PICTURES

1. Fairy Tale Character Siting: Use a picture of a famous landmark or park to write a news article about the siting of a fairy tale character. See page 163 for the full lesson. Pasting the fairy tale character onto the picture is half the fun!

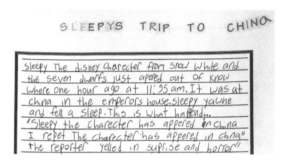

SLEEPYS TRIP TO CHINA

Sleepy The disney charecter from Snow White and the seven dwarfs just apered out of know where one hour ago at 11:35 am. It was at China in the emperors house. Sleepy yawne and fell a sleep. This is what happend...
"Sleepy the Charecter has appered in China I repet The charecter has appered in china" the reporter yelled in suprise and horror"

2. Science Fiction: Use a scenic picture to go along with the writing prompt titled "Exhausted Electronics" on page 139.

Hawaii. There were maps, journals and magazines. How come Serena never noticed this!? "These are my mom's books!" The toaster chuckled. "Well, what do you think I do at night? Sleep? Ha! No, I read. I've been planning this trip for months! I'll pack my bags, take a plane to Paris, France. The

3. Descriptive Introduction: Use a scenic picture to write a descriptive introduction to a fictional story.

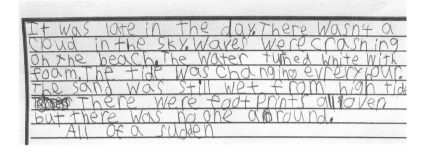

It was late in the day. There wasn't a cloud in the sky. Waves were crashing on the beach. The water turned white with foam. The tide was changing every four. The sand was still wet from high tide. There were footprints all over but there was no one around. All of a sudden

4. Diamond Poem: Use a picture of a landmark from around the world to write a diamond poem. (See page 169.)

Wall
great, big
standing, breaking, blocking
mountains, rocks, Show, bricks
Stretching, splitting, staying
Old, long
China

5. Haiku: Use a picture of scenery to write a Haiku poem. (Find the guided writing lesson on page 151.)

big rocks sitting still
see through water nice and cool
lots of big green trees

185

6. Personification: Use a picture of scenery to write personification around it.

ANIMAL PICTURES

7. Non-fiction: Use any animal picture to write non-fiction.
You can find the full guided writing lesson on page 165.

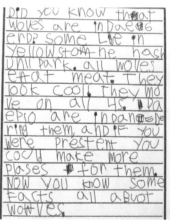

8. Comics: Use an animal picture to write a comical monologue, dialogue or conversation involving 3+ characters.

ANY PICTURE

9. Descriptive Words: Use any picture to write a 5 Minute Descriptive List. Students have 5 minutes to write whatever comes to mind when they look at the picture. They love this exercise and often ask to do the exercise more than once!

10. Rhyme: Use any picture to write rhyme. I've been teaching summer camps for 8 years now. Every year there's a poetry camp and every poetry camp entails a calendar picture lesson. Returning campers love it, remember it and look forward to it! Students can write rhyming couplets (two lines) or quatrains (4 lines).

Two big elephants
behind four boulders
Are they hot today
or are they colder?

Additional Art Accent Ideas to Get You Started

MARKERS ONLY

When using markers, students simply draw a design that goes with their story. Here are some ideas to get you started:

Red: Dripping catsup or spaghetti sauce, candy canes, hearts, cherries, etc.
Orange: oranges, sun's rays, pumpkins, etc.
Yellow: sun's rays, lemons, bananas, stars, etc.
Green: grass, limes, frogs, etc.
Light Green: dripping slime, grass, leaves, etc.
Blue: rain, blueberries,
Purple: grapes, grape jam, berries, plums, etc.

Black: Zebra stripes, cow spots, a soccer ball, etc.
Gray: clouds, rocks, robots, etc.
Pink: hearts, berries, jelly fish, bubble gum, etc.
Brown: mud, dirt, footballs, etc.
Combination of colors: Tiger stripes, giraffe spots, watermelon, a panda's face, a burger, ice cream, popcorn, a tent, etc.

GLITTER

To use glitter, first place the story in a flat, rectangular container or box. Then, use white or Elmer's glue to draw the design around the border. Shake the glitter over all of the glue. Lift the paper and let the loose glitter slide off. Set the story aside to dry completely. Students can even write a title with the glue and glitter! Here are some glitter ideas to get you started:

Silver: snowflakes, silver hearts on red marker, coins, etc.
Gold: golden egg, drops of gold, gold coins, etc.
Red: Christmas ornaments, hearts, candy canes, etc.

Green: Christmas ornaments, leprechaun tracks, etc.
Blue: fairy dust, magical waters, rain drops, etc.

  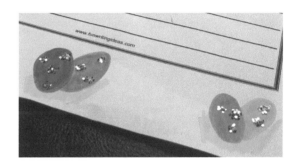

GLITTER GLUE

Glitter glue is easy to use and has a charming outcome. It takes the longest to dry, so it's important to allow 24 hours for this easy art accent to be complete. The glue is very thick and goopy when you apply it. Then, as it dries, it flattens out and leaves a sparkling finish.

Some ideas for glitter glue include: silver on blue for snowflakes, gold on green for Jack and the Beanstalk, pink on light colored marker to represent anything magical. One lesson that my students completed was a myth about a "god of laughter". They used glitter glue to spell, "Ha! Ho! Hee! Hum!" all around the border of their writing. For an Easter egg prompt, they formed pink glitter glue on a purple border. You can also write a title using glitter glue.

  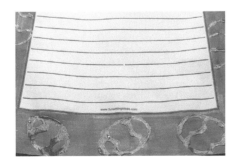 

GOOGLY EYES

Googly eyes are another big hit. If you're working with a large group of students, you will need to ration them out. Inform the students how many googly eyes they are allowed to use. Otherwise, they will go hog wild and use them all, leaving none for the last few students. ☺ Googly eyes stick best if you use a glue stick or put white glue on the paper first. Then, place the googly eyes onto the glue. Allow time for the eyes to dry, otherwise they will slide around and smear marker that the students have colored. Here are a few ideas to get you started:

Tiny eyes for:	Medium eyes for:	Large or Gigantic eyes for
Mud mites	Aliens	A human or large animal
Snow mites	Jelly fish	A giant or monster

PIPE CLEANERS

You can do a lot with pipe cleaners! Students can really twist them into almost any shape. In the images below the students shaped the pipe cleaner into a magical bubble wand and a magical bracelet. They added beads, then wrote a story about the magical item.

 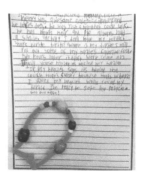 

One time, however, we wrote about the Never-Ending-Syrup-Sundae. Students used the pipe cleaners to form tubes that squirted syrup onto their ice cream. In this case, they used glue dots to stick the pipe cleaners onto their border. You can find the Never-Ending Syrup Sundae guided writing lesson on page 176.

PUFF BALLS and COTTON BALLS

Fuzzy puff balls will only stick if you use a glue dot. Students can place a glue dot on the border of their writing, then place the puff ball on top of that. Because the puff balls are thick, I usually create guided writing lessons that only require 1–3 of them. One example includes the gumball machine lesson found on my website www.funwritingideas.com. In another lesson, students wrote a spinoff story involving the mythical Phoenix's egg. So, puff balls can represent magical gumballs, eggs, rocks, etc.

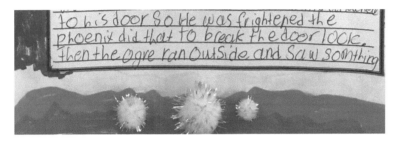

A Phoenix's egg between two other eggs

SEQUINS

Sequins can represent beach shells, gems in a tiara, a magical seed in a watermelon, gold in a pot, etc. Like puff balls, sequins will only stay on the paper if you use glue dots. Students place the glue dot on the border of their writing, then press the sequin onto the glue dot.

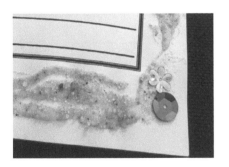   

STICKERS

First, students can use ABC stickers to write titles. Second, you can create guided writing lessons based on the themed stickers that you have. Students love stickers! If you have a limited supply, you will definitely need to ration them out, otherwise the students will use them all! Try collecting stickers from any one and everywhere. They serve as a very popular art accent that motivates students to write and rewards them for their work!

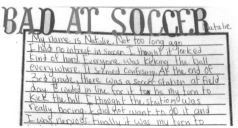

TEMPERA PAINT, PLASTIC PAGE PROTECTORS and MOD PODGE

This art accent is a bit strange, but so easy and creates a neat result! It can be completed in 2 easy steps!

1. Lay a plastic page protector out on a mat. Brush tempera paint vertically or horizontally on one side of it.
2. Spray Mod Podge over the paint and let it dry.

When, you place the child's story or picture in the plastic page protector, it will shine through the paint. The picture below is of a serval behind "grass." You can find the Serval's Personal Narrative guided writing lesson on page 133.

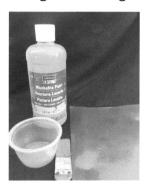

<u>Ideas for various colors of tempera paint:</u>

Red: catsup, tomato sauce, blood, lava, etc.
Orange: orange juice spill, lava, Gatorade, etc.
Yellow: sunlight, lemonade, etc.
Green: grass, slime, poison, etc.
Blue: rain, water, the sea, toothpaste, etc.

Purple: grape juice, a melted popsicle, Kool Aid, etc.
Black: ink, oil, soda, etc.
Gray: stormy weather, cement, etc.
Pink: bubble gum, medicine, etc.
Brown: mud, chocolate sauce, syrup, gasoline, etc.

WHITE CRAYON and WATER COLOR PAINT

I first learned of this art accent on http://www.blackfootartcenter.blogspot.com (Weston, H. 2–15). It's another super easy art accent that yields intriguing results. My students used this for the Puddle Jumping lesson found on page 161. It can be completed in 2 easy steps.

1. Use white crayon to draw a design around the border.
2. Brush watercolor paint over the border. The white crayon will show through!

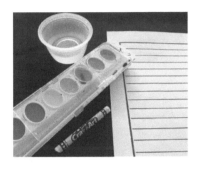  

Ideas for various colors of watercolor paint:
Red: apples, cherries, etc.
Orange: pumpkins, orange slices, etc.
Yellow: sun rays, lemons, etc.
Green: grass, limes, etc.

Blue: rain, puddles, waves, etc.
Purple: snowflakes, berries, grapes, etc.
Black: spiders, insects, etc.
Gray: stormy weather, rocks, etc.
Brown: chocolate chips, mud puddles, bricks, etc

WATERCOLOR PAINT and SALT

Here is a third easy art accent that surprises students. Simply brush watercolor paint around the border. Then, immediately sprinkle salt over the wet watercolor paint. The salt crystalizes and dries into a sparkling, snowy, icy like pattern.

TINY AMOUNTS OF ACRYLIC PAINT

Next, we use small 50 cent bottles of acrylic paint from Walmart. I suggest having one of each color that your students might use. Have students use Q-tips or small brushes to paint simple designs around the border of their writing. Students can even write the title of their story using the acrylic paint.\

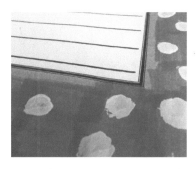 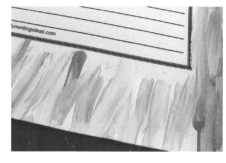 

Ideas for various colors of acrylic paint:
Red: candy cane stripes, hearts, etc.
Orange: fire
Yellow: the sun's rays
Green: grass
Blue: rain

Purple: purple polka dots
Black: zebra stripes
White: snow spots on blue marker
Pink: stripes or streamers
Brown: a lion's mane on yellow marker

BUBBLE WRAP

Bubble wrap serves as an excellent art accent for stories involving scales. The image below was from a fictional story about an alligator. To complete the art accent, simply glue bubble wrap to the border. Then, use a small amount of acrylic paint to brush over it. This forms a scaly like skin.

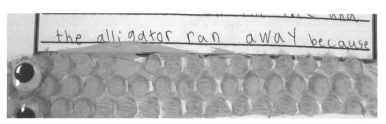

CLOTHES PINS

Tiny clothes pins are crafty and cute! Students can use them to hang a sign at the top of their writing. First, use cardstock when printing the lined paper. Second, students punch holes in the top two corners. Third, they tie yarn through each hole. Fourth, they cut small pieces of paper to form the sign. Last, they use tiny clothes pins to clip the letters to the yarn. We added this art accent to a persuasive ad for our camp bake sale.

SAND

Students can glue sand around their border. When using sand, it must go on last. First color the border or paste googly eyes and sequins. Then, place the story or essay in a flat plastic container. Use white glue to mark where the sand should go. Next, sprinkle sand on the white glue. Last, lift and tilt the paper to let the loose sand slide off. Students can use this easy art accent with any prompt about the beach, desert or sandbox!

 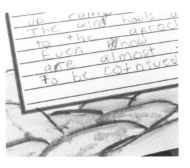

SEEDS

The last material that I'm presenting in this book are seeds. They are heavy, so for this art accent you'll want the students to write on cardstock. After completing their writing, students add seeds to their border. To add seeds, they first place their writing in a flat plastic container. Then, they apply white glue around the border to mark where the seeds will go. Next, they sprinkle seeds on the white glue. Lastly, they lift and tilt the paper to let the loose seeds slide off. You can use this easy art accent with a non-fiction prompt about seed dispersers or any other prompt about seeds.

My students wrote a science fiction story titled, Solar Seeds. They were eating sunflower seeds and then suddenly gained a super power related to the sun. You can find this guided writing lesson on page172.

Does this list cause you to generate ideas of your own?
If so, write your ideas here:

_____

_____

_____

_____

_____

_____

_____

_____

_____

_____

SECTION 7

PARENT REVIEWS

(Actual names have been changed.)

The primary purpose for writing this book is to equip parents, teachers and tutors to build confidence in young writers. I hope so much that after implementing these strategies, you, the parent, or the parents of your students, will begin to say the same as the parents below.

Jake was so proud of what he'd written and couldn't wait for me to read it! What a joy to see both of my boys so thrilled with writing. Somehow you've made what was a dreaded thing fun!
—Mother of a 1st and 4th Grade boy

Thank you SO much for sending the word lists. I used them today to start figuring out where Josh needs some work. It's super helpful to have a concrete plan of where to start and what to do next.
—Mother of a 2nd Grade boy

These ideas are great! I will practice them with Kelly today. Her writing and tolerance for it is improving greatly!
—Mother of a 4th Grade girl

Gabriel came back so excited about your class. He really enjoys it. Yours is the class he's most excited about. Since I can barely get him to write his name, that's saying something!
—Mother of a 4th Grade boy

Steven loved writing class yesterday! What a fun idea. He was really proud of his writing and pulled it out to show me as soon as we got home. I'm continually thrilled, and surprised, this year to see how much he enjoys writing!
—Mother of a 3rd Grade boy

Before your class, my boys really struggled to write down their opinions and summaries. It took them so long to write even one simple sentence. I was so amazed that they started to like writing and felt comfortable expressing their opinions on paper. They used to fear writing. Their writing skills have improved so much!
—Mother of 7- and 8-year-old boys

Frequently Asked Questions

1. How can I help my older students?

   First, start on page 53 and begin by finding out which high frequency words they can and can't spell. Then, start them on a list of sight word sentences found on pages 86–107.

   Second, while your child progresses through the sight word sentences, go to Section 4, found on page 115. There you can begin guiding them to complete a composition. Have your child write a composition 1–2 times per week. Start off by having them write 2–3 sentences per section and progress to 4–5 sentences per section.

2. How can I help my English language learner?

   First, make sure the student can complete all 12 steps in Section 2. Use many visuals to go along with any vocabulary that they are learning. Next, begin Section 3: *An Easy and On-Going Spelling Strategy*. Here, they will learn how to use and spell high frequency words, sentence structure and new vocabulary.

   Once they are comfortable with the routine of learning sight word sentences, go to Section 4, found on page 115. There you can begin guiding them to complete a composition. Have your child write a composition 1–2 times per week. Start off by having them write 1–3 sentences per section and progress to 3–5 sentences per section.

3. What materials are good to use when writing?

   For your youngest writers, I recommend thick markers. For older writers, I strongly recommend using pen so that students don't feel the failure of erasing. Instead, they move forward by drawing a simple line through their mistakes and continuing on. I also encourage using markers, colored pens, spiral pens, sparkly pens, spy pens, any kind of pens that get the kids excited about writing!

4. My child refuses to write, what can I do?

   Definitely reread Section 1 of this book to help tackle this problem. The most important points that I make and explain in that section are:

   A. Set clear expectations: Show the child how many words or sentences you want them to write, write alongside them and wait until they finish it.

   B. Give strong support: Write with the child until they lower their resistance and/or gain more confidence. Draw letters side by side or write sight word sentences side by side. Have them speak a story. Write out their spoken words and then have them copy those words on their paper.

C. Incorporate the interests of the child: The sentences, stories and essays that you guide the child to write should include their interests, such as their favorite activities, movies, books, characters, games, sports, foods, friends, etc.

D. Double the rewards: Show the child that you're serious about helping him or her with writing and also serious about rewarding them for their hard work! For one 3rd Grader, I set clear expectations for his handwriting. It was illegible and needed to be corrected. We wrote thousands of letters and then rewarded that hard work with a pizza party (his choice)!

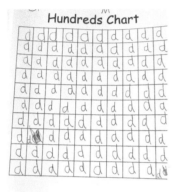

As we were eating the pizza, I pointed out to this student that we probably wouldn't want a sloppy pizza delivered to our door. Imagine if we opened the box and the toppings were stuck to the top of the box, the cheese had slid off to the side, the pieces were torn or upside down. Yuck! We'd surely call, complain and ask for another pizza done right. It's the same with handwriting. How we write is how we present ourselves and our work. We want people to be able to *read* what we have written. Handwriting is important!

5. My older child has horrible handwriting. Is there a way to change that?

I believe there is. My suggestions are as follows.

First, decide which letters are the most illegible. Plan to focus on those. Don't expect to change, correct or improve all the letters of an older child, just the ones that really need it. You can find proper letter strokes for capital letters on page 38 and lowercase letters on page 48 of this book.

Second, make sure the child is drawing *counterclockwise O's* which will set them on the right track for capital letters O, Q, C, G, S and lowercase letters c, o, a, d, g, q and s.

Third, make sure the child is *starting at the top and drawing down* for their first line in the lowercase letters, h, b, r, n and m. This helps them write more smoothly and fluidly.

Kids Win at Writing!

If you are concerned about the positioning and height of your older child's letters. Have him or her practice writing the letters on notebook paper. They can start by writing **large** capital and lowercase letters (Image 1 below). Then, they can write **small**, normal sized capital and lowercase letters (Image 2 below). This helps them draw the correct height, size and position of each letter. Have the child work on the letters that are most difficult for him or her.

Fourth and finally, set a goal, complete the task with the students and then celebrate! I had 3 students work together to write 4,500 letters to earn a pizza party. If you're working with one child, you might make a goal of 1500. This is how my 3 students completed 4,500 letters and steps that you can follow as well:

A. Again, choose the letters (only capital, only lowercase or a mix of both) that you want each individual student to work on. The letters can be different for each child.

B. Next, give each student notebook paper or 2–3 blank <u>hundreds charts</u> (Image 3 below).

1. Large capital and lowercase letters

2. Small capital and lowercase letters

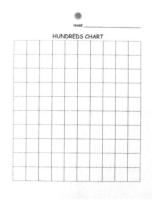

3. A blank hundreds chart

Have each student write the letter that you want him or her to write 100 times in the blank hundred's chart or on notebook paper. Do this for each letter. The student may need to practice some letters more than others, etc. Please note, 3rd Graders can EASILY complete three 100 charts in just a few minutes. This activity isn't as arduous or daunting as it might seem. Have the student(s) complete 2-3 100 charts each day until they reach 1,500 points each.

C. Third, gather points from the letters that they're writing in their writing games, activities and stories.

Note, this activity may feel tedious for the parent, teacher or tutor! HOWEVER, it's so worth it because the kids are excited about the points that they're earning! More importantly, they become mindful of their handwriting when writing words, sentences and stories.

Here's how the point system works. Every time the student writes one of their focus letters correctly in a word or sentence, they get TWO points for it. If they still write the letters incorrectly, they have to rewrite those letters. *Then,* they get ONE point for each rewritten letter.

You can tally points as they write, or tally the points as soon as they're done. Once you figure out how many letters they need to correct, write it down on a piece of paper and the number of times they need to write each letter again. For example, after reading all of the practice sentences that a student completes in any one activity, you might give him or her a page that looks like this:

20 o's

16 a's

28 d's

11 g's

9 h's

The student will write 20 lowercase o's next to 20 o's, 16 lowercase a's next to the 16 a's, and so on. Keep adding up the points until a single student gets to 1500 points or a team of students gets to 4,500. Then, CELEBRATE!

You'll probably need to complete this activity and celebrate several times. Celebrations can be a pizza party one time and an ice cream party the next. Write and reward as often as a student needs to write his or her letters correctly and confidently. Hard writing work is so important to their lives and future, thus, it deserves happy rewards!

REFERENCES

Bond, K. 2012. "Reindeer Sandwiches-Kid Friendly Holiday Lunch," *Aspottedpony.com.* December 10, 2012.
http://www.aspottedpony.com/fun-for-kids/reindeer-sandwiches-kid-friendly-holiday-lunch/47581.

Buffett, W. (n.d.) "Warren Buffett Quotes," *Azquotes.com.* (n.d.) https://www.azquotes.com/author/2136-Warren-Buffett/tag/writing.

Carolina Tiger Rescue: The information listed for the Serval Personal Narrative writing lesson on page 133 was gathered from in person tours (2016–2017) at the Carolina Tiger Rescue, www.carolinatigerrescue.org.

Common Core State Standards Initiative. (n.d.) "English Language Arts Standards: Reading Foundational Skills K–5," *Corestandards.org.* (n.d.) http://www.corestandards.org/ELA-Literacy/RF/

Common Core State Standards Initiative. (n.d.) "English Language Arts Standards: Writing K–5," *Corestandards.org.* (n.d.) http://www.corestandards.org/ELA-Literacy/W/

Common Core State Standards Initiative. (n.d.) "English Language Arts Standards: Language K–5," *Corestandards.org.* (n.d.) http://www.corestandards.org/ELA-Literacy/L/

Duke Lemur Center: The information listed for the lemurs writing lesson on page 136 was gathered from in person tours (2014–2017) at the Duke Lemur Center, www.lemur.duke.edu.

Fellows Echoing Green. (n.d.) "Mario Jovan Shaw," fellows.echoinggreen.org. (n.d.) https://fellows.echoinggreen.org/fellow/mario-jovan-shaw/

K12 Reader (n.d.) "Reading Instruction Resources: Spelling Words," www.k12reader.com (n.d.) www.k12reader.com.

Kidadl Team. 2021. "50 Best Malala Quotes from the Activist and Nobel Peace Prize Winner," *Kidadl.com.* November 4th, 2021.
http://www.kidadl.com/articles/best-malala-quotes-from-the-activist-and-nobel-peace-prize-winner.

Weston, H. 2015. "Raindrops and Puddles," *Blackfootartcenter.com.* March 24, 2015.
http://www.blackfootartcenter.blogspot.com/2015/03/raindrops-and-puddles.html.

ABOUT THE AUTHOR

I don't have horses but had a blast guiding students ages 5-11 to write stories and poems on a horse farm a few summers ago. Horses. Farm Animals. Art Accents. Writing. Writing Games. Finishing a book. It was a perfect combination for a summer camp.

Making writing fun and active inspires and strengthens young writers. I hope so much you find this book useful as you peruse and gather ideas to motivate your own students and guide them to becoming comfortable and confident at writing and reading.

Over the past 22+ years, I've been teaching language learners and observing young writers in very diverse settings. The last 8 years particularly, has been committed solely to offering year round writing camps and classes to students in Grades K–5, all the while home-schooling my own 4 children.

As a result of my observations and my passion to see young children grow in their confidence in writing and reading, I wrote this book to serve as a resource for parents, teachers and tutors.

If you have questions or are looking for additional support, feel free to contact me, Angie, directly at writingwondersandmore@gmail.com or sign up for live support online at writingwonders.com.

CPSIA information can be obtained
at www.ICGtesting.com
Printed in the USA
LVHW010319180622
721315LV00015B/133